LOVERS LEAP →

CEDAR VALE HILL

GOVERNMENT PEACH ORCHARD

OLD ROAD TO GARDEN

ROCKY GLEN

GIRLS SCHOOL (LATER)

Camps

MAThews House

AgenTs House

OLD salT Well

Mashankashe Lodge

Osage Indian BOYS AND GIRLS school

STone LAUNDRY

cenTiPed

STone BAKE ovens

Skimmer and Simcock (LATER)

HILL Side

Road To SOLDIER CREEK

Osage Woman

SWamP

Pecan TRees

Indian GRave

Government PasTure and Farm

PeRSimmon TRees

—MTA—'32

Karen L. Kramer

WAH'KON-TAH

Major Laban J. Miles

WAH'KON-TAH

THE OSAGE AND THE WHITE MAN'S ROAD

John Joseph Mathews

Illustrated by May Todd Aaron

Norman
UNIVERSITY OF OKLAHOMA PRESS
1932

IN MEMORY
OF MY FATHER
WILLIAM SHIRLEY MATHEWS

CONTENTS

Introduction
13

THE TRAIL TO THE AGENCY
Chapter One
19

THE AGENCY OF THE OSAGES
Chapter Two
27

THE MAJOR AND HIS DIARY
Chapter Three
33

"WE ARE FED LIKE DOGS"
Chapter Four
43

A VISIT TO CHE-SAH-HUNKA
Chapter Five
58

MYSTERY AMONG THE BIG HILLS
Chapter Six
75

THE MAJOR VISITS WASHINGTON
Chapter Seven
91

THE CEREMONY OF THE DOVE
Chapter Eight
112

BIRTH OF THE OSAGE NATION
Chapter Nine
136

LAME DOCTOR'S CROSS
Chapter Ten
151
GAME OF HORSE TAKING
Chapter Eleven
172
"THE HANGING JUDGE"
Chapter Twelve
196
DEATH OF CHE-SAH-HUNKA
Chapter Thirteen
224
FIRESIDE "BIG TALK"
Chapter Fourteen
239
THE WHITE MAN'S ROAD
Chapter Fifteen
257
THE MOURNING DANCE
Chapter Sixteen
288
"CIVILIZATION ARRIVES"
Chapter Seventeen
301
THE GREAT FRENZY
Chapter Eighteen
320
EAGLE THAT DREAMS
Chapter Nineteen
330
NOTES ON THE OSAGES
345

ILLUSTRATIONS

Major Laban J. Miles   FRONTISPIECE

The Agent's Residence   29

Osage Agency—map   FACING 40

The Council House   45

A Government Building   119

Osage Woman   153

A Hunting Camp   177

An Osage Grave   231

In the Trader's Store   249

Mourning Dance   291

Civilization   315

Introduction

MAJOR LABAN J. MILES

IN THE year 1878 Major Laban J. Miles came to the last reservation of the Osages as their agent. Following is an introduction of himself taken from his notes.

"*In commencing this little sketch or story of my connection with the Osage Indians, I will say that I can scarcely account for my interest in the Indians, but it started when I was but a boy. I had a relative by marriage who was a Quaker in Minnesota, and I wanted to go with him but could not leave home. In my school days at the close of the term we used to have dialogue. I well remember taking part in them a number of times, and to me one of the most interesting was the dialogue of the story of William Penn—where he went to talk with the king and the king asked how he was going to get possession of the Indian lands and William replied that he was going to buy them of the Indians, whereupon the king returned, 'Buy them of the Indians? You have already bought them of me.' Penn replied, 'Not because you had any right to their lands....' And so the discussion went on. Being a member of Penn's historic church I always took the Penn side of the dialogue. I recall an old adage which was given me when I was much older, by an old gentleman who said, 'There are always two sides to a question—the mule's side and the driver's side.' On the same theory I always believed that there were two sides to the Indian question—the Indian's side and the white man's side.*

"This opinion was greatly strengthened by an incident which occurred on my first night at the University of Iowa. Three young men of my acquaintance, with four others whom I had never met, and myself were to room in a new building which was not yet completed, so they gave us a room in the basement of the university building, formerly the capitol building of the state, to occupy until our rooms were finished—there on some pallets we spent the first few nights of our college life. There had recently been some trouble in the northwest between the whites and the Indian, and there was considerable disturbance in the community in reference to the matter. That night the question came up and was discussed among us young men together in the room, and finally near bed time one of the young men made a little speech, setting out his views and what he would like to do. He said, 'I would like to be a Cavalryman of a thousand men armed with nothing but swords. I would like to have all the Indians of the United States rounded up into one corral; then I would like to ride in and cut and slash, and cut and slash until there was not a red man, woman or child living.' And when he had finished he remarked, 'I think it is time to retire. I've always been used to having services before retiring. Let us have a little season of prayer.' I have never forgotten that night, and have always felt that I was on the opposite side of the Indian question from that young man.

"There came a time in my early life when I felt that I must make a change in my vocation, and I cast

about to see what I would take up. One man in the community in which I lived had been connected with the Indian service, and several others, members of the same church, had been connected with the service for some years, having been appointed under the plan originated by General Grant, during his term of presidency. Upon inquiry I found that an application for the service must be made to the headquarters of the Agency, which was in Philadelphia. So I made application and in due course of time received word that if I would come to Philadelphia my application would be considered. Upon reaching Philadelphia I found that the matters were in the hands of a committee of the church, so a letter was written to New York asking some members of the committee to come down to Philadelphia. After conference with the committee, it was agreed that I was to accompany two of their members to Washington. On the day following our arrival at Washington we had a conference with the secretary of interior, Karl Schurz, and in the afternoon we called informally to meet the president, Mr. Hays.

"After a conference with Mr. Schurz, he inquired of me if I would be in the city the following day, suggesting that I call the next afternoon. In conference the next day we had a long talk, referring only casually to the matter of the Indian service, but as I was about to leave the secretary said, 'I see you have rubbed against the world and I will give you a place in the service.' He added that there was a vacancy a long distance from the railroad, whereupon I informed him that I had a young family and for that reason I did not desire to be so far from the railroad. Then he said, 'You can go home and

I will telegraph you every vacancy and if you find one you are willing to accept you can answer.'

"In the course of two or three months I received a wire from the secretary stating that there was a vacancy at Osage Agency. I accepted the place, asking the secretary to send on the papers which were required by the Department. I then made my fifty thousand dollar bond and went to Washington in July of '78. I received my instructions and left for the Agency. The instructors read that among my first duties at the Agency would be the making of a semi-annual payment, and that the money for the payment would be placed in the sub-treasury at St. Louis. I stopped at St. Louis on my way to the Osage Reservation, and the sub-treasurer gave me the money for the payments, which I carried to the Agency in my satchel."

WAH'KON-TAH

*That which the children of the
earth do not comprehend as
they travel the roads of the
earth and which becomes clear
to them only when they have
passed on to the Great Mysteries is Wah'Kon-Tah*

THE TRAIL TO THE AGENCY

Chapter One

THE IMPRESSION was one of space; whispering space. The curved blue sky met the undulating emerald on all sides among the rounded hills; the emerald becoming darker and softer, the blue becoming pastel as they merged. When a line of blackjacks became the meeting place of sky and prairie, their rounded tops became black and cut definitely into the blue in such a way as to suggest adventure beyond. It was wild space yet it was never silent. In summer the grasses whispered and laughed and sang, changing to mournful whispers during the autumn, then screaming like a demented woman when winter turned the emerald to copper. In the spring the breezes talked confidentially of the mating season, burdened with the scents of the earth and carrying the voices of the curlew, the sandpiper, the killdeer, the meadow-lark and the sonorous booming of the prairie chicken. Nothing could give a stronger impression of wild spaciousness than a buggy, or a horse and rider moving, almost imperceptibly along the trails that led from "the States" to the Osage Agency.

One day in June about the year 1879 two government mules drew a single side-spring buggy over the Caney trail. The buggy crawled over the emerald world like some purposeful bug, appearing suddenly over the brow of a hill, then disappearing in a depression. It would appear again some time later, and remain visible for a short time along a high divide, increasing its speed for a short distance, when the prairie breezes carried off the pale clouds of dust that the mules kicked up, then, as it slowed down again when the trail became rough, the dust clouds curled and eddied around it.

Increasing their speed as the buggy increased speed, and slowing down as it slowed down were six horsemen riding behind. The breeze played with the manes of the ponies and hissed through their tails; it ballooned the figured shirts of the riders. They had let their blankets fall from their shoulders and had tied them around their waists. They seemed a part of the ponies they rode. They carried guns across their saddles; "short guns" they called them. These were issued to the Indian police of the Reservation and to the guards and were made for use from horseback, and were known as Springfield cavalry rifles.

Because these riders seemed to be a part of the ponies they rode, and because they inclined a little forward, they could be identified as Indians. By the fact that they wore roaches with eagle feathers projecting above them, they could be recognized as Osages.

Two of them wore figured bandeaux above which the roaches quivered and the eagle feathers swayed and spun in the wind. Their heads were shaved close leaving the roach which reached from the top center to the rear, in the shape of the scalplock; in fact it symbolized the scalplock and served as a perpetual challenge to the enemies of the people.

They rode silently.

The Major sat in the side-springed buggy which crawled slowly over the prairie, watching the road ahead of him. His eyes squinted in the brilliant June sun. He lurched from side to side as the buggy creaked and groaned over the rough trail. He sat forward with the reins held loosely in his hands, uttering an occasional "Giddap," but failing to enforce his command with the whip when the mules failed to respond. "Giddap" was said mechanically, and was associated with the feel of the reins and the swaying and creaking of the buggy.

The hooves of the mules kicked the sand of the hills with a muffled thud and when they were climbing their shoes struck the platy limestone with a metallic ring. The tires of the buggy rasped over the sandstone and drew sparks from the limestone, or buried themselves in the soft sand which welled up over the rim and flowed through the spokes.

The trail lay across the Reservation like parallel bands that had been dropped; crinkled bands with one end at the Agency in the center of the Reservation and the other at Caney in "the States." It followed the high divide between stream systems where this was possible. It climbed out of the valleys up long hills where the alternating strata of shale, red clay, sandstone and limestone were exposed. The sandstone and limestone formed little shelves. Along the divides it lay almost in a straight line across the prairie, then dropped suddenly into a ravine, where it crossed at some shallow, usually where the resistant limestone was exposed. Then again up a long sandstone hill through dense growths of blackjacks and postoaks, then out onto the prairie again to follow along another divide until it dropped again into the blackjacks, then onto the alluvium of a stream bottom among the sycamores, elms, cottonwoods and walnuts. It passed little stage stations almost hidden among the hickory and second-growth oaks where the freighters changed horses or put up for the night, climbing out again to the limestone prairie, on through sandstone hills, across prairie ravines, to end finally by coming down through the blackjacks into a narrow, elongated valley to the Agency.

The freighters and traders had names for the topographic features along the trail; especially each long hill and each ford. There were Caney Gap, Tinker hill, Clay hill, White Swan crossing, No Pah Wollah crossing and Deep ford. Rounded hills standing apart on the prairie with groves of blackjacks were important as landmarks, as they could be seen for great distances.

On this June day the Major was returning from Independence in "the States" where he had received the money for the coming payment to the members of the tribe. He had placed the money in a little bag in the back of the buggy. He went often for the money, alone, to avoid suspicion and each time upon reaching the borders of the Reservation he felt comparatively safe from bandits. He often smiled to himself over the fact that the borders between the Indian country and the country of the white man should mean for him the line of safety.

On this day he felt a premonition. All morning he had felt unsafe. He knew that the guard behind him were perfectly trustworthy and that they could give a good account of themselves in a fight, but when the trail passed close to one of the thickly wooded ridges, or along blackjack covered hills he felt nervous; he knew that they would have no chance if the bandits attacked from such ambush.

As the day wore on the feeling became intense, and he watched anxiously that part of the trail which climbed in a zigzag fashion, a long hill to a gap. He watched particularly a point of a ridge where the blackjacks grew down the side, close to the trail. As he watched this point fear came to him like a sharp pain, as he said "It seemed that there was a cloud about me."

At the foot of the hill he stopped his mules as though to rest them before the climb. Their rumps were lathered under the breeching and sweat foam appeared under their collars, and their sides moved in and out like feeble bellows.

The guard came up and stood around the buggy but no one spoke. After a short time the Major said "It will be good to take other road, I believe." He abruptly turned his mules and started back along the trail to the point where the other trail branched off; the trail which climbed to the high limestone prairie and was open for a long distance. The guard turned and followed without comment.

When they had climbed to the prairie they could see in the distance a band of horsemen, and as they drew near recognized them as a band of hunters from No Pah Wollah's camp. When they passed near the Major and the guard they raised their hands in recognition but rode on. At that moment the "cloud" suddenly passed away and the Major thought no more that day of his fear, but later came to know that his fears were well founded.

Later the little party passed the stage station on Hickory creek, crossed the Caney river, climbed over the divide and dropped down to Mission creek. Here they prepared to have lunch and allow the mules and horses to rest.

The Major unhitched his mules and loosened the check-reins, then drove them into the water to drink. As he stood there listening to the sniffings and splashing, he watched the many little deer trails that led down to the water and thought he caught sight of a white tail glistening for a fraction of a second in the sun. Suddenly his attention was drawn to the edge of the water by a group of water lilies. As he looked at them he suddenly remembered his first trip into the Reservation. He had his wife with him and they had stopped at this same ford for lunch. He had undone the check-reins on the horses and his wife had driven them into the water to drink as he busied himself about the making of a fire. He had heard her clucking to the horses and looking up saw that she was urging them into the deep water toward this same group of lilies. He called to her but she only pointed to the lilies and continued to urge the horses forward. Before he could get out to her one of the Indian guards had slipped off his leggings and blanket, and in breech clout walked to the head of the team and turned them toward the bank. The Major was very frightened, he remembered, and was telling his wife of the danger, when he noticed the guard was swimming across the stream toward the lilies. They watched him gather some of them in his arms and swim back; he waded out of the water, his bronzed body dripping. He walked up to the Major's wife and offered her the flowers and as he did so the Major noticed that he had taken off his breech clout and stood there naked glistening in the sun. Shocked speechless and looking up into a cottonwood tree the Major's wife accepted the flowers of her heart and Victorianism had been formally introduced to the children of Wah'Kon-Tah.

As these thoughts came to him the Major smiled.

After lunch the party climbed to the prairie, where the clear call of the meadowlark came on the soft breezes. Dickcissels swayed on the tops of weeds and sang in their weak voices, and from the grass roots came rasping, tinkling stridulations. The breezes talked and laughed merrily.

Then on into the blackjacks where the prairie breezes seemed to have become entangled and died. Here life seemed to murmur, almost whisper as the heat devils danced. The leaves rattled slightly, lazily, and made moving patterns on the sparse grass. There were the sleepy voices of birds; the sad call of a woodphœbe, the jerky notes of a brown thrasher, and a mockingbird singing persistently from the top of a dead tree wasting his voice on a somnolent world. The party disturbed a band of deer taking their siesta, but saw very little except the white flags of their tails as they seemed to melt into air among the dark boles of the trees.

It was a relief to drop down into the creek bottom again, where the long grasses were dappled with yellow; where the quiet holes of water looked cool under their arches of elms, and little water-striders skated here and there over the surface as though they had nothing else to do. The constant, shrill buzzing of the cicada was so deafening that the leaves of the cottonwood seemed to move gently, without the usual accompanying whisper; as in pantomime. The white boles of the sycamore, reflected in the water, danced crazily.

Soon the hills began to hide the sun completely and the little party crawled along for some time in their shadows to emerge again into the yellow light of the late afternoon sun. The emerald of the prairie became dark green velvet which merged in the distance into purple.

Later moving through the dark shadows of the blackjacks the party wound down into the valley of the Agency along the road that ended abruptly among a few austere stone buildings.

THE AGENCY OF THE OSAGES
Chapter Two

BIRD CREEK had its source in the high limestone prairie to the northwest, and ran tortuously; marked in its sinuous wanderings over the prairie by a thin line of elms, cottonwoods, and walnuts, finally losing itself in the blackjacks where it cut small valleys out of the sandstone hills; flooring them with deposits of alluvium. In one of these little valleys near the center of the Reservation, were the stone buildings and the traders' stores of the Agency.

Dominating the valley, standing brusquely above the post-oaks was the native sandstone Council House. It was topped by a bell tower. In line with it and facing the hill in the same direction were three sandstone buildings, two-storied, severe. On one side was the building which contained the doctor's office, and other agency offices. Across a dusty road that led to the creek was the doctor's house. On the other side of the Council House was the third stone building which was successively the blacksmith's house, the chief clerk's house, and later a house where room and board could be had. Between the Council House and this building were two traders' stores divided by another road that led down to the creek. They were long, wooden buildings which had sprung up from primitive stockades. Across from the stores at the foot of the hill was a little log-house which was the remnant of the original Agency buildings, and close by was the small building with barred windows, which was the jail, and known locally as the calaboose. Between the line of buildings and the base of the hill where the four roads which led into the Agency met, there was a dusty area, dotted with great post-oaks. This area was the center and the heart of the Reservation. There people met and talked or loafed under the shade of the trees. Teams and saddle-horses stood hitched to the hitching racks in front of the stores or to some convenient tree. Traders moved across the area with the business usually assumed by Americans who sell things. Here the mixed-bloods from the fertile valleys of the Reservation met and talked, exchanged experiences and boasted. Agency employes moved across it from the building, stopping occasionally to talk. Freighters from "the States" shouted their horses or mules to a stop, the commotion sending the yellow dust into clouds. Indians with their blankets wrapped tightly about them partly hiding their heads strode with dignity across the area, or stopped in the center to gaze intently at the hills or the sky, holding their eagle-wing fans above their eyes.

Beginning in front of the Council House and cutting the area, a road led up over the hill. It climbed to a terrace, ran along on a level for some distance, and climbed a second hill, which was known as the Cedarvale hill. On the first terrace almost at the edge, and overlooking the valley was the sandstone residence where the agent lived. Farther up the road were the buildings of the government school, dominated by an immense structure of sandstone which was composed of two austere wings meeting at the center under two cupolas. In

The Agent's Residence

one wing was the boys' dormitory and in the other was the dormitory for the girls. At the very edge of the hill overlooking the upper valley a little frame hospital clung to the sandstone among the blackjacks.

Stern and powerful were these buildings of sandstone; fitting symbols of might. These "guv'munt buildins" inspired respect for the strength of the authority which covered this land of prairie and blackjack. To the Indians these buildings meant the material evidence of the great power somewhere in "the States." They meant the authority of power, yet they meant service to themselves; they were there to serve them, and all people connected with them were there to serve their people. "Guv'munt buildins" and the higher government officials never inspired the awe and the instinctive respect in the Indians as they did in the mixed-bloods and the traders. Through heredity the latter had in their blood the awe of authority and of Authority's symbols, whilst the former had been a free and independent people for ages and in their blood flowed the same spirit of independence and chivalry that flowed in the veins of the medieval prince. Crude chivalry and crude honor perhaps, but honor that was ever placed above death; honor of greater importance than wealth. They had never fawned or adulated nor kept shop. Their tribal laws were severe and based on the rudiments, but they were few.

They came to the Agency to be served. The traders, the employes and the agent were the symbols of that service which the powers had agreed would be theirs.

Immediately back of the area and its buildings were the creek bottoms, the third of the series of terraces that Bird creek had made through the centuries. Here on the edge of the creek, near a ford was the sandstone mill and the government barn. Here among thick groves of elm, and cottonwoods, many members of the tribe camped when they came into the Agency on business or pleasure. Many councils were held in these bottoms and during the period of counciling the rounded lodges of the people extended along the creek for some distance.

It was here that the Major came to meet the chiefs when they held long and vehement councils concerning the rations.

THE MAJOR AND HIS DIARY

Chapter Three

THE MAJOR was alone in his office, the employes having gone home. He opened a locked drawer in which he kept his notes—notes which he intended to use some day. He held the first few pages in his hands, the ones he had written when he first came to the Agency. He was rather ashamed of them. It occurred to him that they were like freshmen poems, written as they were in his first enthusiastic year at the Agency. Since then his attempts to understand these people had begun to bear some fruit. Yet there were facts in these pages well enough but he felt that he had written about these great people as a bureaucrat, or as a government official might write about Indians in general. He could never write about them as he wished to write. In the first place he could not express what he had begun to feel, and in the second place his understanding and friendship with men like Big Chief, Hard Robe and Governor Jo was something that one couldn't write about. How could he make people understand a man like Gray Bird, for example? He threw the papers on the desk and looked at them a long time as though he were deciding their fate, with an expression that indicated he wanted to be just to them. Finally he picked them up deciding he had better not destroy them; better keep them. They were facts that might be used some day. He began to read them carefully.

"*The Osage Indians were removed from Missouri after having agreed to move to the State of Kansas in compliance with the treaty of 1847. However, while the main body of the Indians resided in southern Kansas quite a number of them had gone over to what was known as the Indian Territory before the treaty, and still remained in the Territory for some time prior to and during the period of the Civil war. Many of the mixed-bloods and quite a number of full-bloods who remained in Kansas joined the Union forces during the war, and quite a number of the Indians in the Territory joined the Southern forces and were with them all during the war. From parties in the service at this time I have learned that very little attention was paid to the Indians excepting to comply with the government obligations in a purely official way. They existed almost entirely by the hunt, making two annual hunts, one for the purpose of securing meat for summer and the other for securing robes and furs in winter. There is no record of any open outbreak on the part of the Osages against the whites, and it has been their boast from the first settlement at the mouth of the Osage river in Missouri over one hundred years ago they have never in any way attempted to resist the authority of the government. However, I found, on going to the Agency, that hundreds of thousands of dollars worth of claims had been filed and would be filed, on account of the depredations of the Indians. The claims were at first filed when the Indians agreed to sell their lands in Kansas and move to a reservation that the government should purchase for them in what was known as the Indian Territory. Many of these claims were forwarded to me for examination and report. I took considerable time in attempting to report intelligently on a number of these claims, but found that it took more time than I could spare from the duties of the Agency. From memory I can only give the general character of a few of these claims.*

"One man claimed that he had turned a large number of cattle loose on the Reservation in the fall and was unable to look after them during the winter. When spring came and he had rounded up his cattle he found that many of them were short so the Osages must have killed them as he had found no dead cattle but had found a few horns and other evidences of cattle having been killed. He therefore made a claim for the shortage, asking the government to pay the same.

"Another claim on which I spent some time traveling over the State of Kansas to get the facts as nearly as possible before reporting was that of a man who claimed he had been driving cattle from Texas and when he arrived near the State line he was surrounded by some Indians that he thought were Osage Indians. They proceeded to cut out a number of his cattle and kill them. When he counted his head he was short a certain number and made a claim for the shortage.

"These cases were, in a way, typical of the character of the claims filed, these in the aggregate amounting to hundreds of thousands of dollars. Most of them were for cattle but some were for ponies and horses they claimed had been stolen. I returned from Washington some time later and reported to the Indians that a claim had been allowed for quite a large amount by Congress, and

was to be paid. I told the chiefs that they were eventually going to have to pay for their old sins and they asked me how much was the claim. It was for sixty four head that somebody on the drive with a herd of cattle had encountered the Osages and claimed they killed sixty four head of his cattle. On my telling who it was and where the cattle were claimed to have been killed the Indians said they remembered getting some cattle from him but they only got twenty seven head.

"Undoubtedly there was a great amount of outlawry in those days and doubtless the Osages were liable to criticism for at least a part of the trouble. Many people suffered losses from the gangs that infested the country, many of them not being Indian at all. The department found it impossible, in any legitimate way, to settle these claims so decided to dump them into the court of claims which had been created in the city of Washington. The Osages employed attorneys there to defend them against all such claims, these attorneys receiving salaries, and in a few years they succeeded in adjusting all the claims that had been filed against the Indians.

"Soon after I reached the Agency I received notice that $5,000.00 had been placed to my credit to reimburse the Indians who had suffered losses from the raid made on some Osage people while on a hunt in western Kansas. I called the Indians together and ascertained as nearly as possible what their losses were and made a careful estimate of these losses, making the price of articles lost about the same as such things could be purchased for at the Agency stores. In summing them up I found that they amounted to about $2,500.00, so I returned the remainder to the treasury with the recom-

mendation that the balance be paid to the families of the men who were killed. My recommendation was ratified by Congress and such a payment was made.

"The raid had been made a year or two before I went to the Agency but from the Indians and others I learned that a hunting party had gone out as usual for their summer hunt and as was their habit had taken their families along. The women would cut the meat and help take care of it. They were suddenly fired upon by a company of white people and three of them were killed. The camp was broken up in a panic and when they returned to the Agency the officers had great trouble to keep the Indians from retaliating."

He laid the papers down on his desk and looked at the window. His mind went back to the stories that had been told of the troops, the fifth cavalry, he believed, being camped in the little valley of the Agency. The traders and the agent had been much impressed by the sullen action of the Indians. The people had deserted the camps in the bottom near the mill, and when a tall blanketed figure appeared in the area his bearing implied more than regality; there was something ominous in the carriage of his body. A tense waiting had fallen upon the Agency, as it awoke every morning to the reveille.

The troops had been sent to preclude any trouble that might spring from the Kansas incident, but it was never a pleasant thought to the Major, that in case the Osages had determined that the government was not going to do anything about the matter, and had initiated action themselves, that it would have been the

Osages who would have fallen before the bullets of the cavalrymen; not the perpetrators of the crime.

The Major picked up the notes again. He made his final decision to leave this fifth cavalry business out of them.

"It was generally understood that there had been no provocation and no reason for the attack more than the desire of the white settlers to persecute the Indians. Later on it was generally understood that the State of Kansas had sworn the men of the attacking party in as militiamen and dated the act back, so that these men would be protected by the fact that they were militiamen and thus be protected from prosecution. It is my opinion that the examination made by the government fully warrants this claim.

"During the summer and fall I spent much time in the Indian camps studying their ways of living and wondering how they could be changed for the better. I was very much surprised to find that here was a country occupied by more than two thousand people, in which there was no law covering any crime that might be committed among these people. If a crime were committed between an Indian and a white man they were subject to the United States statutes and were under the jurisdiction of the court at Fort Smith, two hundred and fifty miles distant, and subject to arrest by the United States deputy marshals who visited the Agency occasionally; but for any crime, either civil or criminal, between the Indians themselves, there was no law and the officer in charge of the Agency was supposed to be the mediator and to control the Reservation.

"The department had instituted a system of police,

simply as a means of assisting the agent in keeping order; and had provided for a police court. I appointed the police but the more I considered the matter the more I felt that there was no policeman there to whom I wished to give the position of police judge, so I instructed the policemen that in any disputes that might arise, or in any trouble, either criminal or civil, on the Reservation, the cases should be brought to me. It seems incredible that there was a place in this country where there was a large community in which there was no court, no protection—even against murder.

"So far as I was able to learn from history and from conversation with the Indians, the government had never made any attempt in any way to interfere with their domestic relations. In fact, they had been treated in that respect as a foreign nation over which we had no control, and in our legislation we entirely ignored them as having existence in our body politic. There is no provision in our laws for any restraint or any regulation. As nearly as I could find out such relation had been subject to their own whims; some of their ideas may have come from different foreign countries with which they may have come in contact, others from their own imagination, but their system had no such thing as any legal regulation concerning marriage. As far as I could learn they had practiced polygamy from their earliest history."

The Major sat for some time with several pages of the notes in his hand, then he arose and went to the window.

The little valley was sleeping under its heavy heat. He could hear the cicadas along the creek bottom, but the area in front of the Council House was silent. Here and there in the shades of the buildings and under the Indian wagons, dogs snapped lazily at flies. The horses at the hitching rail in front of the trader's store stamped with sleepy resignation; stamped in the dust until they made little depressions, and their shod hooves had reached solid soil.

An Indian family came leisurely across the area. They had made their few purchases and were moving along toward their wagon. The mother walked in the lead carrying the bundles, and behind her in single file came the three daughters. The father was at the rear of the file, his blanket tied around his waist and his eagle-wing fan held in front of him. He seemed utterly detached from the world. The family reached the wagon and the father untied the horses while the mother and girls climbed into the bed and sat down. Then the father got into the high seat in front, and turned his team to start out on the road which led across Rocky ford and on to the southern part of the Reservation. Six or seven mongrel dogs stretched and yawned, then trotted listlessly along with the wagon on the shady side.

The Major stood at the window for some time, then he went back to his chair. He felt the futility of words to express what he felt. He was afraid of words; he was afraid of being sentimental, but he knew he was beginning to understand these people who were certainly not European, but possibly Asiatic in their origin. Their customs, their conception of God, their quiet dignity and courtesy and sincerity as compared with the aggressiveness and hypocrisy of his own race, made the understanding of them difficult. It seemed to him that they did not assume virtues as did the white man, or attempt to control the destinies of others. They were individualists in that respect, though they lived by the harsh rules of the herd. They had remained a part of nature and had not developed the enervating ornamentation, or that softness and self-indulgence which was called civilization. They often talked in pictures with a classical simplicity.

It seemed to the Major that the two races would never meet, and that there would be no one with sympathy and understanding sufficient to interpret the Indian. He knew what he himself had begun to feel, and he knew what the better class trader felt about them; a sort of respect and admiration that was almost inscrutable. When he thought of this chasm between the two races he invariably thought of the incident of Paw Hunka and a trader.

Paw Hunka had lost his wife. At the burial there was great mourning and many of the people were there. When the people were gathered for the burial of the wife of Paw Hunka, the trader had come with a bill for the many things which were purchased for the funeral. But with the bill he had an official-looking paper, which must have Paw Hunka's mark as well as the approval of the agent, before it became valid. So he chose this time to come to Paw Hunka, knowing that he would be far from this world; detached from all the things of the earth in his great sorrow. The trader knew that the Indian does not pray as the white man prays; with one eye open and his hand around his money pouch, but that he loses himself completely for the moment; his whole soul given up to his grief.

When the paper was pushed into Paw Hunka's hand it was a subconscious annoyance to be got out of the way as soon as possible, and the trader went away with the mark of Paw Hunka and the thrill that comes when financial gain is anticipated. Many of the white men—white men who had not lived long with the Indian, and had not yet learned to respect him,—said that this was very smart, but the Indian believed it to be sacrilegious.

.   .   .   .

In the area shadows were becoming very long. The office building threw its shadow across the dusty road almost to the doctor's house and gradually the shadows deepened, then suddenly the area was disturbed by the creaking and rattling of a freighter's wagon, and the loud shouting of the driver. Then a long silence.

The Major looked at his watch, put the papers back in the drawer and arranged his desk.

As he came out of his office the area was dark. From the traders' stores dim red lights shone like cautious eyes under the oaks. From down in the bottoms came the persistent bark of an Indian dog disturbed by some imaginary enemy.

"WE ARE FED LIKE DOGS"
Chapter Four

WHEN the Major had first come to the Agency the people were having trouble about the rations. Those first months seemed difficult to him, because at that time he was unable to speak the Osage language and found it necessary to speak with the people through an interpreter. There were many councils being held over the Reservation and feeling was running high. The leading men of the bands presented their demands to him but he could do nothing until he had heard from the department, and the Indian bureau seemed to avoid decisions.

The people came to him saying that they were being "fed like dogs" and he felt that they were right when they claimed that the cattle for which the government had contracted with cattlemen were not fit food for dogs, especially after being left on the range all winter. As soon as the trouble arose the government had authorized the use of troops, but the Major spent his time attempting to come to some agreement with the leaders, and he found himself dependent upon the very wise council of We Eh Sah Ki (Hard Robe) and Pawnee No Pah She (Man Not Afraid of Pawnees). The latter was called Governor Jo and Big Hill Jo by the traders. Both were men of great ability and sane judgment.

After payment the Major sent word to all the chiefs that he would talk with them about the rations. When they were assembled for the council he had some misgivings as he spoke to them. He told them that he was powerless, and that he could do only those things which the government allowed him to do but that he personally agreed with them that it was an insult to a great people to be asked to come from over the Reservation to receive rations once a week. He told them however that the coffee, flour, sugar and beef were already contracted for the coming year, and that these rations would be issued on the first day in every week. He said that their demand that the "little house" be opened and all the rations be given out at one time, and that thereafter there should be no more rations, was impossible, though he hoped that the rations would be discontinued by the government as soon as possible. He said that it would be his plan to work with the chiefs in this matter and all other matters which might arise, and not through an appointed "business committee," as had been done previously, and that before the rations for another year were ordered he would council with them but that there was no knowing what the government would do. He said that he would make the wishes of the people known to the government and suggest that the rations be stopped immediately, and he certainly would not make purchases for the coming year before the wishes of the people were known. Finally he suggested that they accept the rations under the circumstances, adding that for more than two weeks the door of the "little house" had been opened on the first day in the week, but no one had called for his rations.

The Council House

During his speech he had noticed that the chiefs were not impressed by his assurances, and he waited for some time after finishing before one of them arose, drew his blanket about him in front, and cleared his throat. He looked very tall. Twice he moved his eagle-wing fan slowly before his face, then clutching it in both hands he said:

"Forever white man will talk. Forever white man will lie. He will look upon ground forever. He looks for white iron of white man as he walks on earth. This money which he pays to us is our money. This money which comes from Washington is money paid to us for our lands in Kansas. Who is this white man to say how this money should be paid? We do not want rations. We are not dogs that we should be fed like dogs." He pointed his eagle-wing fan at the Major and continued: "You tell your people that Osages are tired of this thing; tell them Osages will not be fed like dogs. Tell them that Osages are not many but they know how to die."

When he finished he sat down slowly and began to fan himself with quick movements. When the interpreter arose to translate the speech he thought it discreet to leave out the threat.

Several of the chiefs arose and talked about the rations and it looked as though they did not intend to give ground. The Major had begun to grow nervous, not through fear, but he had begun to believe that the council would come to nothing and there would be real trouble. When We Eh Sah Ki (Hard Robe) rose slowly to his feet he felt that the climax had come. Hard Robe was a great war chief, and people listened to his talk. The great chief stood for a moment looking over the faces of the circle, then he raised his face slightly, and began:

"This man has come among us. He will be here long time as our agent. This man came with friendly heart, I believe. He seems to talk with straight tongue, and I think we had better listen to him. We will see if he keeps his tongue straight. It will be good thing, I believe, if we take our rations now. We will take our rations now and go home to our business there. We will see if this man keeps his tongue straight."

After Hard Robe's speech the council broke up and the Major felt that the matter was becoming settled, if only the government would make some decision.

There were many letters between the Agency and the department, and still there was nothing done about the rations, as the Major and the Indians waited.

One day an inspector appeared in the Agency. He stayed for several days and had long talks with the Major in his office. Everybody was wondering what was going to happen. What he learned about the matter, no one outside the office knew. He walked about like a man who is doing a disagreeable job but very sure of his worth, and it seemed that he must have believed that his mere presence would have the necessary effect upon the Indians, and it is not unlikely that he believed that he had accomplished something, if he misinterpreted the actions of the Indians in ignoring his presence. There was only one incident that indicated that his identity and mission were known.

He had nosed everywhere, and appreciated the slight awe in which the traders and some of the mixed-

bloods held him. One day he was in one of the traders'
stores, talking casually with the trader when a tall
blanketed figure appeared in the door. The Indian stood
there for some time before the trader looked up and
said "How." The visitor ignored him. He suddenly
transferred his fan from his right hand to his left, then
pointing his finger at the inspector, walked toward him
until his finger was within a few inches of the latter's
nose. Then he said, "Ho, big inspector, you have come
to bring us beef, I believe. Where is this beef which be-
longs to us? You have sent us horns, bones and hide of
this beef, maybe now you have come to bring meat." He
turned, and with a quick movement, left the store.

The inspector turned to the trader and asked,
"What did he say?"

"He said you had sent the horns, bones and hide
of the issue beef; when were you going to send the
meat."

The inspector laughed unnaturally "Who was he?"

"His name's Kah'n Sah Hah'r-ee."

"Oh!"

Among the leaders of the tribe was Wah Ti An
Kah. He was very handsome and extremely proud. He
was well over six feet and always dressed in the finest
buck-skin moccasins and leggings. He wore a great beaver-skin bandeau and bear-claw necklace, and affected a
red blanket, in the folds of which he carried a long
knife. His face was like that of a bronze Dante.

His voice was loud but beautiful, and he was a
great orator. He swayed the people by his personality
and his voice, but he usually had things to say. He
would not tolerate inattention to his harangues. He

watched the faces of his audiences closely and if he discovered that they were becoming lax in attention he would stamp his foot on the ground and pointing at them, say: "You do not care. You can say everything is good; everything is all right. You sit like rabbit with nothing in your head. You look like rabbit and think nothing. You sit with nothing on your faces."

His great voice rang out in the councils of his people when they sold their lands in Kansas. Many said that it was through his influence that the Osages came to the Oklahoma Territory, instead of going farther west.

There had been two parties. One under the leadership of Paw Hue Skah, (White Hair) son of the second Paw Hue Skah, and the party led by Wah Ti An Kah. The Paw Hue Skah party was in favor of taking land in the western part of Kansas, where there were still buffalo herds, but Wah Ti An Kah, coming to the councils from a visit to the land south of the Kansas border, where he had spent some time among the prairie and the blackjacks, threw all his force into arguments that the Osages should buy land from the Cherokees.

Before the councils he stood, straight and regal, and spoke thus:

"I have been in south. I have seen much there. There are many trees with black boles where deer sleep when sun is hot. I saw many deer there, and many other things. I said, this land will be good for my people. I said, there is much game in this country; there is much grass and much water. I said, my people will be happy in this land. White man cannot put iron thing in ground here. White man will not come to this land. There are many hills here. I said, white man does not like country where there are hills, and he will not come, I believe. This country is not good for things which white man puts in ground. I said this will be good place for my people. I said, if my people go west where land is like floor of lodge, white man will come to our lodges and say, 'We want your land.' Government will come to our lodges and say, 'We will buy this land for white man; white man wants this land; he will plant things there.' Soon land will end and Osages will have no home; they will be far from place where their grandfather is; from graves of their grandfather. I said, it good for my people to go to this land in south."

In the counciling about the rations Wah Ti An Kah's voice was heard often, doing much to stir the people. Because of this the Major said that he was very loud and lacked the dignity of a true Osage. He spent much time telling the people that the agent was their servant, and that he must do what the people wished; that they were weak if they let the white man tell them what to do.

When the council was chosen to go to Washington about the rations, the chiefs purposely left the name of Wah Ti An Kah off the list. They were afraid that he would harm the cause by undiplomatic speeches. But by some means he got on and after some debate they allowed him to go, though each member of the delegation feared his presence. "What will Wah Ti An Kah do?" they said, "He will talk too much," they told each other.

All the way to Washington Wah Ti An Kah sat

sullenly, ignoring the cities and the strange countryside.

The delegation had an appointment with the commissioner of Indian affairs at 9 o'clock the morning after arrival. Its members waited in the lobby for the carriages to call for them. Each one was dressed in his best leggings and blanket. They pretended that they didn't see the many white men staring at them, but it made them uncomfortable and angry.

As they waited, they noticed that Wah Ti An Kah had not come down yet, and they wondered about this; they thought it was bad. Soon they saw him coming, moving across the floor quickly, though silently and with great dignity. He was wrapped almost to the eyes in a great red blanket, and they could see that his face was painted like one who goes to war. Across the eyes was a thin yellow band of paint and there were many symbols of red and black on his cheeks; "Ho," they thought, "This thing is bad. We wonder what he will do."

They arrived at the place of meeting with the commissioner and were seated by an attendant. Soon the commissioner came in and looked over his gorgeous visitors, casually, but when his attention fell on Wah Ti An Kah, he was held fascinated. He stared at him, seemingly unable to take his eyes from this great man. The people noticed this and they thought the white man very ill-mannered but they knew that he was only a white man. Wah Ti An Kah was very much insulted that he should be stared at in this manner but he said to himself, it is only white man; he has no manners.

With his eyes still on Wah Ti An Kah, the commissioner looked at his watch and rose, then he said,

"Mr. Interpreter, tell these gentlemen that I am sorry that I have another appointment at this time—I am sorry I had forgotten about it until just now. Tell them to make themselves comfortable, and that I shall not be gone any longer than necessary."

The interpreter stood by the desk and translated the words of the commissioner, and over the room there were several "Hows." The commissioner then started toward the door, but in one quick movement, Wah Ti An Kah was before him. He let his red blanket slip from his shoulders and to the surprise of the others, he had nothing on except his breech clout and his moccasins. His great chest was tattooed with many lines and symbols, and on his left shoulder was tattooed the head of a horse. From each side of his beaver-skin bandeau projected small buffalo horns, and around his neck was the great bear-claw necklace which he affected.

He stood there towering like some primitive god of the dark forests. He stood and looked through the band of yellow stain at the man in front of him. With a quick upward glance to the interpreter he said, "Tell this man to sit down." The interpreter looked apologetically at the commissioner, and translated a request instead of the demand. The commissioner sat down and looked up at the terrible figure of the devil. Wah Ti An Kah raised his hand to the intepreter, and said, pointing to the commissioner; "Tell this man this thing. Tell him we have come to talk about rations. We have come long way to talk about this. He says he wants to talk to man who is here in this place. We have come from Reservation many miles—he will talk to us first—

we will talk about rations. We have come at time he said. We are ready to talk. Tell him this thing."

The intepreter translated. The commissioner answered with a smile; it was not a smile of amusement, "Tell this man that the White Father has been considering the rations of the Osage people for some time, and he has been investigating the conditions on the Reservation. He was almost ready to believe that these people were ready to be paid in money instead of having rations given to them, but," and here he looked up at Wah Ti An Kah, "here is a man who has come to Washington with his war paint on. If the White Father saw him this way he would think that all Osages were savages yet and would not know how to use money. He would say that the rations ought to be continued until these people became civilized. Surely this man who doesn't know how to act—who comes to my office almost naked, with war paint on his face, is not civilized enough to know how to use money."

He said this patronizingly, and with a certain air of finality, but he checked the slightest movement to rise and be on his way, as Wah Ti An Kah stood menacingly above him. He looked at his watch as the interpreter translated. The others began to stir and wish that they had not brought Wah Ti An Kah. They believed that he was acting bad.

When the interpreter had finished, Wah Ti An Kah drew himself up to his full height, and placed his hand on his chest "Wah'Kon-Tah has made me as I am. I am glad, I am not ashamed of my body. I do not wear clothes to hide body that Wah'Kon-Tah gave me; clothes that reach up to neck," and he pointed to the large cravat that the commissioner was wearing. "If these things," and he pointed to the commissioner's clothes, "make white man civilized, I believe it is good that this man wears them." Again he returned to the interpreter, "Tell this man we have come long way to talk about rations. Tell him we did not come to talk about white man's road."

Wah Ti An Kah's speech was translated into a very few sentences.

The commissioner took up a pencil and tapped on his desk for a few moments, then he said, "I think that we can assure you gentlemen that there will be no more rations, but you must remember that the rations already bought must be used up, before we can make other arrangements. Your agent will know what to do about this—you must listen to him in this matter and I am sure that everything will be all right."

When Wah Ti An Kah heard this he took his blanket and went back to his chair. The commissioner gave a few words of advice, then asked if there was anything else that the people wished to talk about. When there was no answer he looked at his watch, put it back in his pocket and hesitated. It seemed that he wished to vindicate his dignity which had been damaged, he felt, before these—er—savages; the dignity of a representative of the Great Father. He believed he ought to say something more; something patronizing. While he hesitated, there was slight movement in the room and Wah Ti An Kah rose and addressed the interpreter. Everyone expected a long harangue, and the commissioner believed he was in for a long speech in praise of the Great Osages. Many times he sat bored to distraction during these long harangues; he wished fervently that he had gone when he had started. But to the surprise of all Wah Ti An Kah spoke in one short sentence and sat down. He said: "Tell this man it is all right now—he can go now." The interpreter translated to the commissioner thus: "He said his people have said all that they came to say." The commissioner answered, "Very well," and as he left he hoped that the Osages would have a good time in Washington.

On the delegation's return to the Reservation there were more councils and the Major called all the chiefs together as he had promised. They went over the matter of the rations very thoroughly.They kept insisting that they would not be fed "like dogs" any longer. In this the Major agreed with them but he attempted to make them see that with the rations, the yearly buffalo hunts across the Arkansas, and the deer of the black-jacks they could live very comfortably, but that now the buffalo were very few across the Arkansas and they would have to depend upon beef rations a while longer, supplemented by the deer which they might kill.

Finally they reached a compromise, in which they agreed to have the beef rations another year, and a few articles of clothing, including enough shrouding for each woman, a pair of leggings for each man, and a blanket for each member of the tribe. This would assure them of sufficient clothing for the coming winter.

But there was some suffering when the rations were stopped. White men sneaked over the boundaries and slaughtered deer and turkey by the thousands, and it seemed that the game could not be adequately protected. Later when the grazing leases were given to the cattlemen, there were no provisions protecting the game of the Reservation, and thousands of prairie chickens and quail were killed and shipped out to market. The cowboys and the hangers-on of the ranches killed deer and turkey simply for the sport of killing and they sold quail and prairie chicken at a dollar and a dollar and a half a dozen in the little border town of Hewins.

Fortunately however the payments of the Osages became progressively larger, and they soon passed the stage of actual want. There had never been any reason for lack of food, except that the ubiquitous white man, in his inscrutable desire to proclaim his presence, slaughtered wild life. The great stretches of prairie and the wild blackjack hills, seemed to inspire in him consciousness of his inferiority, and he shouted his presence and his worth to the silent world that seemed to ignore him.

Where the Indian passed in dignity, disturbing nothing and leaving Nature as he had found her; with nothing to record his passage, except a footprint or a broken twig, the white man plundered and wasted and shouted; frightening the silences with his great, braying laughter and his cursing. He was the atom of steam that had escaped from the pressure of the European social system, and he expanded in this manner under the torch of Liberty.

A VISIT TO CHE-SAH-HUNKA

Chapter Five

NE AFTERNOON a runner came into the office. He said, "In camp of Wah Se Se Gah there is white man."

The Major looked up. "You have not seen this man?"

"I have not seen this man. They said I must tell you."

"What is this man doing?"

"I don't know what he is doing. They said I must tell you."

"Why haven't the police brought this man to me?"

"I don't know."

"Good, tomorrow I shall go there to see about this thing."

The runner left the office and soon disappeared along the road that led across the ford by the Mill.

The next morning the Major set out for the western part of the Reservation. His mules were fresh and alert. He crossed the ford by the Mill and was soon climbing a long hill. Quail ran across the road and the grasshoppers ticked in the grass. The blackjacks stood serene and fresh in the morning air, their eastern halves ashy green where the sun hit them while the other half was dark and cool like some metal with a patina.

It was July. The grass was no longer a vivid green but had taken on a golden cast; there was hint of gold about the whole landscape. Mauve flowers on shaggy stems stood tranquilly in the still air. A squirrel chattered from the fresh shade. As the mules topped the hill the crows were strung out in the flight above the trees, raucously proclaiming to a fresh dewy world the importance of all crows.

The buggy creaked and strained and the harness squeaked; the tires rasped on the rock ledges in the roadbed. One of the mules blew loudly through his nostrils.

The Major thought that life was full. He had eaten a good breakfast, and the lunch that had been prepared for him was at his side and still warm. He had the day before him. He would go to the Big Hill country to see the white man who was trespassing and then on to the camp of Big Chief where he would stay the night. Big Chief had sent a runner to the Agency the day before requesting that the Major come to see him as he had much to talk about. Big Chief's camp was in the southern part of the Reservation on the Arkansas river, across from Cedar islands. It would be a long drive on a hot day, but the Major was always glad to see his friend Che Sah Hunka, whom the traders called Big Chief, because he was chief of the Chesho, a grand division of the tribe. His camp was sanctuary to all races of men. They could come to the camp of Che Sah Hunka, if they were in trouble and there stay until the difficulties were settled, safe from attack by their enemies.

The Major anticipated with pleasure his visits to the camp of Big Chief, and as he drove over the prairie he thought of his friend. He thought of the stern face with eyes that smiled, and those characteristics which had endeared him to his people and to the traders. His gentle humor and his calmness were never taken for weakness by those who knew him. There were many stories about the prowess of Big Chief; many stories of his great sense of humor. The Major recalled an incident during the June dances at the Agency.

The dance had begun, and as usual most of the seats were taken by the women and children, and by the agency employes and mixed-bloods. During this particular dance there were some white visitors at the Agency who sat enthralled upon seeing their first Indian dance. They were occupying several places on the end of one of the benches.

During one of the short intervals, Big Chief, who was not taking part, walked into the dance area. He walked with the dignity of an oriental emperor, his beaver-skin bandeau almost touching the branches of the roof. Behind him with eyes cast modestly to the ground came his wife. He walked straight toward the visitors. As he approached they arose as one from their seats, whereupon Big Chief and his wife sat down.

All eyes were on this magnificent chief but he seemed to see no one, and with Olympian indifference to the people about him he sat there and watched the dancers, without approval or disapproval.

There had been no menace in his approach to the visitors. They had arisen instinctively without thinking; as a soldier comes to attention at a command. The roots of heredity are persistent things. The Major had always believed that Big Chief had enjoyed immensely the humor of this occasion, and he often wondered if there had been forethought.

Again he remembered when he had come to the camp of Big Chief late one evening. It was a cool evening in early autumn and the Major remembered how merrily the fire crackled. He and his friend had sat before the fire for some time in silence, then the Major had said that he had come to this part of the Reservation because there had been a gathering of Indians, and he had wanted to see what they were up to. Big Chief replied that it had been nothing and there had been silence again. The Major remembered the sad silence of that evening; the mournful stridulations from the grass roots and the absence of the usual summer voices.

Big Chief had gazed for a long time into the fire, he remembered, and then finally, had said: "My friend, it is bad that you have come to my lodge at this time. I am much worried in my mind about this. But I have thought about it, and now I think it is not so bad. At this time we have very little to eat here. But I have thought about this thing and I believe that since you are here for one night, it will not be bad if you eat that which we must eat for some time." Then there had been another silence.

The Major had not commented on the words of Big Chief. He couldn't have said that he was not hungry anyway. He knew that it was not the fact that there was little food in the lodge, but to be unable to offer food was to Big Chief a great discourtesy to his friend.

Presently the wife of Big Chief had come out of the lodge and offered them some burr-oak acorns and sassafras tea which they ate in silence. Then, after talking for a short time about the people and the condition of the Reservation they had rolled into their blankets.

．　　　．　　　．　　　．　　　．　　　．　　　．

On the high prairie a breeze was blowing and the sweat on the flanks of the mules had begun to dry, one of them snorting loudly when a flock of prairie chickens arose one at a time from the side of the road where they had run from their dust-bath. They kept rising after the buggy had passed, alternately sailing and flapping over the rolling green of the prairie.

Monotonously the mules trotted. A mere speck in all this green expanse that suggested something gold washed; on toward the meeting place of the green and the sky—the edge of the world.

To a lonesome man this definite meeting place of the sky and the seemingly endless green would have given assurance that there was an end; that there was relief from this glorious space where the winds whispered and the tires rasped out the miles, but to the Major with his thoughts there was no loneliness. He wasn't really aware that he loved the prairie and the hills; perhaps he had never thought about it, but he was much like the lover who loves all things which remind him of his girl; a glove, a perfumed handkerchief; the street where she lives. He loved the blackjacks and the prairie because they were the home of a people whom he loved and respected. He often thought that the wild prairie with its temperamental changes of weather was a perfect home for the children of Wah'Kon-Tah, the Great Mysteries which was the sun, the wind, the lightning; that which lived in all things which had life. The just, cruel, vengeful god visualized by these people.

To the Major Wah'Kon-Tah was more than the god of a so called primitive people. In his strict consciousness, he had seen, in his contacts with the children of Wah'Kon-Tah, how many of the credos of his own belief of Brotherly Love had become mere form, and without meaning. In his contact with primitive virtues he had realized this. This realization had broadened him and given him tolerance. He was never the monitor, nor did he like to be didactic, but he often thought he would like to hold the worshippers of Wah'Kon-Tah up as an example to some of the people who worshipped as he worshipped. Perhaps it was only the tendency to defend these people who were called savages; to defend them against those who do not understand, with the most human desire to say: "You see?"

But he could not lose himself in a few years. He was European and understanding of the people came slowly. First through his beliefs and then through his broad sympathy with humanity, and later through an intense desire to understand, he had begun to appreciate them, though in fact he was still the agent, still the government official, and there had been too many generations of the stern teachings of Right and Wrong, for the Amer-European iron in his soul to have dissolved so quickly. But he was no simpering sentimentalist, and therein lay the value of his sympathy and understanding.

When he came to trees again he noticed that the shade formed a circle about the roots; he looked at his watch and saw that it was 12 o'clock. Ahead he could see the elms that bordered Salt creek and he became conscious of being hungry. He could see the gleam of the water for some time before he reached the stream.

Finally on arrival under the shade of the trees he un-hitched his mules and watered them.

He sat by the shaded water and ate his lunch. The cicadas had begun their songs; those monotonous songs that in midsummer give a knife-edge to the heat. For a long time he sat and watched the little water-striders skate here and there over the surface of the cool, shaded water. He had heard that these striders were the symbol of one of the clans, and he immediately decided that he would look it up, or ask some one about it. From the tops of the trees where the prairie breezes played, he heard the discontented voice of the cuckoo.

When the mules were rested he hitched them and drove out onto the prairie again.

An hour later he came into a region where the soil was reddish and the ravines small and dry. There were great tangles of undergrowth; redbuds, wild plums, and dogwood. Then when some large oaks came into view he saw the camp of Wah Se Se Gah. There were some Indians sitting in the shade among the trees. He drove up to the camp, but the Indians seemed not to notice him. He got out and hitched his mules to a tall hickory tree, which had become slick and worn from previous hitchings. He walked over to where several men were sitting and sat down with them. For some time he sat, then he said: "I have come long way. I have come to talk about white man who is here." There was silence. He wondered if they understood him; sometimes he had trouble with the deep guttural sounds of the Osage language. Then again he said: "I have come to talk about white man who is here." Again silence. Suddenly he pointed to a man who was sitting with his back to a tree and said: "You will bring white man here; I have much to talk about with this white man." The man then motioned for a small boy to come to him, and as he came up he said: "Go bring white man here." The boy started toward some lodges at the end of the camp, then he turned around and asked: "Ee Stah Hah?" The man replied "How."

The little group in the hot shade of the trees sat silently. Then the Major noticed the boy coming toward him accompanied by a tall, bearded white man, and as they came near he arose and went to meet them. He thought the man, despite his tattered clothes and his hang-dog expression, had all the characteristics of a cultured person; there was something about the mold of his face and his hands, and there was about him a certain air of carelessness, which was unlike the swagger of the ordinary white barbarian.

When they met the white man said: "Yes sir?"

"I am the agent—have you a permit to be on the Reservation?"

"No sir."

"Do you know that the department demands that everyone living on the Reservation, who is not a member of the tribe must have a permit?"

"Yes, I have heard it."

"We must know who is on the Reservation and their reasons for being here—the department is very strict about these matters."

The man seemed to be dejected, but apparently he was not embarrassed. Suddenly he looked up at the Major with an expression of hopelessness: "Your department would not recognize my reasons," he said, "and I shall not ask for a permit, but in explanation to you I will say that my reasons are at least important to me—and perhaps others. The fact is I have come here as the most likely place for losing myself. I am not sure what power you have here on the Reservation, but if you have the authority to take me down on the creek and have me shot, I should consider it a great favor—in that way I could really lose myself and you would be doing something which I haven't the nerve to do."

For some time they stood and looked at each other. The Indians were pretending that they were not in the least interested in the conversation. The Major saw a log a short distance away from the camp and led the way there, saying: "We can talk over there."

When they reached the log and had sat down the Major said: "Now, do you wish to tell me more, so that I can better consider your case?" The man looked intently at some small boys playing among the trees and said wearily: "Guess it makes no difference one way or the other—might as well—here's the story.

"I lived in the east—name of the state makes no difference either—my name is not necessary to the story. I met a girl of position much above mine—I idolized her and she loved me. Her family raised cain when we were married. I had no money—those things matter in the east—at least it matters to soap makers and needle makers. I heard about the great west, and I came. I lived on a claim for several years and nearly starved to death. Finally my wife died and left me with two little girls—couldn't pay a doctor—she might have lived—that's the hell of it. I couldn't even feed the little girls so I changed their name and put them in an orphan-home. Her family knows nothing about it you see—couldn't tell them after all the things they had said and predicted—you see I couldn't call on them—at least I wouldn't. Well, I changed my name and have been wandering in the Indian country ever since. I like these people—you kinda forget." He paused for a moment and looked at the ground, then as an afterthought he continued: "Now you know the reason why I said that if you would take me down by the creek and have me shot that it would be the best thing that you could do for me."

"Give me some clew as to the name, the whereabouts of your children, or the name of your wife's family—they needn't know that I learned from you." The Major was very much moved by the story.

"No, I'll drift on—no use asking—absolutely no use." He got up and disappeared the way he had come; into the undergrowth of the river bottom. That was the last the Reservation saw of Ee Stah Hah.

The Major walked over to his mules, untied them and climbed into the buggy. As he drove out of the bottoms and through the blackjacks to the camp of Big Chief, he kept thinking of this white man. He believed to a certain extent in pride, but he believed that the man's pride was false, and that he had no sense of duty, and Duty was a sort of stern goddess, unbending, unflinching. Finally he clucked to his mules as though he were suddenly in a great hurry; a defense against the unpleasant thoughts.

It was growing late. The shadows had begun to lengthen and the night-hawks filled the air, dodging here and there in their chase of insects, and the warmth of anticipation came over the Major as he neared the camp.

Suddenly through the half lights of the late afternoon he could see the white dome-shaped lodges, looming white and spectre-like among the dark boles of the trees. The dogs began to bark, and some half-naked boys ran out from among the lodges to see who the visitor might be. But instead of running back to tell their parents, they stood and looked as though they were quite unconcerned.

Before the Major had descended to the camp, Big Chief came out of his lodge and stood waiting, until the buggy was at the bottom of the hill, then he motioned for some of the boys to take the Major's team. He approached and offered his hand; "My friend," he said, "it is good to see you." The two then walked to the front of the lodge, sat down and crossed their legs.

Big Chief's wife appeared at the entrance to the lodge and he told her to prepare some food, then he turned to the Major and said: "Tonight we have some fresh meat, and you will tell my woman how you want it cooked." The Major turned to the waiting woman and said: "My sister, you can cook meat long time for me." The woman said "Good" and turned into the lodge again.

The two men sat silently in the darkness. The bull-frogs were croaking down on the muddy banks of a small stream. The night-hawks had almost disappeared, except for a few energetic ones that gulped insects from just over the tops of the lodges, the air that passed the corners of their mouths during their dives making sounds like one blowing in a gun barrel. A few cicadas still buzzed from the tall elms, and a myriad of insects had started their chorus from the grass roots. It seemed that this part of the river bottoms was replete with life; as though here was the pulse of the universe.

The boys were playing some game like "tag." But silently, like grayhounds at play; a silent running and dodging broken occasionally by a slight altercation. All through the encampment forms were moving; women carrying wood and water and men leading horses, but with a silence that made their movements more purposeful than agitated rushing here and there. Swiftly they came and went, not in the manner of performing necessary duties, but as though these movements were a part of their existence; of being alive, like breathing.

Soon Big Chief's wife appeared with the food. There were lily roots, fried bread, a large piece of broiled beef and black coffee. The Major ate heartily as Big Chief sat like a statue, paying no attention to two lean dogs that came sniffing tentatively close to them, but his wife came out of the lodge scolding and waving a large spoon, and as the curs ran off with tails between their legs she scolded menacingly.

When the Major finished he wiped his mouth with a large red handkerchief. He said "My friend that is good; it is good to eat at lodge of Che Sah Hunka." Big Chief answered: "I am glad. Today my mind has been troubled." The Major waited for him to continue. Big Chief moved his position slightly, then began to talk in a deep voice: "My friend, I have said that my mind was troubled. But now my mind is not troubled. You have come to lodge of Che Sah Hunka. I will tell you what troubled my mind.

« 69 »

"Yesterday my people came together to talk about business. When they came together there was nothing for feast. That was bad. They came to me and they said: 'There is nothing for feast.' That is bad, I said, if there is nothing for feast. I remembered that there was cow which was visiting our cows. I said this cow should not be with our cattle. I said this cow does not belong here. I called some young men and I told them this: 'Go get that cow that is visiting our cattle, and kill him for feast.' Then I was worried about this thing. I said the owner might come and there would be trouble. But now my mind is not worried about this thing. Since you have come to lodge of Che Sah Hunka, I am glad and this trouble has left my mind. It was like dark cloud, but it is like clear sky in morning. You have come and it is good. I understand in white man's law that if man ate of meat from cow that had been taken, that it would be bad for him too. Now you have eaten this meat and you have gone against white man's law too, and my trouble that was like cloud is gone. I am glad you have eaten meat of this cow."

The Major smiled and he imagined that he could almost see the eyes of Big Chief smiling in the darkness. He wondered if the cow had really been a stray or if it had been from Big Chief's own herd. In any case he enjoyed the joke that his friend was having at his expense.

In the silence that followed the Major enjoyed the hot, heaviness of the evening. In his deep sense of well-being, the thoughts came and went but none stayed to disturb him.

Suddenly he realized that his host was preparing to

talk. He saw him pick up a short stick and begin to make marks on the ground in front of him, then as he made little circles with the stick, he said in simple Osage so that the Major would understand: "My people are like these marks. They make their road in circles. They do not know where this road will end. Some day they will take white man's road. I know this; but now they are Indians. They do not know what they want, my people. My mind is troubled about this thing. Some young men try to talk like white man; they try to act like white man. But they talk like white man who talks like crow, and they act like white man who acts bad, I believe. It is not good for young men to talk like white man who talks like crow. They send our young men off to school and there they learn to talk like white man who knows how to talk, I believe. I believe that is good. But at this school they make our young men do things like white man; but he is Indian. At this school they make things of iron, and they make things of wood. This is not good, I believe. I am troubled in my mind about this thing. I do not know if it is good for Indian to learn from white man. Indian knows many things, but white man says that these things are not good. I believe white man does not know many things that Indian knows. One time Navajo came to my camp. He had many blankets, and young men stood around and said: 'that is good.' This Navajo made pictures of horses and dancers and braves, and trees when wind blows, and young men stood around and said: 'tompa, that is good; tompa, that is beautiful.' But my mind is troubled about my people. I think they are like dog who has lost trail; they run in circles saying: 'here is trail, here is trail,' but trail is lost and they sit down like dog that has lost trail, and wait with no thoughts in their heads." Big Chief paused and the Major waited.

Quiet had settled over the camp in the river bottom. Occasionally a horse sneezed, and the hobbled ones could be heard moving with short jumps as they grazed. A barred owl sent his booming call into the night from a nearby tree, and another answered him from up the creek, like an echo; then again, and again the answer. A lone whippoorwill talked like a persistent, petulant child. A nearby insect sent his almost metallic rasping from the grass, and a frog gave one "garumph" and fell silent.

Again the low guttural voice of Big Chief broke the silence: "This mourning dance. I am much troubled about mourning dance; I believe it is not good. Much trouble has come to my people because of this mourning dance, and I am much troubled about this thing. Before white man came it was good to have mourning dance, but now it is bad, I believe. Some day Indian will take white man's road; slowly they will take white man's road, and I think it is good if they do not have mourning dance. Slowly they will leave their customs, my people, and I believe that mourning dance should go now. There has been much trouble between my people and white man because of this mourning dance. I think it is time they should stop mourning dance."

"How," said the Major, "I believe it is good too."

"Some day," continued Big Chief, "I shall go away. Soon, I think I shall go away. My people will say: 'It is Che Sah Hunka who has gone away, and we shall mourn for him.' They will have mourning dance but

I do not want this. I want you to say when I am gone: 'There will be no mourning dance for Che Sah Hunka.' Say to my people: 'Che Sah Hunka does not want mourning dance; I am his friend and he told me this thing.'"

A pang came to the Major as he sat in the dark with his friend. Somehow he felt that what Big Chief had said about his death was true. Indians were uncanny about such prophecies. Death to them was a mere matter of transition; there was no doubting it; they had faith and they were not afraid. They spoke of the end as they might speak of going to sleep. Not particularly in anticipation, but as a matter of course; as fate weaving its pattern in which night and sleep followed day and activity. The Major thought of them as fatalists, and he had a feeling that Big Chief's prophecy would come to pass. He said: "My friend you will live long time as councillor to your people."

"I shall go soon," he persisted. "For long time I have wished to do many things for my people. I cannot do these things now. For long time I have wished to be governor of my people, but now I believe it is too late; I have lived long time."

The conversation was ended. Big Chief arose and walked into the lodge and the Major followed. There had been a fire burning in the center, and the bed had been prepared on each side; the Major's bed between the fire and the entrance and Big Chief's bed on the other side of the fire. Big Chief's wife and boys slept back of him in the rear of the lodge.

They were soon rolled into their blankets.

The Major lay for some time listening to the noises

of the night, and as he lay, thoughts of his worries as an Indian agent came to him. He thought of the payments, and the trips across the wild prairie to the railroad towns in Kansas. He decided he would take steps immediately to have this matter adjusted by the department. Then his thoughts came around to the trespasser and his children, and he consoled himself with the thought that he would not give up until he had found the family of this man's wife; until he had brought about the happiness of the people interested. With this determination he felt happier, and he thought of his conversations with Big Chief and became vaguely unhappy again; he told himself that Big Chief would live a long time yet.

The thoughts became less definite, and began to fade as though in the distance, where they merged with haze. He was startled by the long mournful howl of a wolf coming from back among the hills, and instantly every dog in camp barked and howled in a different key. A horse snorted, and from down the river, he heard a woman scolding the dogs and they suddenly became silent. A cool breeze came into the lodge, like a breath that had been grudgingly released from the heat-blanket, and had come wandering up the valley, exploring here and there. Finally the sustained, almost audible hum of the silence faded, and sleep came to the Major; untroubled sleep in the lodge of his friend.

MYSTERY AMONG THE BIG HILLS

Chapter Six

EARLY the next morning the Major left the camp of Big Chief. As he wound his way up through the blackjack-covered hills, he wondered what would be waiting for him at the office. Every day brought something new, especially when the department became suddenly cognizant of some unimportant procedure which they had ignored previously. At such times there were many letters and routine cant, and the Major thought that the department was not unlike a whimsical, temperamental woman.

The matter about the money for the payments came to him again like a slight shock. The time for the next payment was approaching, and he had received no definite instructions about the number of guards he should take with him. He felt weak all over when he thought of his great responsibility to his bondsmen, especially since the fear of bandits, "which was like a cloud" over him, had been experienced on his last trip over the Caney trail, made with the currency. The mules were trotting along the rough road, but he tapped each one on the rump; an action on his part always indicative of annoying thoughts.

Soon he came out onto the prairie. The green expanse was in a different phase from the one of the day before, with its hot winds and its heaviness of midsummer. On this day the cool winds were almost screaming in the tall grasses, bending them, twisting them in merry, whimsical play, while great white clouds in the forms of castles, prancing horses, elephants and dragons moved across the sky; forming and reforming; dragons and castles and prancing horses becoming sailing ships and impossible piles of cotton, their mauve shadows moving across the green prairie; moving down into ravines and up hills, until losing themselves in the blackjacks and making of them a black and mysteriously interesting wood, in the land of phantasy.

The thoughts about the matters at the Agency soon left, and those things which loomed, became gradually less important. He allowed the mules to drop into a slow walk again; there seemed to be no urgency. Big Chief began to fill his thoughts, and a warm, flowing sort of happiness came over him, and he felt a desire to get back to the office and to the notes which he kept in the locked drawer of his desk. He was in the mood to express what he thought and understood, about Big Chief and his people. He almost convinced himself that the world waited to hear about his friend.

His thoughts toward the department became kinder, and the restrictions under which he worked, gradually lost their importance and he was almost ready to excuse the people in far off Washington in their misunderstanding and their whims, feeling that if they could be made to understand as he understood, all would be well. He began to feel that if he could express himself as he desired, he could make the department see that it was making a mistake in listening to the wild shouting of a few half-civilized whites along the borders of the

Reservation, whose only interest was to get the Indian lands; make it see that it was being misled in showing concern over the fancied rights of a few squatters and settlers, and turning deaf ears to the calm, dignified claims on justice, which the original Americans were making. A people who were concerned only in holding inviolable that which belonged to them, so that they could gradually adjust themselves to the overwhelming conditions that were being thrust upon them; attitudes and conditions so foreign to their natures. A people who asked nothing more than to be left alone, to enjoy that which was theirs by right of purchase. He hoped some day to make the government see that the civilization of the Indian would be nothing more than a travesty, as long as they came in contact chiefly with the white barbarian of the west; certainly they could not hope to become civilized by imitation of the white men with whom they came in contact on the borders of their Reservation, and as trespassers.

In periods of such optimism, the Major could put himself in the place of the department. He appreciated the checks and balances, and the restraint of initiative, in the various departments, and he once wrote boldly in his notes that the government was only the mirror of the people; of people who thought of nothing else except the mad exploitation of the natural resources, which included the senseless destruction of the forests and the game; things which the Indian had considered as gifts from Wah'Kon-Tah, and as such were revered. In such periods of optimism, he could almost sympathize with the white men to whom he referred as the low white who attempted to get the ear of the government, by whining about homes in the new lands of the west. In fact, during these periods he believed that understanding was possible, and desired by all right thinking men, and he used his own standards as the criterion of man's action, never taking into account biological processes. The great hosts of Europeans swarming to America had for him no biological significance, and that quick, impossibly sudden adaptation was the only solution for a few Indians on a reservation, in a period when a nation was in the throes of expansion and exploitation; a nation which had no time to be protective, only in the case of growing business enterprises.

The Major was a Friend. He had been taught how to live; to worship Duty, Justice and Honor, but best of all he had been born with a deep sense of humanity. If he set standards for his own life, what matter if he became annoyed at people who could not live up to these standards, as long as his humanity, a thing that was not taught, flowed out to them. He seemed to attribute humanity and understanding to all men, taking the attitude it was only dormant and needed awakening, so that it might function. He believed that the swarming European who thought of gold and land, and razed forests, would eventually come to an understanding of the Indian people; they need only understand them as he understood them, to experience the same emotions he experienced.

His desire to express himself was partly from the joy of having explored and found something unique and strange, and partly to bring about understanding, and one of his greatest annoyances was the fact that he couldn't express himself as he wished. He wrote his few notes under great restraint, and he recognized the result as being a sort of military report. He was afraid of being sentimental, and he had a deep fear of words.

He thought there was nothing more sickening than the "trash" that had been written about the Indian; the "poor Indian," and his treatment by the government. It seemed to him that when one became bitter against the department for some reason or other, he immediately wrote a book about Indians, in which the government was represented as blundering, ignorant and soulless. He was afraid of books which mentioned the "noble red man," and made no distinctions among the vastly differing tribes; as though one would refer to a Frenchman or an Italian only as Europeans, attributing to all of them the same characteristics and tendencies.

It was mid-afternoon when he entered the little valley of the oaks. The dust from his buggy rose into a thin yellow cloud, then drifted on the wind, and finally settled on the buck brush which covered the side of the hill. He waved his whip to a small group of men who were standing in the shade of a tree. He tied his team to a hitching-rack, and brushing the dust from his clothes, climbed the stairs to his office.

As he came in one of the Big Hill Indians was waiting for him. He was a sombre fellow, who was always finding faults with something, seeming to thrive on discontentment. He came to the Agency only when he wished to complain about some other Indian, or to inform the Major that hunters were again in the country of the Big Hills slaughtering the game. He hated all white men and he never lost an opportunity to inform against them.

The man from the Big Hill country looked at the Major with a frown. He pulled his blanket close about him and said in a voice full of menace: "I have come to talk about thing which is bad. You do not know about things that happen in Big Hill country. You do not know these things."

"I am one man—I cannot know everything—I haven't got eyes to see all over Reservation at one time."

"You do not try to find out about this thing, I believe. You do not know about this thing which is happening in Big Hill country."

"I cannot know about these things—I cannot be everywhere at one time—I cannot see over Reservation. If you know this thing which I don't know, you ought to tell me, I believe. You ought to tell me so that I can make it all right."

"You pretend that you know everything, but you do not know this thing which is happening in Big Hill country."

"Have white men come to your country? Do white men come across river and kill fawns, so that you can trail them by blood?"

"You do not know. I believe you don't care about Indian."

"Do Pawnees take white man's ponies and say that Big Hills did it?"

"In Big Hill country there are many things which you don't know about." Saying this he got up and went out.

For several days afterward the Major could not get this visit off his mind. He wondered if the situation was of real importance and if it would warrant another trip to the western part of the Reservation. There had been a gathering of Indians, which the police had reported but he found it had had no significance other than a social gathering.

In looking over his mail the Major found a letter summoning him to the United States court at Wichita, Kansas, and one from the special agent whom he had asked to get information for him from the department, as to the nature of the guard he should take on his trips for the money to pay the Indians. The special agent stated that the department felt that it should not specify as to number of guards to be taken on these trips.

For several minutes he sat with the letter in his hands, and thought of the dangers which he faced on such trips across the Reservation with a bag full of currency, and the great responsibilities to his bondsmen. The time for the next payment was approaching and he felt nervous; he felt very much alone. At such times he was almost bitter against the department.

. . . .

Some days later the Major was driving through the fetlock-deep sand in the Arkansas river valley. He had picked up his mules that morning at the livery stable in Arkansas City, on his return from Wichita, where he had attended court, and he had started on his way to the Reservation early that morning. It was a beautiful morning and he was happy; happy because he felt a certain relief from the worries about the transportation of the money for the payments. He felt relief not because the situation had been cleared in any way, but because he had come to a decision about the matter himself. A decision which perhaps resulted from a conversation which he had with a United States marshal during the sessions of the court.

A marshal came up to him one day, and after a few words of conversation asked him how he had gone into the Reservation with the money the June before. The Major told him of the premonition and the decision to take the trail across the high, open prairie. He told him of the cloud that had hung over him that morning, and which was dissipated only when he saw the band of hunters from No Pah Wollah's camp. The marshal then told him that he had arrested a gang of bandits in western Kansas for the robbery of a freighter, and it had come out in the examination of these men that they had been baffled in June when they had got a group of men together for the purpose of robbing the Major of the payments. They said that they did not know where he would come into the Reservation, so they had divided the band, and distributed them at all points along the borders, and of all the locations they believed that the one at the Caney Gap was the most important one as they had learned that he had gone to Independence this time. They said that they were very much surprised, when they heard through one of their spies that the Major was making the payments that June as usual, and they could not understand how he had got by them.

Upon hearing of this the Major had made up his mind. He had telegraphed for a ten days leave of absence, and expected the reply when he reached the Agency. He would go now by way of the Kaw Agency, thence to the Big Hill country and attempt to learn about the thing that had troubled Little Wolf, by seeking out some of the policemen, or asking some of his friends about these mysterious happenings.

As he jogged along over the high plains of the Kaw Reservation, he felt sharply the dangers which had attended his trips for the money to the various railway stations across the Kansas line. He remembered one time when he had come over the road he was now traveling, with the money hidden in nail kegs.

He had come to Arkansas City with several of the employes of the Agency, for the purpose of getting some lumber to put up buildings. He had driven his mules and had followed the wagons. While the wagons were being loaded he thought that he might as well get the money and save a trip later. While no one was looking he emptied the nail kegs, then placed half the nails back in the kegs. He distributed the money among the kegs, then put in the rest of the nails and closed them. Later they were loaded on the wagons with the other materials.

On the return trip he followed the wagons until they reached Timber Hill, five miles west of the Agency. The Major, then feeling that the nail kegs were quite safe, whipped up the mules and drove on home, where he had dinner. He waited for a long time but did not hear the rumble of the wagons. After two hours had passed he became very nervous, and went down to the office. He waited there for some time, but was afraid to evince his nervousness. Finally he went to the window and saw one of the men who had been with the wagons walking across the area. He hurried down the stairs and hailed him, attempting to appear calm. He asked the man what had happened to the wagons, and the man told him that soon after he left them an axle of the lead wagon broke and after several attempts to repair it, they decided to unhitch and come into the Agency, and take a new axle out with them the next morning, adding that "nothin' would bother anything, no how."

The Major recognized a dilemma. If he went out to the wagons that night, people might become suspicious; he didn't want anyone to know that he had the money in those nail kegs. If he didn't go there was the danger that some one would take the lumber. The only assurance he had was that it was quite unlikely that anyone would come along that road before the next day.

He had slept very little that night, and was up early the next morning, waiting with intense anxiety. Then he heard the rumble of the wagons as they crossed at the Mill ford. On seeing the teams plodding up the hill, he went out to meet the drivers and directed them to place the kegs on his back porch, saying that they would not become rusted there. He had been very much upset about the nail keg incident.

The time he had to bring the blacksmith of Coffeyville into the secret that he was carrying the money, was not so upsetting and certainly there was more zest attached to the incident. He had kept his departure from the Agency very secret, and in order not to attract attention, had taken just one guard with him. Being ever on the alert at such times, he noticed a man at the hotel, whose actions had aroused his suspicions. He felt sure that this man was interested in the money.

During his stay he kept the little black satchel close to him, awaiting time for departure. On the day before the start he went to the shop of the blacksmith, whom he knew very well, and told him of his suspicions. After a long discussion they came to an agreement. The Major came back to the hotel with an empty satchel, which later was filled with old papers.

The next morning while the suitcases and other bundles were being loaded in the buggy, he kept his eye on the strange man, and after everything else was loaded, he slipped the little black satchel into the seat. Out of the corner of his eye, he saw the man lift the bag as though he would determine its weight. Thus his suspicion was confirmed.

When he was in the buggy and was ready to start, the hotel man said according to plan: "Well, Major, when you comin' up for the money for your Indians," and he replied, "I don't know." He waved good bye to the group in front of the hotel and whipped the mules into a trot. Suddenly the blacksmith came running out of his shop and shouted, "Oh Major, you're about to forget your axle-grease." He stopped the mules, turned around and drove over to the shop, where a much smeared keg was loaded into the front of the buggy.

His mind was made up about the money, and he tapped each mule lightly to indicate that he had come to a decision.

He came to a high point, where the trail led down into a heavily timbered valley and where the Arkansas and Beaver creek joined. The river had deposited a floor of deep sand, and among the great oaks that sprang profusely from this floor, was the Kaw Agency. He made frequent visits to this agency in the oak-shaded, sandy valley; usually he stopped for several hours to make an inspection, but on this day he stayed only a short time. Soon his little mules were climbing the steep, limestone hill, which marked the Osage-Kaw boundary. Sparks flew from the tires, as he was jostled from side to side by the platey stones, and bumped by the strata that formed ledges in the trail.

When he reached the top, he whipped his mules into a trot across the wind-tossed grasses of the high prairie; a hot wind that came from the south burned his face like the air from an oven, lifting the dust that the mules kicked up and forming it into a cloud that looked like smoke. Horned larks flitted ahead, barely keeping ahead of the mules' feet; they seemed to be playing a game. Prairie chickens ran from the trail where they had been dust-bathing.

Far to the east he could see the line of trees which bordered the upper waters of Salt creek. A line of dark green, lying on the brighter green of the prairie, like some gigantic snake, above which, high in the wind-swept sky, a pair of golden eagles circled, as though they were about to attack the monster.

When he reached the reddish hills and the sandy valley of the Big Hill country, the Major began his investigations. He talked with many of the people, but all were silent. This caused him to realize that the matter must be grave indeed. Finally he drove to the lodge of a man whom he had appointed policeman. He was greeted warmly, and sat for some time with his host, neither man giving intimation that he knew what the "main talk" would be.

It was dinner time and the odor of cooking meats was in the air. The two men sat as though they were unaware of each other, waiting for the meal, both knowing that the time for talk was never before one had eaten.

The wind had died, and the heat among the hills was like steam. The sun seemed to be making a last effort to make life unpleasant by seeming to linger just above the high cottonwoods and the elms of the river; its slanting rays heating spots of the earth that the vertical rays had left untouched. Several disconsolate dogs lay panting in the shade of the Major's buggy, and for once the spirited little mules appeared lifeless, as they stood under a cottonwood tree. The cicadas sang monotonously their song of heat.

After the meal the Major and his host sat for some time. Then the Major spoke: "I have come to talk about thing which has made my mind troubled. We must talk of this thing now. Tonight I shall go back to Agency. There will be moonlight."

"How."

"One day Little Wolf came to office. He said there were things going on here which were not good. He said he knew this thing." There was a long pause, then the host said: "I don't know."

"Little Wolf told me about this thing. My mind is troubled about this thing. Government has sent me here to see that everything is all right. I cannot see all these things which happen on Reservation; I am one man, but I have appointed good men like you to help me. Good men who are not afraid. But you do not know about this thing. Some day people at Washington will say, 'This man is not good man for agent; he does not know all things which go on in that place; we will tell him to leave.'" The host moved slightly; then he said:

"I believe that it is all right now. I believe you can go home and worry no more about this thing. You have nothing to worry about now, and my people have nothing to worry about either; it is all right now."

The struggle within the man was evident to the Major, and he wished that he did not have to put him into such a position, but he could see that the situation was more serious than he had at first imagined. There was his duty as well. He attempted to keep urgency and curiosity out of his voice: "If this thing is all right now, there is no danger for your people and there is no danger for me. There is nothing to do about it but I believe that it will be better if I know about this thing."

"My friend, do not ask questions about this thing. Do not ask certain young man who has scar on face; do not ask young man who wears many colored thing which he got from Creeks, about this thing. Do not ask this young man about a very good gun which he has. They say this gun is best gun white man can make, and has much metal on it which shines like white iron. It is worth many ponies. Do not ask this young man to talk about this gun, and everything will be all right. The danger will go away then."

With a start the Major realized what had happened in the Big Hill country. Some weeks ago a policeman had brought two white hunters to the Agency, whom he said had been slaughtering deer and turkey. The Major had told them they were not to come into the Reservation again, and made them pay a large fine. He told them that they would be escorted out of the Reservation by a policeman. They had seemed so contrite; they had paid their fines so readily, and had been so glib in protesting their innocence, insisting that to be escorted out would be humiliating, that he had allowed them to make their way alone to Cedarvale, across the border, after making them promise that they would never come into the Reservation again. He remembered distinctly a new gun which one of them had; a splendid thing of the latest model, mounted with silver wherever silver could possibly be put. He had handled the gun and admired it.

The story was plain. These hunters who had seemed so honest and repentant; who had seemed so frightened when he told them that he could not control the Indians when they became incensed about the slaughter of their game, had not gone to Cedarvale. They had gone back to the western part of the Reservation to continue their slaughter. He hated lying, and these white men had lied, and he believed that retribution was certainly a part of Justice.

He rose to his feet and brushed his clothes. He looked down at his host, who apparently was not aware of him, and said: "It is good. We will not talk about this gun any more. I shall not talk with this young man who wears many colored thing." His host got quickly to his feet, and the Major extended his hand and said "How." He walked to his buggy and climbed in. His host followed him and said: "Next time you will stay in my lodge." He backed his mules away from the tree, and before starting, he said to his host: "Next time I shall stay in your lodge."

He followed the trail across the prairie. The moon was climbing out of the earth like a great brick-red plaque. It seemed to struggle out of the hot earth to get into the cool sky of the evening; a scorched thing which accentuated with its redness the heat of the August night, although as it climbed higher, and changed into a small white disc, floating over the prairie, the night breezes would whisper merrily in the grasses, and long before reaching the Agency, the Major would feel the need of a coat.

THE MAJOR VISITS WASHINGTON
Chapter Seven

N A FEW days after his return to the Agency the Major found that his request for a leave of ten days had been granted, and he immediately left for Washington. He took train at Coffeyville, Kansas. On every hand he saw the enterprises of the Amer-European, and nothing, not a hint that the American, the true American, had once occupied this land. Many of these people whom he saw working in their fields and turning up arrow heads with their plow, had never seen an Indian; to them he was still the savage of the "Penny Terrible," the scalper of virtuous white men.

As the fields, the farmsteads, the streams passed his windows in kaleidoscopic manner and the train rolled in and out of hustling cities, the blackjacks and the prairies of the Reservation seemed far away. It was not difficult to realize that after the Civil war men were too busy building great enterprises and spanning the continent with railroads; too busy opening the great west; plowing sod and building factories, and dreaming dreams, to think of a handful of Osage Indians in a wild country below the Kansas border.

In the cities, squat, hairy men from the islands of Greece; Germans, Slavs and Italians had taken the place of the Missouri, the Kansa, the Illini, the Osages and the ravaging Pawnee. From all over Europe they had come; from the gutters of the cities as well as from little white villas hanging on the mountain sides; from the monotonous flats of north Germany, from the crags of Sicily and little villages in the nestling valleys of the Alps; from the midlands and fenlands of England, from shanties in Ireland, and from villages of thatched-roof cottages in France and Belgium; escaping from the terrific pressure of social stratification in Europe to expand in America through the safety valve of immigration.

As these thoughts came to the Major's mind he checked them immediately, believing them intolerant and partisan. He really believed in the land of opportunity. He thought it was worth it all if a few of these immigrants could make their names glorious by this chance of expansion and thereby add to the glory of America.

But soon his thoughts came back to himself and the reasons for this train ride to Washington. Suddenly he realized with a start that this visit might mean the end of his associations with the Osages. Yet he must do something about this tremendous responsibility toward his bondsmen. Characteristically, some weeks previously he had made an irrevocable decision.

On arriving at Washington he went immediately to the office of his friend, the commissioner of Indian affairs.

"Well, Major," the commissioner said, "I thought you had a leave—what can we do for you?"

"Well, one of three things is going to happen."

"What are these three things?"

"Well, here I am down in a wild country, forced to go from sixty five to seventy five miles every payment to get money with which to pay the Indians. You don't realize the wildness of that country. There are perfect places for ambush, and let me tell you there are some pretty mean gangs of white bandits on the borders of that country—ignorant criminals who would do anything. You know that I am under a heavy bond and that I have a great responsibility to my bondsmen. Sometimes I sneak out of the Agency alone to get this money, sometimes I take Osage guards with me, but you see I want to be relieved of this responsibility, that's why I say that one of three things is going to happen: You either give me instructions as to the character of the guard I shall take, or second, I get permission to make the payments in checks, or third, failing instructions or permission I am ready to quit, and let someone else make the payments."

The commissioner looked at the pencil he was holding. He picked up some papers and placed them carefully on the side of his desk, then he looked up at the Major and said, "We place the money to your credit in St. Louis. It is your job to disburse it. You intimate that you will pay by checks. What are you talking to me about it for?" The commissioner paused, then he looked up at the Major significantly, "Do you understand?"

"I understand. I guess that's all. I'll go back right away. Guess I'm still agent—well, goodby."

As he passed through St. Louis on his way back to the Agency, the Major called at the sub-treasury and informed them what he was going to do. Then he filled the little black satchel with blank checks and took train to Coffeyville, where his little mules awaited him.

His spirits were high again as he drove into the Reservation. At the top of the first long hill he stopped the mules and sat there looking over the world of gold washed green, broken by blackjacks whose tops cut the horizon; not sharply but with curved lines like the lines of the prairie. There was no sharpness about the landscape; no abrupt pinnacles or barren rock masses, but flowing lines reaching to the blue that curved down to meet them.

As he sat there the wind moved the duster-tails of his mules and whispered in the grass. High over the blackjack ridge a group of turkey vultures wheeled in perfect grace. The Major always thought of the phrase "distance lends enchantment," when he saw these masters of aerial grace high against the blue. Many times on his trips over the Reservation he had watched them as they gorged on the carcass of a deer; some of them standing around gorged and disgusting while others spread their great black wings and reached their bare red heads into the fetid mass, their wing tips and their breasts greasy with fat. In the spring these birds guided the Indians to new born foals and calves, and they often guided the hunter to his wounded deer when it was too late, and searching parties looking for a lost traveler, on seeing these birds circling could say, "There, he is in that clump of blackjacks on the point of that hill."

Several days after his return the Major was busy in his office.

There were always Indians from their camps in the various parts of the Reservation standing around the office building. They held the attitude that it was theirs and was there to serve them, and they used it. Many of them were like their discontented white brothers. For everything that went wrong they blamed the agent and they came to him to talk over the matter; matters which they could have solved themselves, but in their state of doubt as to their status, and their worry over the strange new laws of the white man they wished to be safe before taking action. As a matter of fact many of them sullenly refused to take any responsibility at all, and came running to the Agency in order to place the responsibility on the agent who represented the government that had placed upon them these strange, half-understood restrictions. They were a proud and sensitive people and were almost as bound by traditions as people of the European civilization. They admitted no superior and certainly held in contempt many of the uncouth white men with whom they came in contact; those of them who had not gone with the delegations to Lawrence, Kansas, or to Washington, believed that these white men with whom they came in contact on the borders of the Reservation, and in the Reservation, were true representatives of the white race. They considered most white men boastful and ill-mannered and when they found exceptions they were disagreeably surprised. So in sullen vindictiveness they brought all their troubles to the agent whether trivial or important.

It is not far-fetched to compare them to the people of Judea whose laws the Romans altered or displaced, and whose traditions they sometimes smashed when they conflicted with Roman laws. As the people of Judea came to the procurator with their bickering so the Osages came to their agent. It would not have been difficult to visualize the Major standing hesitant, encircled by silent but determined Osages, demanding some readjustment or the punishment of someone whom they believed had attempted to destroy traditional belief. But the Major would not have washed his hands as did a certain procurator of Judea. Unless the matter was too trivial he always found some solution in his sincere attempt to play the rôle of friend.

One day one of these Indians who had been standing around the doorway or leaning against the window ledges, came into the office. He sat for some time and the Major could see that he wanted to talk about a matter which he thought grave. He recognized him as a man from the southern part of the Reservation who had his camp on Hominy creek. His name was Shi Kuh. The Major knew very little about him except that he was one of those Indians who held a grudge against the white man and who resented any interference in his affairs; "one of those mean fellas" as the traders called such Indians. Shi Kuh's visit would not be a pleasant one, the Major felt, but he said nothing as was the custom. Shi Kuh spoke in menacing Osage, "I have come to talk about my girl," he said.

"How," said the Major.

"I have come to take him back to my lodge. You will let him go."

The Major thought for a minute, then remembered this little daughter of Shi Kuh. A bright, round-faced little girl whom he had sent to Haskell at Lawrence, and who after returning from Haskell had gone to the Mission and continued to live there. She seemed to have no desire to return to her home. "That is good," replied the Major, "I shall have him come here and we shall talk about this thing."

When the little girl came her father began to insist that she return home again but she sat silently like some little statue of bronze, her hair combed straight back, parted in the center, and each pigtail tied with a checked ribbon. To her father's requests she shook her head in a way that she had learned at school. The Major was touched by this tall, dignified father pleading with his daughter to come home, but he thought it best that he remain silent, knowing that Shi Kuh thought that the white man's influence was bad.

After some minutes the little girl consented to go, but at the door she turned to the Major and said in English, "I'll go all right, but he must promise to bring me back when I want to come."

"Tell him that."

But when she asked her father if he agreed he was very subtle in his answer. They left the office together.

Some weeks later when the Major came down to the office he found a note on his desk from the little girl. She wrote that she wished to come back but that her father refused to bring her back and would he please send someone down for her. The Major felt that he ought not interfere further so he ignored this appeal. However, several weeks later another note came in which the little girl stated that her father had locked her in the little log cabin which the government had built for Shi Kuh but which was never used. She added that her father was attempting to marry her off and insisted that the Major send someone for her immediately. Yet he felt that he should not interfere, though he became very annoyed with Shi Kuh for attempting to marry off a mere child.

For some time he had planned some drastic action to break up, if possible, this custom of child marriage. He had appealed to the department but they had replied that there was no law warranting such action. Now this incident made him more determined to put an end to the custom, yet he felt that until he had made some regulation he could not interfere. During the next few days he thought much of this little girl in her fathers's camp twenty miles south of the Agency.

One afternoon some days later the doors of the office opened and the little girl came in and drew a chair up close to his desk. She was filled with the excitement of her daring but there was no indication of it on her bright little face. "My father," she said in English, "wishes to make me marry man I don't like. Today when my family come in the wagon to the Agency to trade, I just jumped out and come over here to see you, and I ain't goin' back neither."

"Very well, you are welcome to stay here but when your father comes you will have to talk with him—I'm afraid I can't interfere."

She looked at the Major with big black eyes and though he knew that her heart was beating in fear and doubt, and that she was at the highest pitch of excitement, he could see nothing but calmness in her round face.

After a few minutes they heard the stairs creak under the steady tread of Shi Kuh, and presently his great height filled the door. He came to the middle of the room and stood, then he began to argue with his daughter to come with him. But she sat shaking her head, telling him that he talked with tongue of white man; that he had told her things which were not true and that she would not go back with him. This made him very angry and he started toward the desk to take her but the Major arose and said, "Wait, you do not think of me in this thing. I am your agent—I have given my word to government that when anyone comes to me for protection, I shall protect him. This little girl has come to me. It make my heart heavy to say that father cannot take his own daughter. But this father knows that this little girl is also person, and that it would not be good to leave him when he has come to me for protection."

The Major then called one of the police and told him to take the little girl up the hill to the school. After they had gone the Major sat down again and watched Shi Kuh as he stood rigidly by the door; he watched him walk to the window where he gazed intently at the policeman and his little daughter as they climbed the dusty hill. Then suddenly he turned from the window, his eyes blazing and approached the desk. "It is good for you," he said, "you will call policeman but I shall come again. Then when I come I shall bring my gun."

The Major remained seated. He knew that sometimes Indians bluffed but his years with them had taught him to know when they were not bluffing. Shi Kuh continued: "Next time when I bring my gun I shall take him back with me and there will be no agent to say anything about it." The Major knew that a policeman was standing out in the hall, but he knew that it would only make matters worse to call him, so he said: "You do not understand my side; you do not think of me. Sometime we shall talk about this." This seemed to incense Shi Kuh more and with a quick movement he drew a knife from his blanket. The Major stood instinctively and put up his hand not as a movement of protection but as a signal to speak, "Shi Kuh," he said, "they did not tell me that you would kill man who has no knife." At this he threw open his coat and continued, "You see I have no knife; I cannot defend myself."

Shi Kuh stood for sometime then he laid the knife on the table. He walked to the window again and looked out on the dusty area in front of the office. He stood for a long time, then he came back and sat down. The Major waited for him to speak. He looked steadily at the Major for a short time, then he said: "It is good; you have given your word to these people at Washington that you will protect Indian. These people at Washington will not give that word back. My girl he comes to you and you must protect him. It seems good. But if he goes away from Reservation you will tell me."

"That is so; no one will leave Reservation until I have talked with parents."

"Good. Your mind will be troubled no more about this thing." And Shi Kuh left the office wrapping his blanket about him with dignity.

When the lists were made of those who were to go out of the Reservation to school, the little daughter of Shi Kuh asked that her name be placed on them. The Major told her of his promise to her father. She said nothing; she showed no emotion, though her disappointment was undoubtedly keen.

When the wagons were started on the long, dusty trip over the trail to the railroad station in Kansas, the Major followed them in his buggy. He thought of the heavy hearts that were in those wagons, but he felt that it was best for them; one of the unpleasant things in life; the stern dictates of Duty. He always felt a pang when he saw those brown faces at the windows of the buildings at Carlisle and Haskell, and he realized that for some of them this was the greatest tragedy of their lives. He realized that the cases where teachers were broad enough to understand, or attempt to understand those mysterious minds placed under their care were very few. But for the benefits which he believed would come to them he felt that a few months or years of unhappiness would bear fruit in the Indian's preparation for the final contact with the world of the white man. Especially he forced himself to think of this when he remembered those faces at the windows. He wouldn't let himself think of these austere buildings as prisons though they actually imprisoned many sensitive spirits, and spiritual imprisonment was more tragic to the Indian than physical suffering. He often wondered what their dreams were; he wondered about this when he saw a lone, slim boy sitting on some log or rock a little way off the campus. He thought he must dream of the pony's mane blowing in his face as the wind swept over the prairie, or of silent moonlight nights when the white lodges in the valley were the homes of ghost people. He imagined them listening from their bare dormitory beds for the coyote's chorus from the prairie, or the haunting call of the barred owl. He could appreciate the poignant homesickness which must flood the boys when they saw the V's of canadian geese against the red of sunset. It was a loneliness like the long howl of the gray wolf over the white world of winter. An iron loneliness of bare, cold walls and white man's idea of discipline; the loneliness of perfect misunderstanding.

As he followed the wagon over the trail the Major submerged his feelings that sprang from sympathy and understanding and made himself think only of Duty.

When they arrived at the station to his great surprise he found the little daughter of Shi Kuh. He told her that he could not take her as he had made no provisions for her, but she assured him that she had money and could pay her own way; that she had borrowed money from some of the employes and would pay it back. He told her that she must immediately write to her father telling him that she had run away and had come to the station, and that he had required her to write the letter on account of his promise. She sat down on one of the boxes, and with pencil wrote a letter, her dark face bent low over the paper, placing the point of the pencil in her mouth after every sentence.

On his return to the Reservation the Major gave the letter to Shi Kuh, translated it and explained to him all that had happened. For a long time Shi Kuh stood and looked at the letter. Suddenly he seemed to awaken from some deep thought and to realize that the Major was present. He folded the letter carefully and placed it in the beaded pouch which he always carried suspended from his left wrist. He placed it in the pouch very deliberately and then slowly drew the strings. His face was unreadable. This incident seemed to have no effect on him. He pulled his blanket together in front then extended his hand to the Major and said, "How." He turned and left.

The Major sat for a long time and looked at the window. It was his habit to stare intently at the long, narrow window when he was deeply moved, perturbed or angered. He was thinking of Shi Kuh. He knew that behind that stern, unmoved exterior there was a father's heart that was leaden; a spirit that was stunned. He knew that this austere man, on his long trip through the blackjacks would sing one of the social songs of his people. From his high wagon seat he would sing in a low voice as he beat the rhythm on the wagon bed with his whip butt. He would lose himself in this song so that he would not think of his poignant sadness.

Years later the Major inserted in his notes with his usual severe restraint, this paragraph: *"I learned, long after I had left the Agency, that this little girl had married a Pueblo Indian who had attended the school, and with him she had gone to the Pueblo Reservation. From the Agency officials I learned that she is still living there but that she retained her rights with the Osage people, and her children have been enrolled with her people. I never learned whether or not her anxiety to return to school was on account of her interest in the Pueblo Indian boy, but I have that impression."*

After thinking over the affairs of Shi Kuh and his little daughter for several days, the Major came to a conclusion on child marriage. He had really studied the matter for two years, but as usual was loath to interfere in the customs of the tribe. Now, however, he believed that the time for stopping this practice had arrived, so he issued an order that no girl should be married while a mere child, and if this order were violated she must be placed in school and remain there until she was fifteen years of age.

He explained this order very carefully to the Kaw people, whose custom it was to marry their girls very young. He told them that he had made the order for the good of the girls and for the good of the race. He told the Osages that they were a great people, tall and courageous and handsome, but that he had a great fear in his heart that some day they would become smaller. He told them that girls married when they were still children could not be mothers of big men, and that their tribe would become small, and sit around the lodges like women afraid to go out.

There was no comment on the part of either tribe; they took this order as they took all orders, in complete silence. Later if after considering the matter they thought the order to be offensive, they would hold councils over the Reservation and come to the Major with their conclusion. But fortunately with such counsellors as Hard Robe, Pawnee No Pah She and Big Chief, the Major was not worried about an order that was as logical as he believed this one to be.

He had heard nothing from it until one day news came to him that a little girl of ten years had been married in a camp about ten miles from the Kaw Agency. He drove out to the Kaw Reservation immediately and talked to the father and mother about it. He told them what he had explained to the tribe as a whole, and when they showed disinterest, he told them that he had power to cut off the family's rations.

Two weeks later the father brought the girl into the Agency and placed her in school.

The Major had begun to think that his plan was working, when he was shocked to find that one of the chiefs of the Kaws had come to the Agency school and had taken his little girl out, and married her to a man about thirty years of age. He wondered whether this was simply a bluff on the part of the Kaw chief to test this new order, or whether it was open defiance, but in any case he meant to stay by his guns because he believed that he was right in this matter. He also wondered about cutting off the rations which belonged to this chief, especially since he had no authority from the department; he wondered, strictly speaking, if even the department had a right to cut off rations which represented money that the government paid to the Osages and the Kaws for their lands in Kansas. He had been unable to find anything gratuitous in the government's relations with these people; these people had paid their own way. He was of the opinion that there existed no precedent for legally depriving one of something which was already his, and the department had already stated that the domestic customs of these tribes were outside of its authority.

But the Major felt that it was a bad thing, and he would take a chance because of his intense interest in these people, and he was still under the influence of the Rights and Wrongs of his inheritance and the Duty of his Credo. Or perhaps it was his humanity which sprang to life when Shi Kuh's little girl fled to his protection. After all, he believed that it was a small concession for these people to make to one who thought always of their interest, but in any case since he had taken up the spear and shield he knew these people well enough that he dare not lay them down until he had come to some settlement.

He was undetermined whether to call another council of the Kaws, or whether to carry out this order by depriving this chief and the husband of the little girl of their rations. He decided on the latter and the rations were cut off, and the next day he received word from the chief, that he was father of his own daughter and intended to do that which pleased him. He told the messenger to tell that man at Osage Reservation that a Kaw chief spoke; that a Kaw chief did not need rations of white man.

If the reply of this chief had been moderate as the Major had expected it would be, he would have resorted to milder means of carrying out the order, but when he received this reply he felt injured; injured innocence, a perfectly human reaction when one has had only the welfare of the tribe in mind. But from this slight injury grew annoyance, and then anger, and he immediately gave an order that there would be no more rations until this little girl was brought back to school. In this order he included the whole Kaw tribe.

Here was the iron hand of the conquering race. In his resentment of the chief's reply the Major became the Reformer, the military man with all the pride of the epaulettes of authority. The iron in his soul was not dissolved. Suddenly piqued by an insolent reply, he became the self-righteous parent whose children have shown indications that they do not appreciate all that he has done for them, do not appreciate his interest and love, and he brings into play authority and might. Child marriage became to him a grievous wrong; a terrible thing. He did not stop to think that he had no authority behind him for action, and it seems that for the moment he had forgotten justice; justice in her subtler phases. He was using as a weapon that which he had no right to use. This was purely the assumption of authority; the actual interference in domestic customs, where courtesy had kept him from interfering previously. He seems to have forgotten his courtesy in this sudden assumption of a rôle which was part patriarch and part conqueror, one who determines Right and Wrong with all the intolerance of strict creed and pride of race.

He had not heard from the Kaw Agency for three weeks when a runner came to him saying, that some of his people wanted to see him at their Agency. When he arrived he found quite a number of them camped along the bottoms of the Arkansas in the usual places. When they saw him approaching the camp, a man walked out to him indicating that he wished to speak. The Major stopped his mules and the man came up to him and said, "My people are hungry; they want to talk about this thing."

"That is good. My heart is very heavy; my heart is broken up over this thing. Marriage of this little girl has made our hearts heavy. Tell your people that I cannot talk with them about this thing. Tell them this little girl has not come back to school." The man turned and walked back to camp.

The Major was determined to hold his position; his bridges were burned. He was happy that there seemed to be very little resentment, and he was very anxious to have the affair over. He believed that the tribe as a whole was not much concerned about the matter at present, but if it were not settled soon there was a possibility that it might be.

As soon as the spokesman left the Major got into his buggy and drove to Arkansas City which was a short distance from the Kaw Agency.

The next day he returned and drove up to the government school building. As he stopped his mules a crowd of Indians gathered around his buggy and asked him what he was going to do, but there seemed to be no resentment or anger.

The Major got out and tied his mules to the hitching rack and was preparing to speak to the people when the chief came up to him and said he was ready to bring his daughter back to school. When the Major told him to bring the little girl the chief went back to his camp and returned with her. The Major took the little girl by the hand and led her over to the superintendent, telling him to send her to the matron. Then he turned back to the crowd. The employes of the school were standing in front of the building wondering how the affair was going to come out. They stood back some distance and waited with that hopefulness which a crowd watches the progress of something possibly tragic—held by a strange fascination.

The Major waited, then the chief stepped out from the crowd, drew his blanket around him and spoke to the Major and his people as follows: "My friends you have made my heart heavy. It was small thing but with it came heavy hearts. It was small thing and I bring my girl back to school. It is good. My heart is heavy to see my people suffer for this thing which I did." Having finished, he strode majestically away.

The slight rustling in the crowd which followed the ending of the chief's speech was stilled suddenly and the man who had married the little girl came with quick and determined movements to the front of the crowd and stood before the Major. They stood facing each other for some seconds, then the man spoke: "I am husband of this girl. His father gave him to me and I have something to say about this thing." Then he turned to the crowd and said: "This man is not our friend. He cannot be friend of Indian if he does these things. He thinks he can tell us what to do. He cannot do this. He is not our chief. He is here to see that everything is all right among our people. He is not here to tell us what to do about these things. For long time we have done these things. He must think we are afraid because you people have come to him and said, 'We are hungry—we wish to talk about this thing.' I wish to say this. It will be bad for him if he is not careful. Some day you will see many big black birds with red heads flying high in circles above Agency. You will say, 'Maybe someone's horse fell and died.' But if you will watch these birds some of these days, and you see them light near Agency, you will go there and find dead Indian agent." He turned to the Major, his eyes blazing with wrath, then he turned and walked away.

The Major looked at the crowd and thought he ought to say something after this abuse and the threat. He said to the crowd, and partly to the retreating figure of the man: "I have no fear of this talker. This man is coward. Only coward would marry little girl and make him into woman. Wah'Kon-Tah will surely punish this man for his great wickedness to this little girl." He heard no exclamations of approval, but he did not wait for them. He turned to the superintendent of the agency and said in English, "Go kill a beef, open up the commissary and give these people something to eat."

That night as the Major traveled the well known road between the Agencies he was not wholly pleased with himself. He did not then seek justification for his actions in making this order, but seemed to be waiting for the approval of Duty which had not come. He was secretly glad that this had happened at the Kaw Agency instead of at the Osage. He believed that he could not have given such an order to the people of Big Chief, Hard Robe and Pawnee No Pah She, and he believed further that such an order would not have been necessary after counciling with them. The feeling that he had strained the bond remained with him for a long time, even though the Kaws seemed as friendly as ever after this incident.

Years later however he seemed to find some justification for his action and inserted in his notes these lines:

". . . . This happened almost fifty years ago. The man who married the girl has long ago gone to the Happy Hunting Grounds, and I have traveled that road between the Agencies many times, both day and night, and am still here to tell the story. There are some compensations, as since this occurred, one who is now a woman long past middle age has thanked me for being permitted to live free and marry the man she wanted."

THE CEREMONY OF THE DOVE

Chapter Eight

HE OSAGES were ever aware of Wah'-Kon-Tah; they were ever conscious of his omniscience. They beseeched his protection and placated his anger. Like many people of other races they were under the influence of a class of men who played the part of mediators between them and Wah'Kon-Tah. These men lived on the credulity of the people. Sometimes they were the repositories of the sacred rites, and went through very strict training in order to be initiated into the priesthood. They were called medicine men. In some tribes their hold on the people was very small but in others it was all-important. In some cases they had degenerated to small tricks of sorcery and held sway over the credulous mass, but the more intelligent men of the tribe, like the leaders of Greece and Rome, did not always believe, but were ever ready to use these men to hold their power over the people.

Thus the medicine men held sway over the more credulous of the Osages, and though their power was not tremendously important, they inspired awe, and to them was attributed inscrutable powers in magic.

The Major had never talked of the medicine men and their crude remedies and panaceas, or of the mysterious rites of the Osage creed, though he often wondered about it, and one day he came face to face with the work of a medicine man.

A man came to the office of the Agency physician and said that he was sick and that he would like to be cured by white man's medicine. The physician examined him carefully but could find nothing wrong with him, and sent him away telling him that he was all right. A few days later he came back and told the physician that he must be mistaken; that surely something was wrong. The physician carefully examined him again and found him in perfect condition. Then he asked him where the pain was and the man replied that there was no pain but that he was sure there was something wrong. He said he didn't know where wrong was but he was sure that it was there somewhere. The physician was perturbed, and immediately called the Major. When he came into the physician's office he saw sitting in a chair by the window a man who seemed quite unconcerned and untroubled, as though he had just dropped in for a friendly call. But when the Major began to talk with him he ascertained from the inflections that he was worried. The Major said in Osage, "My friend you have come to white doctor; you say you are sick. Doctor says you are not sick."

"It is certain that I am sick."

"Where is this great pain."

"Great sickness is there but I cannot find it—but it is there, I believe."

"Why do you come to doctor when you feel no pain? What does medicine man say about this thing? Does medicine man say that you are sick?"

"He does not say that I am sick, this medicine man."

"What did he say?"

"He said one night he had dream. He said his mind was much troubled about this dream. He said Great Spirit came to his lodge. He said Great Spirit seemed very angry—he had war paint on his face, medicine man said. Medicine man said he felt afraid. There was voice, and this voice said, 'When grass on prairie is this high (holding his hands about three inches apart) I shall come to lodge of Osage; I shall call name of this Osage.' I said to this medicine man, 'What Osage?' This medicine man said, 'You are Osage which Great Spirit will call when grass is this high.' (Again measuring height of grass.) I am much worried about this thing. All time my mind is troubled about this, and my heart seems like bird that is dying."

"This medicine man," said the Major, "did he say he would go out in hills and fast and talk to Great Spirit about this thing?"

"He said that he could make everything all right, and Great Spirit would not call my name when grass is not high in spring. He said that if I give him bay horse, that he would ask Great Spirit to let me live. My mind is much troubled about this thing. I came to white man's doctor. He said that I am all right. I told this medicine man about this. He said Great Spirit came again when night was very dark, and clouds had eaten stars. He said Great Spirit said, 'I shall come to lodge of Osage when grass is not high; I shall call name of this Osage.' When this medicine man said, 'What Osage?' he said he would call my name. My mind was much troubled again and my heart was like bird that is dying. I came to Agency on my horse. Where there was green of prairie I saw nothing; where there were trees I saw black spirits, pointing to me with their fingers, like old women. I said I must be sick. White man's doctor he said I was not sick again, and I said I do not understand this thing—I must be sick. And this medicine man said he would talk to Great Spirit and let me live. But I do not want to give this bay horse. It is good horse, this bay horse, and my heart swells when I ride him to tomsheh feasts, and people say, 'Tompa, there is good horse.' But I don't know what to do about this thing."

The Major said: "Something tells me that this medicine man does not know about this. He wants your bay horse. Don't give him this bay horse. Go back to your lodge and do not think about this thing. Do what this doctor told you to do—he is good man, this doctor. Do not eat too much at tomsheh feast—do not drink white man's whiskey. Be good man and Great Spirit will let you live long time."

"That is good. I shall do this thing. I shall pray when east is red like blood. I will not go to these feasts. I will not drink white man's whiskey which makes my head sick." He got up with a quick movement and went silently down the stairs.

GRAY BIRD

Some days later Gray Bird, one of the men whom the Major had appointed as policeman, came into the office. He was a stately Indian, with the savage, alert movements of a wolf. His eyes seemed to see everything. He was very proud of his height and his fascinating proportions, and dressed in perfect harmony with his magnificence. His fringed leggings were always bright and fresh and his moccasins plain. Around his shaved head he wore a red bandeau, above which his roach appeared and quivered when he walked. His shirts were well made and had red figures, and on his blanket were many designs. When he talked he seemed to express some sort of wolflike energy by jerkily fanning himself with his eagle-wing fan, the butt of which was wrapped in buckskin with a thong hanging down. Over his left arm he carried a long, beaded pouch, possibly one he had got from the Sioux, as it was undoubtedly of Siouan make.

They had a mutual admiration, these two men. The Major admired Gray Bird's intelligence and his subtle humor, and he liked to watch him riding over the prairie like some red god. He was always amused at the extra dignity which Gray Bird assumed when they rode into the little town of Coffeyville; dignity that seemed proper to a guard, as it seemed totally unaware of the glances of the citizens. Gray Bird, on the other hand, admired the Major because he sensed his sincerity and felt that he understood the people, but perhaps not a little of this admiration was due to an incident which occurred in front of the Major's house, when the Major first came to the Agency.

Tze Xobe Sabe, a sullen bad-tempered man of the usual gigantic proportions of the Osage, had one day become angered with his wife, and had hit her in the face several times. The Major had, in a flash of anger, caught Tze Xobe Sabe by the scarf around his neck, and struck him a terrific blow on the chin. Such an insult to anyone else might have had a dangerous sequence, and there might have been the flash of a knife from the folds of a blanket. But Tze Xobe Sabe was a bluffer, a tempestuous bully, and this blow brought only respect for the giver. The Osages loved courage, and when this courage was evinced by a big man they were the more impressed. They worshipped size. They looked with contempt upon small people, and were proud of their name, the Great Osages.

Gray Bird sat down on a chair, pulled one foot up under him, and began to fan himself. "My friend," he said, "tomorrow they will make medicine man and we shall go see this thing. You will come to my lodge tonight; tomorrow we go to this place."

"Yes, I will come to your lodge tonight, and tomorrow we shall go to this place. It will be all right if I go to this place? I do not know this because I am white man."

"That is good. You are my friend and it will be all right."

The Major was quite anxious to see this ceremony of the initiation of a medicine man, and he sent to the barns to have his mules brought around so that he could leave as soon as possible, knowing that Gray Bird had ridden in to tell him about this ceremony and to invite him especially.

"Good, I shall come to your lodge tonight. You will be there long time before me. You have good horse."

"That is good. I shall be there when you come." As he said the last word he was up with one of his wolflike movements. From the door he turned and said, "I have good horse; I shall ride fast."

"Wait my friend, do not go. How shall I find this place where your lodge is?"

Gray Bird stopped. He raised his hand and made a sinuous motion as he said: "You know great river that keeps Osages from Pawnees? It is near this river, by spring that boils. There you will find lodge of Gray Bird." The Major remembered this spring near the winding, sand-choked Arkansas, in the southwestern part of the Reservation. He said, "Good, I know about spring that boils." Gray Bird disappeared through the door.

After lunch the Major set out for the lodge of Gray Bird. It was early autumn and the summer voices were almost stilled. The cicadas in their monotonous heat song had passed on, but there were a few isolated insect songs from the grass. However in comparison with the palpitant buzzing and rasping of summer, there seemed to be an ominous silence, as though the voices were stilled in expectancy of change. The air was clear and the sun genial without being hot. The distant hills took on deeper hues and seemed in the cool atmosphere to become sharper; a general deepening of the pastels of summer. Already several species of hawk had begun to quarter the prairie ravines and sail lazily over the black-jacks. As he climbed to the high prairie west of the Agency he saw several eagles making wide circles against the blue. All was peace and ominous stillness. The breezes seemed not to whisper merrily in the dying grasses of autumn, as they did in the emerald grasses of summer, and there seemed to be a touch of sadness in their spasmodic talking.

The Major flicked his whip several times at a great black horsefly on the flank of one of his mules, but being unsuccessful he stopped the team and got out, smashing the fly with his hand. Then he had to pull out

A Government Building

his handkerchief and wipe off the blood. He went to the head of the mules and looked far to the north. When he was driving along he thought he had seen dust floating against the horizon, and now as he stood there he was sure. It rose from the prairie and then hung like pale smoke. The longer he looked the more convinced he became that it was a herd of buffalo, although he knew that they almost never crossed the Arkansas from the high plains of the Kaw Reservation. He wanted to drive across the prairie and see about the dust, but he thought of the many ravines and steep escarpments of limestone and flint which lay in his path—the edge of the flint hills. He got into the buggy and clucked to his mules, but kept watching that cloud of dust.

Presently, far across the prairie, he saw a horseman riding along the edge of the hill. Soon he was joined by another. He could see that they rode like white men. And he realized the cause of the dust. They were cowboys starting out on the autumn roundup. Each year cattle from Kansas strayed into the Reservation, or were allowed to stray there by their owners, and in the autumn the cowboys came across the line to round them up. It was a precarious situation. The cattlemen had no right to allow their cattle to come across the border, and the Major felt that trouble was avoided by the tolerance of the Indians, especially when he could remember how the Osages used to take toll from cattlemen who found it expedient to drive their herds across the corners of the Reservation. He would never forget those wild horsemen with eagle feathers spinning in their roaches, and shirts ballooning in the wind as they seemed to flow down the hillsides and across the ravines. A mad cavalcade of many colors; riders bending forward over their horses' heads with the manes brushing their faces. The thunder of hooves and the clouds of dust, as they surrounded the herd shouting "Beef! beef! beef!" The Major had always thought it needless to wonder whether or not they got their beef from the trespassers.

Such incidents, he believed, were the basis for many of the claims which cattlemen had filed with the department against the Osages; such incidents and the feeling that the department would believe almost any lie about the Indian. In this way many of the cattlemen hoped to receive compensation for cattle which had died, or which they had never owned, and were careful to make it appear that there had been a raid on their herds outside the Reservation and not as a simple demand for toll.

The Major came finally to a clear stream bordered by elms, then turned down it toward the river. Dry cottonwood leaves floated and turned on the surface of the clear water, and the elms had begun to drop their leaves. Along the sides of the hill the sumac bushes were becoming crimson, though not flaming; they had just begun to attract attention. A band of white-tailed deer started off through the trees as the buggy creaked its way over the rocks, but they stopped suddenly and facing the Major watched his movements with wide-eyed wonder, but not too concerned to stamp occasionally the vicious autumn flies from their slender legs.

Soon he came to thick timber; the kind that grows in the rich alluvium of river valleys. Then very soon in a group of big oaks he saw the large lodge of Gray Bird looming among the dark, gray boles of the trees. There was tranquillity in this timbered valley; Gray Bird choosing to live away from the village with his two wives. His horse was hobbled and was busily grazing near the spring, the hair still stiff and whitish from sweat.

At the noise of the Major's approach Gray Bird came out of the lodge, and behind him came his wives. Though they did not smile, their faces showed expressions of welcome as the Major drove his mules under a large tree and unhitched them, taking a sack of oats out from the rear of the buggy with which to feed them. On these trips he always carried feed for his mules as the Indians provided no food for their horses.

Gray Bird came up to him and said: "My friend it is good that you have come." They went into the lodge where the usual fire was burning in the center. The lodge of Gray Bird was a large one, about thirty feet long by fourteen feet wide, the Major thought, but this space did not seem too large for the many things which it contained. There were piles of corn and vegetables, and quite a large pile of jerked beef, which had been taken down from the rack back of the lodge, where it had been drying. There were lounging pallets covered with skin, and many black pots and other utensils. There was an atmosphere of activity, as the women were preparing for the ceremony which was to take place about four or five miles distant, the next day.

The sun was almost set and the air had the sharpness of autumn. The fire in the center of the lodge seemed cozy as it crackled under the large pot in which vegetables were cooking. One of the women spread a blanket near the fire and Gray Bird without ceremony sat down drawing his feet under his legs, with his characteristically quick movements. The Major sat down on the other half of the blanket and they began to talk of things which had happened since their last visit together. The women busied themselves preparing the supper, placing it on another blanket on the other side of the fire. It consisted of the usual broiled beef, vegetables, fried bread and black coffee. Suddenly with what seemed like one movement Gray Bird was on his feet, and with a wave of his hand to the Major said, "How." They moved over to the other blanket where their supper was set and ate in silence.

After he had finished Gray Bird wiped his mouth with a great red handkerchief. He looked over at the Major, and with little wrinkles gathered at the corners of his eyes, said in English: "My women don't cook good, ain't it." The Major smiled in appreciation of the joke and the two wives giggled.

The men arose and went down to look at Gray Bird's vegetables and corn. The Major thought there was about half an acre, and that there was enough corn when dried to supply them for the winter, as they had no children. The sun had set and the air was uncomfortably cool, and the silence was almost complete except for the quavering complaint of a screech owl. The flaming western horizon could be seen through the large trees. As they came back toward the lodge, Gray Bird picked up some soft wood for the fire, which during the time between supper and bedtime must be kept fed with light wood so there would always be a bright blaze by which to see.

When they reached the lodge the women had prepared the beds, one for the Major between the fire and the entrance, and one for Gray Bird on the other side of the fire. Their own beds they prepared in the rear of the lodge back of their husband. They sat for a few minutes in silence, then Gray Bird said: "My friend, tonight it is good that we go to sleep. Tomorrow will be making of medicine man. When we come back tomorrow night we will have much to talk about."

The Major enjoyed talking to Gray Bird, but tonight he felt tired and the warm fire had made him drowsy. But after rolling in his blanket he lay awake for some time watching the fire die; watching the miniature explosions when the sparks flew out in all directions. Just before it died into glowing coals it suddenly brightened and revealed the dark form of Gray Bird rolled in his blanket. He heard Gray Bird's horse as he jumped in his hobbles from grass tuft to grass tuft, and the fretful movements of one of his mules. He thought he heard the distant, long-drawn-out howl of a wolf, but he was not sure. Then suddenly a barred owl startled the silence with his booming voice. After this the silence seemed to become more intense, and during this intenseness he fell into sound sleep.

The Major awoke when the east was just turning red. He looked over at Gray Bird's bed but saw that it was empty, and it suddenly dawned on him that Gray Bird had got up to greet the sun with chant. In his drowsy semi-consciousness he thought that he had heard the chant; perhaps from some high place near the lodge.

This prayer to the rising sun had always fascinated him; like most Indian customs it seemed to have such a simple beauty, that fascination which the paganism of Greece and Rome held for people, he thought.

He arose and walked out in front of the lodge. He saw one of the women coming with wood. He walked toward the spring to wash. The morning was sharp and the air carried the delightful scents of the bottoms; of frost touched walnuts and the very pleasing aroma of dying vegetation; an odor almost pungent. The little pool into which the spring flowed had a thin coating of ice around the edges, ribbed and veined like the web of a spider, and as the cold water touched his face youth seemed to flood his body and he felt inexhaustible.

Breakfast over, the four of them set out for the meeting place. For some time before they saw the lodges, they could hear the slow, muffled beating of the great kettle drum. A slow continuous TUM-tum-TUM-tum-TUM-tum-TUM-tum. Like the cosmic pulse; the pulse of the prairie and the blackjack hills.

When the party arrived they found that perhaps a hundred Indians had gathered, and were moving around in a shady grove. In the center of the grove an open lodge had been erected, in which the drummers had already taken their places, the chanters standing near them.

TUM-tum-TUM-tum-TUM-tum—then the singers broke out into a low chant, in harmony with these heart throbs of the earth; chanting their prayers to Wah'Kon-Tah, so that he might know that his children were gathered here for grave purpose. The chanting was spasmodic but the drum beats continued on as an undertone to the activity.

Aside from the rest was a group of medicine men, their faces painted with lines and daubs, which were symbolical of many things. Their faces were not masked, as they were not playing rôles in which they represented mysteries; they were simply praying for the attention of the Great Spirit. Several of them carried sacred bundles and rattles; dried bladders in which small pebbles had been placed. Among them stood the man who was to be initiated, and occasionally the group would break into a chant.

A short distance away from this group was a post about four feet high, and perched upon it was an elongated dove. No ordinary dove ever grew to such proportions, and the Major guessed it was the result of sewing two stuffed doves together, so that they gave the impression of one very long one. The dove faced the east. He seemed to have none of the timidity of a live dove, sitting with frightened glances and close-drawn feathers. Yet he did not resemble the usual, crudely mounted dove, with pop eyes and legs coming out from under the tail, seeming to droop from some incurable illness. This symbol faced the sun unblinking with an air of aloofness and gravity which fitted him perfectly for the rôle he was playing.

Soon the people began to take their places, assembling back of the dove, and as they assembled the medicine men began to chant again and the drum beats swelled slightly in volume, as though to remind the applicant of the responsibility that was about to be placed upon him. As the drums beat this warning to him, the medicine men began to chant fragments of the songs he must learn. As the chanting stopped the drum beats became more subdued, rising at intervals to keep this applicant's mind on the seriousness of his position.

Presently the medicine men came and sat down back of the drummers, followed by six witnesses who came in sedately and sat down in a row behind the medicine men. For some minutes everyone waited, during which time there were certain formalities among the medicine men. Gravely they sat there, and leisurely they performed certain things which the ceremony demanded; grave formalities to the slow throbbing of the drum.

The sun climbed higher and cast deep shadows on the tall grasses, that had begun to turn brown at the top. Soon all movement had stopped and everyone had found his place, and there was a period filled with expectancy. The Major saw several of the men he didn't know, turn questioning eyes toward him; slyly and cautiously they threw these glances thinking that he did not see them. To one less observant it would have appeared that he, the only white man present, was totally ignored.

Then the drums throbbed louder and the singers began to chant. One of the witnesses got up slowly and walked toward the dove. He carried in one hand a bundle of little sticks, about the size of a pencil. Solemnly he came before the dove and stood motionless for a few seconds. Then with great gravity he addressed the dove thus: "Fly away to Wah'Kon-Tah and tell him. Tell him worthiness of this one who wishes to become medicine man. Tell him I know this thing. Tell him this.

One time we were in country of Kaw across river. We were hunting. Wounded bull was charging warrior whose horse had stepped into hole. This man rushed up and stabbed this bull. Tell him I know this thing." Saying this, he threw down one of the sticks at the foot of the pole. He stood like a statue while the singers chanted with increased volume, and the drums became louder and more insistent.

During this interval when the drums beat louder and the chanters raised their voices, Wah'Kon-Tah was being given time to consider these deeds.

Suddenly the drums fell back to their throbbing, and the singers lowered their voices and chanted softly, and the witness began to talk to the dove, "Fly away to Wah'Kon-Tah and tell him. Tell him this. One time we were on great plains far to west. There were many buffalo that season. There were many tribes there hunting buffalo. There were Pawnee and Cheyenne and many others. This man wounded bull and this bull ran toward where woman was skinning buffalo. He killed this bull. He looked for his wife to come but he was far behind. He thought he would get on his horse and go for more buffalo. He saw woman standing there. This woman was not skinning buffalo. He said to this woman, 'You cannot find arrows of your man?' and this woman said, 'I have no man.' This man answered. 'Take that.bull I have killed. Look well at my arrows. When you find arrows marked as they are marked, you will know that I have killed buffalo. You will know that buffalo is yours when you find my arrows.'"The witness threw down another stick and the low chanting swelled; the drum beats became louder.

After some time he had thrown down all of his sticks, and he came gravely back to his seat. As soon as he was seated several men in charge of the ceremony came up to him, and gave him a blanket and some leggings. These things had been agreed upon as payment for his services in testifying for the applicant.

When the drum beats had become low again and the chanting became a murmur, another witness got up and went up to the dove, also telling of the deeds of the applicant.

When the sun stood in mid-sky, there was a recess, and there was much to eat; great pieces of beef that had been broiled over a fire, soup, fried bread and black coffee.

All afternoon the ceremony went on, and the people sat gravely and watched. The singers chanted, and as an undertone was the slow pulse beats of the drum.

The sun swung toward the west, and the shadows lengthened on the grass. Then the sun set in a blaze of red and the air became chilled. The drum beats stopped, and the people seemed to melt into the darkening woods; silently, and with dignity they disappeared, leaving the open ceremonial lodge, standing silently in the chilled twilight.

Back at Gray Bird's lodge the Major again fed his mules, and the women prepared something to eat, and prepared the beds as they had done the night before. The Major and Gray Bird sat silent for a long time, the fire lighting their faces. Then Gray Bird said: "My friend this ceremony which you have seen. I believe you think it is not good. You are my friend. I will talk about this thing that is in my mind. Long time ago I went through this ceremony. It cost me many ponies. It cost me forty ponies, I believe. I found my witnesses and I said to them you will say this thing for me. And they said yes we will do this thing for you, but you must give us this or that, and I say good. Every time I had to give something to medicine men. Every time I had to pay for these services. I learned songs and all these things that have been known by our people for long time. But I know all this and my mind has not changed. It is still like fog in morning, and many things I do not understand. Many things which trouble my mind. But these medicine men, they do things which are magic, and people say that is good. Medicine man tells people to do these things and people say that is good we will do it. For many years it is like this, but I do not know about these things."

For a long time they sat, then Gray Bird rose quickly to his feet. He stepped to the entrance of the lodge and went out, and the Major could see him through the door, as he stood looking into the sky. Then he came back and unceremoniously rolled into his blankets. The Major rolled into his blankets on the other side of the fire. Gray Bird's wives had gone to bed sometime earlier.

Soon Gray Bird began to stir, and rolled over on his back. He seemed to be thinking about something. He began to talk: "My friend I have thought much about this thing. I have thought much about spirit of man. I don't know what white man thinks about this. I've heard white man say much about brain but I don't know. I do not believe that home of spirit of man is in head. I will show you what I mean.

"Sometime when I go hunting I kill deer. I come back and I am very happy. I say there will be plenty of venison. But soon I pass lodge of woman. This woman has lost his man. This woman has some small children and there is no man to hunt for him. I stop at lodge of woman who has last his man and I cut off big piece of this venison. I say I have brought you something to eat. As I walk away my heart swells. I put my hand on my heart and I can feel it swell. I feel happy and I am glad to see anybody. I feel of my head. But I cannot feel any change in my head. It feels same. My heart is only thing that changes. Then I go out hunting again and I kill deer. I am happy. Soon I pass this lodge of woman who has no man. I say my heart is heavy for this woman. I look at venison and I say we need all this venison. I walk on and I do not cut off piece of this venison for woman. My heart seems to become very small. I put my hand on my heart and it seems to have gone away. I can feel nothing there. I do not want to see anyone. I am not happy. When I put my hand to my head I do not feel anything. It has not changed. That is what I think about this thing. Home of spirit is in heart. This I believe. I would like to know what white man thinks about this thing."

The Major thought for some time. He remembered the study of this matter under a very dear professor, who referred many times to the great English philosopher, Doctor Locke, and his ideas of the relationship of mind to matter. He felt that he had never been able to come to any conclusion about the problem. In fact he had forgotten about it in the busy life since his university days. He suddenly realized that here was an Indian in the Osage reservation, with no books in the long winter evenings troubling his mind about matters which scientists over the world had discussed. He remembered that he had also thought such things important during his university days, but one out in the world seemed to worry very little about it, and when he answered Gray Bird's question he said: "This thing you have asked me is very difficult. I believe that I do not know about this. But I believe, that which you believe about this thing is good."

There was another silence, then Gray Bird continued: "A thing has been bothering my mind since you were here." This time the Major knew by the inflection that the matter was not grave, and he waited for a joke. "My wives, I do not know about them. In other times when wood is needed for fire, they go out and get this wood. They hitch up team and go out and get this wood for fire. If I wanted horse they would go and get horse and have it ready for me. Many times when I would come home tired they take horse, and take off saddle and put it away. Now I do not understand. When wood is small they say to me, 'There is very little wood—you must get some wood.' And they say when I come to lodge and ask them to put horse away, 'We are busy—put it away yourself.' My mind is troubled about this thing—I do not know about this."

The Major had noticed that the women had been listening to their conversation all evening, and after Gray Bird had stopped talking he could hear suppressed giggling in the back of the lodge. He raised his voice a little and addressed the women, "Wetunka, what is trouble?" One of the women spoke. "He thinks he is great man now, our husband. Many times he has gone with you to these places to get money for payments. He has become very proud and has changed much since he goes with you to all these places. He comes to us and says he must have shirts. He says to us he wants shirts in many colors. He says he will not wear shirts which we make from skin of deer. He must have shirts which trader sells. We must spend much time dressing him when he goes to these places with you. When he goes to dances it is good. We dress him in all of his things and paint his face. But this thing when he goes many times to Agency, and when he goes many time to these places with you he must have many new shirts. He must have shirts to take along with him so he will have shirt to put on when he gets to these places. All day we are busy making these shirts for him. We cannot do other things when we are doing this."

There was humor in the situation as the four of them lay there in the darkness. Gray Bird could laugh at himself and his playing the rôle of dandy, and no one enjoyed the situation more than he. He was thinking of his wives' baffled attempts to play their part of the tradition, in keeping their warrior well equipped. The wives on the other hand, saw the humor of this great man who was only a boy, with the vanity of a boy. The delightful situation pleased the Major immensely. He had always remarked Gray Bird's magnificence on the trips out of the Reservation. He always rode good horses and his body was straight, and everything he did was with those quick movements of the wolf.

Gray Bird broke the silence in English. He spoke English only when he wished to make some satirical observation to some other Indian or to a close friend, "My wife he not good, ain't it?" The answer which he seemed to be expecting came promptly from one of the women who spoke also in English: "Hunh, shuh, he's crazy. I bet you don't blame us that-a-way; it's his fault. He ain't got no right to say things like that." There was no sound of laughter, though the atmosphere was charged.

Gray Bird turned over in his blanket and silence came into the dark lodge. The fire had died down, the wood used for the purpose of lighting the lodge had burned quickly. Outside a heavy, autumnal silence crept over the great oaks. A chill silence under the blinking stars.

BIRTH OF THE OSAGE NATION

Chapter Nine

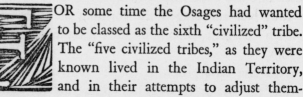OR some time the Osages had wanted to be classed as the sixth "civilized" tribe. The "five civilized tribes," as they were known lived in the Indian Territory, and in their attempts to adjust themselves to the new life they were to lead, had organized themselves and had a government of their own through which they transacted their business with the department. This method appealed to the mixed-bloods of the tribe and was more or less agreeable to the full-bloods as they were at that time friendly with the tribes which formed this organization. They traded with the Creeks for sweet potatoes and after a period of bitter wars were friendly with the Cherokees. They were not hereditary enemies as were the Pawnees. In fact the tribes that composed this government were tribes which had been removed to the Indian Territory from the southern states, and the Osages had not come in contact with them until they had become neighbors on the east.

They had met with these five tribes in council about the matter and had urged their councillors to make every attempt to bring about inclusion in this government, but as usual there was much confusion, indecision and half-heartedness on both sides. The Osages were never included as the sixth "civilized tribe."

The government of the Osages was and had always been by the chieftain rule. Each band had its chief who was hereditary, and as in all hereditary rule there were some great chieftains and there were naturally some with meager qualifications. But after the removal of these people to the Reservation south of the Kansas line the department, in attempting to break up this rule, had encouraged the forming of other bands of which energetic, ambitious men accepted the chieftainships.

After the failure of this council with the tribes to the east, the Major thought the time ripe for the organization of the tribe in order to bring in a more democratic system, though as a matter of fact they were almost communist in their community ownership of the land and cattle. But he felt that many of the qualified hereditary chiefs could be displaced by the more intelligent men; men who were natural leaders. It was not a question of control entirely, but he believed that inasmuch as they would sooner or later be taking their places as citizens, that a method of self government modeled after the European idea would be a training school for them, and make their eventual adjustment easier. Then he thought he could shift the settlement of many of the difficulties that were always arising, to this government. He had found that the settlement of these small difficulties was quite a task. More so because no matter how trivial the dispute he called both sides to the office or went to the different encampments and listened attentively to them, making it a rule to come to no decision on the matter until he had heard both sides. He found that he had to devote one day each week to these complaints.

The police system had been formed and he believed that it was working satisfactorily. In the policemen whom he appointed he failed to find that swagger of small authority that he had noticed among the Amer-Europeans; that crude vanity and childish display of many of the marshals and policemen of the cities and the stage drivers of the far west. These Indian police were proud to be designated as the policemen of the Reservation and went about their business with honesty and the silent dignity so natural to them, but remaining loyal to their tradition as Osages. There were many dilemmas but the Major understanding them often aided them in satisfying their honor.

Always in thinking of the Indian police the Major thought of his friend Gray Bird and his appointment as policeman. Soon after the appointment the Major went to visit Gray Bird for the first time at one of his camps west and south of the Agency. Gray Bird had questioned him very closely as to his duties. The Major told him that the instructions were of necessity indefinite but that he should hold himself ready to come to the Agency at any time he was called and that he should see that no crime was committed. "How," he had said, "I will do this thing—when you call I shall come. This short gun," he said, pointing to the carbine, "I shall carry with me." The Major had said that that was the reason why he had been given the "short" gun.

Sometime later the Major had been called to the camp of Gray Bird's band by a messenger who said mysteriously that there would be trouble there in a few days. When he arrived he went immediately to Gray Bird's lodge and found him ill on his blankets. He stayed by him some time, talked of many things, then said: "I have come to talk about thing which I have heard."

"How," Gray Bird had answered, looking straight into the Major's eyes.

"They say that there will be trouble here. I should like to know about this thing."

"It will be nothing, this thing. There will be nothing to trouble your mind."

"I hear these things and I don't know. I have come to you to know about this thing."

"That is good. I will tell you about this thing. One day my wife was at spring. Young man came out of bushes and made signs to my wife. He made signs for him to come with him to bushes. My wife told me about this thing. I said that is bad. I sent one to talk with this young man. I said tell this young man that I am sick but soon I shall be well. I said tell this young man that 'short' gun and Gray Bird will settle this thing. Many friends of this young man came to my lodge and there was much talk about this thing. I said this is bad and I shall attend to this with 'short' gun. They came back to my lodge, these friends of this young man and they brought with them many ponies and tied them to stakes by my lodge. I said I will settle this matter with 'short' gun. I was sick. I took my knife in my mouth. I crawled out to these ponies and cut ropes. My head was very heavy. I thought trees were dancing. I stayed outside with my head on ground. Soon trees were not dancing. I crawled back to my bed. Then I believe the friends of this young man sent runner to Agency to tell you about this thing. But there is nothing for you to worry about."

The Major repeated: "I am worried about this thing. There will be great trouble about this thing. My heart is heavy." Gray Bird looked at him with unbelief, then seeing that the Major was serious, thought for some time, but seemed to be unable to give expression to the thought which passed through his mind. The Major appreciated the conflict of duty and the traditions of the tribe. He wished to aid Gray Bird in his dilemma but he knew the character of Gray Bird and he scented failure. The Major spoke again: "There will be trouble about this thing. My heart is heavy." Again Gray Bird looked at him, then he said:

"How. That is good. We do not understand this thing together. You give me this 'short' gun to see that everything is all right. If you want this thing to go on here you take this 'short' gun with you when you go home. I am not policeman now."

"I do not want this gun. I see this thing. You settle this thing when you get well." There was a pause. The Major got up and prepared to leave. "I hope you will be well again soon." He left the lodge.

All the time he had been in the lodge of Gray Bird the friends of the young man had been hiding close by, and when he came out and got into his buggy to drive off they followed him. When out of sight of the lodge they rode up on each side and he stopped the mules. "Ho," said the leader, "what will he do about this thing, this Gray Bird."

The Major looked at each one of the young men, then said to the leader, "It is bad this thing. This young man your friend wishes to live. It will be good if he leaves this part of Reservation."

When Gray Bird was well again the young man had gone.

In the order for the establishment of the police system the department had also ordered that there should be a police court but the Major had thought it would be better to have the organization of this court in connection with an executive branch and let it be composed of men of their own choosing. He could not find an orderly way of doing this so when two young mixed-bloods came to him he suggested that they undertake the matter. They consulted with the people of other Indian nations where this plan had been in effect and then set out to prepare a constitution, being assisted by officers of the Cherokee Nation. After a year of work they had the constitution ready and submitted it to the vote of the people.

This constitution provided for the division of the Reservation into five districts with as nearly the same number of people in each of the districts, each district having three members elected to the National Council, and provided for a chief executive who would be called Principal Chief, who was to be elected along with an assistant chief, supreme judge, and other officers composing the judicial division of the proposed government.

The Major believed that this constitution would be much more democratic and would give the people of the tribe a chance to learn to cast their votes, and in general prepare them for the time when they would become citizens of the United States. He was pleased when it was voted on by the members of the tribe and accepted, and the officers provided for therein were duly elected and qualified. He was afraid however that the mixed-bloods would take the matter into their own hands and follow too closely the ways of their white brothers, in which case the full-blood, in silence and dignity, would withdraw and take little interest. He thought it would be ideal if the Indians could absorb the Amer-European method instead of changing completely. He wished that they might build upon this system, yet retain their own identity. He, like many political idealists, could see a great structure arising from the coalescing of these two races, and though it would be humorous to think of the Indian influencing the millions that were pouring into the United States, he thought it would not be impossible to build such a government in this small community; an experimental farm for government.

He had always loved the simplicity of Indian oratory, and thrilled to those gestures of dignity and gravity. Such simplicity struck him forcibly after hearing the harangues of Amer-Europeans in the florid style of that period.

The Major dreamed many dreams as he drove over the prairie, but of these dreams no one knew. If he hoped fervently for this little government among the blackjacks, it was because he loved these tall people of the hills and the prairie; because understanding them, he believed that if they were allowed to develop in their own way, and retain their admirable characteristics, that they might add brilliance to the brilliance which he felt surely would someday be America's.

And thus the Osage Reservation became the Osage Nation, with the executive, the judicial, and the council, and when all was ready he submitted it to the department at Washington. The department was noncommittal, however, and failed to approve it. The congress also refused to approve it, but the constitution of the Osage Nation lived, and when matters came up for the consideration of the tribe, instead of submitting them to the chiefs they were submitted to the council, and the action of this council was taken as the action of the nation, and their actions were approved by the department when the department saw fit, reserving the right to disapprove or ignore anything which the council might pass. But to the Major the government of the nation was a reality and the council took over some of the responsibilities that had been his.

The new council immediately provided for a whipping post, which seemed to the Major and many of the other people of the nation a rather archaic provision, but there was no difficulty about it. Then they provided a regulation requiring all children of school age to attend school a certain number of months during the year, and as a penalty provided that the annuities of the parents should be stopped if such children were kept out of school. The Major smiled with pleasure at this regulation when he considered that the council was composed mostly of full-bloods who have a natural aversion for anything that seems to imply coercion. He was certainly gratified with the results. Prior to this regulation, the employes of the Agency school were obliged to go out over the Reservation and beg for children. They were more or less successful in getting the boys but the parents usually would not allow the girls to leave home.

When this regulation by the national council was submitted to the department it was approved immediately and the next autumn when school opened all those parents who still persisted in keeping their children at home suffered the penalty of having their annuities held up. When these people came into the office to protest they were informed that they had not complied with the regulation of the council. At first they felt the injustice of this regulation but when they clearly understood that the men whom they had elected as councilmen had made this regulation they brought their children into school.

The Major felt as they did; that the council was using a weapon which was not theirs to use, as this money belonged to the people and there could not be anything conditional about the payment of it. However, he was overjoyed that the council, composed mostly of full-bloods, had made the regulation for their own people. It made him glow with pride when he believed that this action by an Osage council was the first case of compulsory education among the Indians; education in the Amer-European sense of the word, though for generations the boys of the tribe had undergone training and education that was Spartan in its severity.

White men brought whiskey into the Reservation and sometimes sold it to the Indians but there were not many full-bloods addicted to the drinking of whiskey, though several of the traders and mixed-bloods drank freely, and the council believing that there might be a possibility that another law, confirming the federal laws, might not be out of place, made a regulation which was promptly approved by the department, that any member of the tribe who had been seen drunk, or who was in the habit of drinking, would be punished by the holding up of his annuity until the habit was corrected. But to the Major, drinking among the Osages had never been a problem. He realized that there were few who drank to excess, and he was glad to see such a regulation passed, though he believed that it was not of great importance; except perhaps to high officials in the government who frequently sent their sons and their special friends to some position in the Reservation, or asked permission for them to stay there so that they could not obtain whiskey, and as the Major wrote in his notes, *"Be free from the civilizing influence of the white man and under the protection and care of the wild Indian."*

It seemed to the Major that the Indian would never be left alone to work out his own destiny; it seemed to him that until the last foot of Indian land had fallen into the hands of the land-greedy hordes there would be chaos. These people who swarmed the west were restive and dissatisfied, and most of them white barbarians if they were compared with people of their own race who had reached the latest stage in civilization. But because they were white they took great pride in the fact that all white men were assumed to be civilized, apparently because of their whiteness. These barbarians waited on the borders of the Osage nation for something to happen; they continually filtered into the Reservation, spending their time cursing the government because it would not take this last dwindled Reservation from the Osages and throw it open to settlers. They shouted to the tops of their brazen lungs for congress to allow them to enter and felt abused when they were forbidden. No trickery was of too little importance for them to try or no lie insidious enough. During the Major's trips into Kansas on business, these people would tell him vindictively that soon they would be taking claims in the Osage.

Many of these people had settled temporarily along the border, and were accustomed to letting their cattle drift across. There was no provision wherein the Osages could get revenue from this grazing, and the Major recognized these drifting cattle as constituting a perpetual menace to friendly relations between the Osages and their white neighbors in Kansas. So when some of the cattle men wanting to enjoy this privilege of grazing their cattle in the Reservation, applied to the national council for permission to lease tracts along the border, the Major was highly pleased.

After long conferences with the council, arrangements were made by which leases were granted on tracts of land lying in bands south of the Kansas line along the Cherokee boundary on the east and south and along the Kaw boundary on the west. These tracts were leased for a stipulated sum per acre, and with the provision that they should be fenced by the lessee. When the leases were signed by the principal chief of the tribe, the Major immediately forwarded them to Washington, but was later notified by the department that there was no law which would warrant the approval of these leases, and since there was no action by the department the tracts were taken over by the lessees, and they began to fence their respective acreage. After the inclosure of these tracts gaps were left on the State line and along the Cherokee-Osage boundary, and the Major asked the department for permission to close these gaps, which authority was granted him. Thus the first barbed wire was brought into the Reservation; a four barbed iron wire, and there was much speculation about this novelty.

This action soon brought about much excitement among the adventurers waiting on the borders of the Reservation like vultures, and feeling became so intense that these citizens of the United States, armed with the power of the vote, began to atract the attention of the department to the matter of grazing leases. They began to spread propaganda that the cattlemen were being favored in the leasing and fencing of land on which the citizens of the United States had no claim whatever. But inasmuch as such leases were detrimental to their plans for the eventual repossession of old claims, from which they had been evicted by the military when the Osages had bought the Reservation from the Cherokees, they assumed the rôle of virtuous homeseekers; the department was supposed to take a paternal attitude toward homeless people. So intense was the feeling of these homeseekers that they often threatened the lives of those people who had been instrumental in bringing about the arrangement between the Osages and the cattlemen.

After these leases had been occupied for some time, a congressional investigation was authorized, and along with the representatives from other tribes of Oklahoma and Indian Territories who had given leases, the Major and the council were called to Washington where they appeared before a committee of the senate. There was a week of questioning; a week of misunderstanding of the real situation as far as the Osages were concerned, but the leasing of the Indian lands was discussed exhaustively. The Major never heard anything of the report of this committee, nor of any act by the senate as a result of such a report. But there came to light certain things which contributed to a general understanding that the investigation was brought about not in the interest of the Indians and the leasing of their lands, but through the agitation of a group of adventurers who were seeking to open up several reservations for settlement; one of the results being that there had been effort on the part of a group of men to take possession of some lands in Oklahoma that were supposed to be public lands.

The major came back from Washington with full determination to protect as far as he was able, these people of the blackjack hills, and help them to resist all efforts of the department to require them to be allotted and their surplus lands thrown open to settlement. He looked with hope to a certain young Sioux who had been adopted by the tribe, and several mixed-bloods and inter-married whites, whose abilities in politics and leadership were apparent. These men, he believed, could stand as a buffer between the politicians who symbolized the government and the full-bloods whom they could never understand. He believed that these men, being as they were, in the transition stage, could understand both sides, thus enabling them to defend and protect their own people until such time as they might become adjusted.

On the limestone prairie the blue stem grass was the best obtainable for the fattening of steers for market. The cattlemen knew this and felt themselves fortunate in that they were able to make grazing leases with the Osages but they made the mistake of attempting to winter cattle in this country, and during the first years suffered great losses, some of the lessees finding it necessary to turn back their leases. Later, however, they grazed their herds during the summer, shipping them out in the early autumn.

The Indians watched with interest the great herds strung out along the prairie, surrounded by shouting cowboys, and almost hidden in dust clouds. The herds were driven out of the Reservation to the railroad terminus at Elgin just across the border in Kansas, where they milled in great stock pens, bawled their discontentment and kicked the pale dust to the heavens. These great pens extended over the Reservation boundary so that the cattle could be driven into them without crossing the border, thus avoiding the quarantine regulations of the state of Kansas.

These great herds from the Reservation made of this little town the greatest cattle shipping point in all the world, and with true Amer-European love for the biggest and best the citizens were inordinately proud of their town, and felt warmly toward all that appertained to the Osages and their Reservation. This warmth did not cool when the cowboys, shouting, eager and thirsty, "hit town" and shot out windows, or at deputy marshals, or at each other, or slept across the tables of the many saloons, with no other obligation than intense loyalty to the boss.

To the mixed-bloods and the few whites at the Agency this little town was the symbol of the "outside," with all the glamour that was then supposed to be civilization's. This little town symbolized "up in the States" to the people of the oak shaded valley, and "goin' to Elgin" was like a trip abroad where everything could be bought that the heart might desire.

LAME DOCTOR'S CROSS

Chapter Ten

HEN payment time arrived people came in from all parts of the Reservation. Families of mixed-bloods came at this time to make visits to their relatives who lived at the Agency. Full-bloods came with their wives and families and their dogs. They camped along the creek bottom or on the hill by the agent's house. They set up their lodges and the poles for their jerked meat, and stayed several days or several weeks, just as the whim struck them. Those who camped on the hill came to the cistern at the residence for their water, while those in the bottoms got their water from any convenient well.

During the day they wandered along in front of the traders' stores, or stood and priced articles of apparel, or other things which claimed their interest. They stood around the Council House or the agent's house, or loafed in the shade of the oaks in the area. Groups of them would sit for hours and talk with many movements of their long, graceful hands, and always at the end of some long tale, they would say, "Ho—ooo." There were times when there was humor, and laughter would come at the end of some recital. Their humor was often boisterous, though their laughter was always quiet and restrained. Though often their humor was based on what the Amer-European believed to be man's frailty when confronted with natural urges, it was more subtle than the obscene jokes of the freighters.

The Indian was not inhibited by the moral hypocrisy of the period, and his appreciation of man's fall from dignity in the inclinations of the flesh, approached the French appreciation of the bedroom difficulties of a general or a statesman. Their laughter had none of the braying of the freighter, nor were their glances or their voices burdened with secretiveness. Oftentimes the loud guffawing of a freighter would float over the still night air of the little settlement, and set the dogs to barking in every quarter, so hearty was his appreciation of some pointless but sufficiently obscene joke.

The time of the payment was the time of greatest activity in the Agency. Besides the tall Indians from every part of the Reservation, there were deputy United States marshals; the traders busy with their merchandise; employes of the Agency, clerks, teachers, etc. There were always freighters just in from Coffeyville, Independence, Elgin or Arkansas City, who stood around telling tall tales, or sat whittling up the shingles which had been torn from the roof of some government building under repair. Dogs slunk here and there, nosing everything, in perennial hope of food, or lay stretched in the dust dreaming dreams, which sometimes made the skin of their mouths draw back showing their teeth, as they whimpered softly.

Dark-eyed French mixed-bloods bantered and joked in groups, ever conscious of their attractiveness; turning as one man, as someone's "har'd gurl," or some other female employe, walked by in skirts that swept the dust. These mixed-bloods, with their French verve and

Osage Woman

their Indian agility and their devil-may-careness, over-whelmed the hearts of Elgin and Chautauqua Springs, and other towns and homesteads along the Kansas line. No Don Juan ever loved as passionately, or as carelessly and indiscriminately as did the mixed-blood young bucks of the Reservation; it is doubtful if a Don Juan ever escaped so charmingly and irresponsibly from the results of such amours.

And during payment time things invariably happened. The young bucks rode their sweating ponies to Elgin, and visited the many bars. Sometimes they secured whiskey from some of the freighters, or from other sources, and rode through the Agency shooting and giving great war whoops. Many of them drank quietly but effectively, and many were as continent in such matters as the full-bloods, but nearly all of them were harmless. They were not desperados or criminals. The country was wild and the carrying of guns was taken as a matter of fact, and the great wind-swept spaces stirred their energy and was inviting to the hot blood of the merged races.

There was little social life and no distractions, except the gossip of the Reservation. Sometimes there were dances at Chautauqua or Elgin, and all the young people of the Agency attended. The men pranced and strutted like turkey cocks, and the girls simpered and giggled, ready to send some swaggering cowboy or mixed-blood on his way if he had "whiskey on his breath." There was never any offense, unless in the case of someone who had become too drunk to remember his natural courtesy, in which case there was always any number of wild cavaliers from the blackjacks to defend outraged virtue. Their chivalry was crude though sincere, and often they anticipated with pleasure such incidents, especially if the offender was not of the Reservation.

When the activities of the drink-excited mixed-bloods were restricted to the Reservation, they burned up their energies in different ways. Some were quiet and pugnacious, some were quiet and jovial, but there were some, who, when they reached a certain stage in their glorious victory over the prosaic dullness of the Agency, began shooting out lights. The Major, sitting with his family in the stone residence on the hill, would suddenly drop whatever he was doing and listen to the yells that floated up from the valley. If he heard a certain high, long-drawn-out yell, he would turn back to his work with the remark, "That is La Chateau—he's all right." But on hearing the short, staccato yelps of a charging Comanche, he would say, "That is Petit Blanc —he will be up the hill in a minute—better turn out the lights."

One of the quiet drinkers was a courageous, scar-faced mixed-blood, who had an appointment as United States marshal. When there were no horse thieves or outlaws to be taken to Fort Smith, life for him seemed to lose its zest. At such times he went quietly to the government barn, and sat in the hay with his bottle. There was something about the acrid odors of the stable that was gratifying to his senses; something soul-filling in the hazy hum of the flies and drone of the wasps in the rafters. As the whiskey warmed his veins and filled his thoughts with vague figures, there was something satisfying about the way the sun beams with thousands of dust specks dancing in them, played across his legs, or glinted on the barrel of his rifle.

He drank quietly until the bottle was empty, then his lip would curl and he would laugh cynically to himself. Life became suddenly a sort of inferior comedy filled with grim humor. He believed that he had many enemies, and he sneered in the consciousness of his own superiority over them.

Finally late at night he would get up steadily enough for one who had drunk so much, throw his Winchester over his arm and walk straight to his home. He would walk quietly up the steps then pound on the front door and await with curling lip and cynical smile, until he could see through the glass of the door, his wife start down the stairs in a nightdress, with a coal oil lamp in her hand. Always when she reached a certain step he would draw his revolver and shoot. The stairs would be enveloped in darkness and the lamp shattered. There was no outcry from his wife; she knew that her lord was drunk.

On the day of the payment the Major would come over to the Council house and stand at a little window on the west side, which looked out on a passageway between the Council house and a trader's store. Ho Lah Go Ne (Good Voice), the crier, would announce in long drawn out call, the readiness of the agent to make the payment. The Indians and the mixed-bloods would gather and wait until their names were called, then each one would walk up to the window as he heard his name, and receive his money. The traders would begin checking over their goods in readiness for their purchases, or open their books in preparation for the payment of back accounts. All day the traders and their assistants would move among their bolts of calico, coils of rope, shiny implements and fresh black harness, always solicitous and friendly. They would greet their old friends from Salt creek, from the Arkansas river, from Pond creek and the Caney river, and there would be much talk and many signs with the hands. In the evening in the camps on the creek bottom blankets would be spread and there would be gambling, and there would be small family feasts, and from the camps would come the delightful odors of campfires and broiling beef. On racks back of the lodges, the firelight would show the jerked beef, which hung like pale, pink ribbons, cut with dull scissors.

Here and there in the valley, dull reddish lights would appear. Sometimes a cavalcade of young bucks would race through the dust on their ponies, shouting and laughing. Sometimes a mixed-blood would raise his voice from out in the darkness, and give vent to his inexpressible ecstasy, created by the fumes of forbidden whiskey.

Sometimes when the people came together for payment, one of the things which made up the life of the Agency among the blackjack hills, was the slow throbbing of the drum, carried up from the creek bottoms as some medicine man attracted the attention of Wah'Kontah to a dying tribesman.

LAME DOCTOR

During the payment time many of the Indians who lived some distance from the Agency would come in to see the Major either on friendly calls, or to talk over some matters of business. At such times his office was filled with mixed-bloods who lived on ranches over the Reservation, who wished to talk over their difficulties with him. The full-bloods would come into the house unceremoniously and look for him before he had arisen in the early morning. They came to pay friendly calls, or to talk over things which they thought ought to be rectified, and often sullen, independent Indians, to whom the traders referred as "mean Injuns," would stalk with dignity into the office, or come to the door at the residence, and ask why he had not done this or that. To each one he gave his attention and made every attempt to settle the matters brought to him.

One afternoon he noticed an Indian lounging in front of the office whom he had not seen for some time, and who came to the Agency only during the time of payment. He knew him to be one of the "mean Injuns," and had heard much of him as a leader of marauding parties, especially against the whites who lived on the border. For some time he had wanted to talk to this Indian, as he was afraid that there would be serious consequences if he continued to live up to his reputation of being wild. But he had never had the opportunity to talk with him, for Lame Doctor, as the traders called him, was arrogant and aloof and would not deign to come to the office of the agent.

While he was thinking of Lame Doctor and his reputation among the traders, and of the stories the other Indians told about his raids, the Major looked up and saw him standing in the doorway, as though he would say, "Well, what are you going to do about it?"

The last of the visitors was just leaving and he

motioned Lame Doctor to sit down. The Indian looked at the chair, then at the Major, then he walked over and sat down. The expression on his face was one that seemed to have been cast in bronze; hard and soulless. The Major sat waiting for him to speak, and as he waited he wondered how he would approach the subject of Lame Doctor's activity. Finally Lame Doctor spoke without the least trace of emotion: "I have come to talk about thing which troubles my mind. I want to talk to you about this thing."

"How."

"For long time I have thought about this. I come now to talk with you about this thing. My mind is much troubled."

"How."

"I have thought about this thing and I know it is good. I have come to tell you. I have made up my mind to take white man's road."

"That is good. My heart is glad about this. You will find this road good road."

"If I take this road of white man, I shall need clothes which white man wears." The Major thought he recognized the trick. He said: "We have these clothes of white man in 'little house.' Government has sent these clothes for Indians who take white man's road. But many Indians who have these clothes do not wear them. They do not take white man's road. They visit Creeks and give these clothes for sweet potatoes. Perhaps there are no sweet potatoes in lodge of Lame Doctor, and he will take these clothes and trade them to Creeks for sweet potatoes. How many sweet potatoes would clothes of white man bring to lodge of Lame Doctor, where there are no sweet potatoes?" Immediately the Major saw that he had made a mistake. He had made a joke of the suggestion because he thought that one of Lame Doctor's reputation could not possibly have good intentions, and when he saw the expression on Lame Doctor's face change ever so slightly, he felt annoyed with himself. He saw Lame Doctor make a move in preparation for leaving and he arose from his chair and came and sat down by him. "I did not know," he said, "I thought you were making fun of me, but now your trouble is in my heart."

"I talk with straight tongue about this thing. My heart is heavy. You do not believe me when I come to you and talk with straight tongue. Am I woman that I should do this thing? There are many people who know Lame Doctor. Ask these people who know Lame Doctor if he would do this thing. Ask these people if Lame Doctor would trade with Creeks for sweet potatoes, with clothes of white man. My heart is heavy if you do not believe this. My mind is troubled if you laugh at this thing."

"Ho, that is good. Your trouble is in my heart. If you tell me this trouble I will help you."

"For long time I have thought about this. I have thought about taking white man's road. I said I will take white man's road, and this trouble will go away."

"Good. You will tell me this trouble now."

"It will take long time to tell about this thing which troubles my mind. About this thing which troubles my mind I have told no one. If you have this trouble in your heart, you will listen to this thing which I tell you."

"Ho, I will listen."

"Long time ago I was little boy. When I was about this high," (he held his hand off the floor, and the Major judged that he must have been about eight or nine years of age) "many of my people were out in country to west. Every year they go there to hunt buffalo. Many times leaves have become red on trees and my people go there to hunt. There was much buffalo meat in lodge of my father. One day he said to me, 'My oldest son we go to find deer along stream.' We found many deer along stream. Sun was not high. We saw white men who were hunting deer. There were three of these white men with hair on their faces. They talked with my father in talk of hands. I said I do not like these white men. Suddenly these white men caught my father's arms and tied him to bush with some rope. These three white men went off and turned around. They shot my father with their guns until he lay dead. His head would not touch ground. He was tied to bush with white man's rope. My heart was like drums at dance. I ran away and hid, but white men did not want to find me. Soon they rode away and I came out. I saw blood drop from my father's mouth. I said my father is dead. My throat was very dry but I did not want water. I could hear my heart beating like drums at dance. I said I will go to camp. But I could not find camp. I started running. I ran for long time. I said I am not tired. Sun went down, and I kept on running. Soon it was very dark but I did not feel tired. I was running. I could not see, but I did not fall. I said I am not tired. My father is dead I said. These white men killed my father, but I said I do not know where camp is. For long time I was running in darkness but I did not feel tired. Soon

I heard barking of dogs and I said camp is there. People were dreaming I believe. I come to my father's lodge. It was dark and cold. I went to bed but I did not sleep. Always I could see my father. I could see his head that did not touch ground. I could see blood that dropped from his mouth like leaves of sumac. For long time I lay there with my eyes shut, but I could see head of my father that did not touch ground. Soon I was very angry. I said why did I run away? Why didn't I kill these white men who killed my father. Pretty soon I heard voice, and I was afraid. Pretty soon I was not afraid, and Great Spirit came to me. He put ban on me that I should kill ten white men. I must kill ten white men to avenge my father. Many times leaves have come to trees since that time. It is long time, but that ban is still on me. Great Spirit has never taken that ban from me. All my life I have tried to keep that ban. I have said I will avenge my father. I must kill seven white men. I have already killed three white men. Now it is different. There are white men all around. Some of these white men are good white men I believe. It is not so that all white men are bad. At Fort Smith there is man who will hang me if I am caught before I kill seven white men. It is bad for one of my people to let white man hang him with rope."

For some time Lame Doctor sat motionless. Then the Major spoke, "My friend I listen to your story with heavy heart. I have thought much about this thing. Your trouble is in my heart." The Major placed his hand on his chest, then he continued, "It was bad for these white men to kill your father. Wah'Kon-Tah will punish them I believe. It was evil spirit who came to your father's lodge that night long time ago, I believe. I believe it was evil spirit who put this ban on you. It is bad thing that you have killed these three men. Many times you must pray to Great Spirit for forgiveness I believe. He will punish men who killed your father."

"I will think about this thing. I will think much about that which you have said. I believe that it is not good that I kill these seven white men."

Sometime later the Major received word from Lame Doctor that he wished to see him. He drove immediately to the Arkansas river where Lame Doctor had his lodge, and when he arrived Lame Doctor seemed glad to see him. After the meal they sat by the fire and talked of many things as was the custom, before coming to the "main talk." Soon Lame Doctor said: "I have thought much about this. I have thought much about the things which you have said. It is good if I join church of my people. But my mind is bothered. To join church of my people it will take much beef. It will take much beef to feed people who will come. It will take many presents for medicine men. I am poor man. All my life I have had this ban. Many people have come to me and they have said, 'It is bad thing, this thing which you are doing. It is bad thing to kill white man. White man will say that all Indians kill white man.' I did not answer them, and they said much about me that is not good. I am poor man. I can give no beef for feast. I have no presents for medicine men. I have thought much about this thing. I said perhaps my friend will help me do this. I said he will give these things for me."

The Major did not expect this turn in events, though

he sat gravely for some time. His intense interest seemed to drown the humor in the situation. He spoke: "My friend I am poor man too. I do not have this beef and these presents which you talk about. I have seen these feasts. I believe you can pray to Wah'Kon-Tah without these things. I believe that Wah'Kon-Tah will see things that are in your heart and it will be all right."

"I do not know how to say these things to Great Spirit."

"You must pray to Wah'Kon-Tah and he will see that your tongue is straight. He will see what is in your heart and will forgive you. I believe that it is not necessary to give these presents to medicine men. I believe if you go out on hill and pray to Great Spirit it will be all right."

For some time they sat there in the darkness. The Arkansas was in flood tide, and the odors of mud and rotted vegetation came to them on the air currents. With the exception of the spirited chirruping of a tree frog, the night voices seemed sleepy. Then Lame Doctor spoke again: "I do not know about this thing." Again the Major attempted to make him see that it was within himself that the trouble lay, and that he could clear his conscience as soon as he had something to cling to; some faith to which he could turn, but it was difficult to make this man see this. It was difficult to wean him from the traditional rites of his native religion, and make him see that the medicine men were not necessary as mediators. He attempted to think of some simile which would make this clear to him but none came to his mind.

They sat thus far into the night, and just before they

rolled into their blankets Lame Doctor said: "I will think about these things which you have said. I will think about all which you have said about this thing. I don't know about this."

Some months later the Major heard that Lame Doctor was camped about six miles west of the Agency, and the conversations coming to his mind, he suddenly felt a desire to talk with him.

He found Lame Doctor's camp at the edge of Timber hill, at the head of a small ravine where water was plentiful. He drove up to the lodge and Lame Doctor came out, showing in the expression of his face that he was glad to see him. When they were seated on some blankets under the shade of a tree, Lame Doctor said: "It is good that you have come. I have thought much about this thing that you have told me, and my heart is light when I think about this. The Great Spirit has taken away this ban I believe. My heart is light. I feel it swell when I think about this." They sat for a long time and talked of the Great Spirit and his children, and of the white man and the white man's God. They came to the conclusion that they were the same; that there was one God for all people, but that the Indian saw him one way because he was an Indian, and the white man saw him another way because he was a white man. They concluded, these two, under the shade of a blackjack tree on the edge of the prairie, that the Great Spirit could look into every heart and see what is there, and that if the heart is clean like the June prairie after a rain, there is no need to talk to the medicine man.

The next time the Major heard of Lame Doctor was during the time of the autumn payment. He had eaten his evening meal and had started down the hill to do some work in the office, so that he might be in readiness for the disbursement on the following day. He stopped suddenly in the thick dust of the road, when he heard the throbbing of drums as they came floating up from the creek bottoms. He stood for some moments to listen, then continued the descent.

It was dark in the little valley and there was no one visible of whom he might ask the meaning of the drums, so he decided to go down to the camps. He turned down the dusty road to the bottoms. He could smell the delightful odor which is the blending of campfires and cooking meats. He thought the camp seemed very quiet as he approached; not even a dog announced his coming through the darkness. He could see the fires light up the lodges, and once someone came out of a lodge and the fire inside was visible for a second, making grotesque shadows on the rear walls. The drums beat incessantly; with a monotony that was fascinating. A dark figure stood out suddenly as it moved among the lodges, and the Major addressed it, saying, "How."

"How," said the tall dark figure.

"I have come to see about this thing. I have come to see who is sick."

The figure answered: "It is Lame Doctor who is sick. He is there," and he pointed to a lodge standing off to itself.

The camp seemed to be full of medicine men, and the Major could hear the chanting of the prayers coming from the lodge indicated by the dark figure. He came to the door of the lodge and looked in. There was an air of heaviness on the inside. The chanters sang the prayers lugubriously, and the drums seemed to plead hopelessly. He thought of the drums on other occasions. He had always thought it remarkable how many of the emotions of man, the simple beating of drums could express. They could express the ecstacy of full-blooded victory; they could express the calm well-being of the social dances, and they could excite men to battle. Then, as tonight, they could make an inscrutable appeal to Wah'Kon-Tah, the Great Mysteries; softly, sadly, as when the heart beats become prayers.

He saw Lame Doctor lying on some skins on the other side of the fire, and of all people in the lodge, only Lame Doctor noticed the entrance of the great bulk of the Major. "How," he said feebly. "It is good that you have come." And he motioned the Major to sit down with him. Then he waved his arm to the medicine men and they stopped the chanting and left the lodge, and as they left the Major noticed that each had a present that had been given him for his services. Lame Doctor saw that he had noticed these presents, and he said: "I have little time here. It is good. I am ready to go away. Great Spirit has taken ban away I believe. Great Spirit has forgiven me."

He paused for a moment as though to gain strength, then he pointed toward the door with his eagle-wing fan: "I did not tell them to come. My wife told them to come. They came because he wanted them to come. I am not troubled about these things. I remember the things we talked about. I remember the things which you have said. Tonight I shall go away."

After saying this he lay quietly, with his gaze

fixed on the domed roof. After a while the Major began to look around the lodge. The flickering flame suddenly showed the figure of Lame Doctor's wife; a silent, motionless figure lit up by the whimsical flame dance; her shadow on the back wall of the lodge, going through the antics of an evil spirit. Her figure as she sat there was like some symbolical statue in an ancient temple; a symbol of human grief, accepting the inevitable from the hand of Wah'Kon-Tah. The Major thought that this motionless Indian woman in the lodge of her dying husband, was the embodiment of all that man has said of the cutting of human ties by death. He wondered about the thoughts of this woman who was unaware of his presence, and a great sadness came over him, and he felt that there was something lodged in his throat. He looked again at the figure on the skins, but it had not changed its position. He suddenly made himself believe that he had duties elsewhere, and he arose and left this dark lodge upon which Wah'Kon-Tah had laid his hand.

He made his way up the dusty road, turning at the corner of the traders' stores, then climbed the hill to the residence. He had decided that it was too late to go to the office. When he arrived home, his wife met him at the door: "Thee has been working at the office?"

"No," he said, "it is Lame Doctor—he is dying—I have been down there to see him."

"Oh," she looked solicitously at him, then she said, "Thee is upset."

"No—wouldn't call it that—I—he'll probably die tonight."

They walked upstairs together.

The Major lay in bed. He could not sleep. He could hear the pleading drums down in the bottoms, and though he knew that they were subdued, the sound was carried along on the stillness of the autumn night. He thought of Lame Doctor lying there uncomplaining, awaiting the will of Wah'Kon-Tah. He thought of the firelight playing spasmodically on the slightly bowed figure back in the shadows of the lodge. On the stillness the coyotes sent up their chorus from Cedarvale hill. Querously they yapped to the night, as though they too were wondering about the mysteries of life and the thing called death.

It was during the darkness just before dawn that the Major awoke from a half sleep. He was suddenly wide awake and listened intently, then he heard it; it came on the cold air like the hunting cry of the wolf, yet it was like the wolf call only in that it was sustained at a high pitch, but unlike the cry of the wolf, it seemed to carry all that men had thought through the ages, of life and death and the sorrow of the human heart; this cry of the mourner which came from the blackjack hills across the creek.

He dressed quietly without disturbing the household, and went down to the lodge of Lame Doctor, where he met the wife as she came out. She came up to the Major and said: "It is good that you have come. My heart is heavy. Last night my husband told me that he wanted his body given to you. He said you would bury it in grave of white man. He said he wanted this thing. My heart is heavy. He is Indian, my husband. He will go to heaven of Indian. But they will say in heaven of Indian, 'Who is this man? Who is this man who has not marks of band on his face. Who is family of this man, who has no marks on his face. Surely this man has no people.' My heart is heavy about this thing. I have thought about it. I said it will be good if I can paint face of my husband. I said my husband will be lost in heaven of Indian if I do not do this thing. I said it will be all right if we paint face of my husband; if we wrap blanket around my husband. He wanted to be buried in white man's grave. I said it will be all right. I said we will paint face of my husband and he will not be lost in heaven of Indian."

The Major replied: "That is good I believe. We will have white man's coffin made. We will take your husband to burying ground. You will wrap him in his blanket. You will have his face painted with marks of tribe. You will have his face painted with marks of band. I believe that he will not be lost in Happy Hunting Ground."

The wife of Lame Doctor turned and went back into the lodge.

Already the Indians had begun to gather to prepare Lame Doctor for his long ride to the Happy Hunting Ground. The Major turned and left the camp in the bottom. The mourning chant from the hills across the creek had ceased, and the sun was tinting the stone buildings with delicate pink, and on the air was the pleasant odor of wood smoke, as he climbed slowly up the hill to breakfast.

GAME OF HORSE TAKING

Chapter Eleven

THE AUTUMN payment over, the Major again turned his attention to the business of the Reservation.

Along the creek bank there was nothing to indicate that there had been camps, except the framework of the lodges standing deserted. The air had become sharp and the brilliant sun that flooded the blackjacks brought out a hundred mad hues. Reds, yellows, browns, purples; these had been painted by the whimsical hand of some giant. The insects had begun to buzz in the sunshine with a purposefulness which they had not shown during the summer, and among the people of the Agency there was an alertness of step and an interest in things, which had taken place of the drowsiness of the long summer. Ax strokes rang out on the hillside as people gathered their winter supply of wood, and in the afternoons and during the night, wild geese, flying in V's honked high above the valley.

Around the stoves in the traders' stores there was talk of deer and turkey and tales of former hunts, and each one of the group guessed he'd do a little huntin' maybe. Sure fine meat, venison. They wondered if the Indians would make their semi-annual hunt for buffalo across the river—like as not they would, they guessed, but they sure thought there would be trouble some of these days with all the tribes there together, and the herds becoming smaller each year. One of the loungers spoke up from the counter where he had been standing, "Ole Big Chief nearly got into trouble himself last fall— out there huntin'."

Then someone from behind the stove said, "How was that?—didn't hear about that."

"Well, him and his band was camped out there some place—anyway they was huntin' buffalo. Seems like they was close to a band of Cheyennes. You know they ain't no love lost between the Cheyennes and the Osages—never has been. Well, the way I heerd it, the Cheyennes had lost a warrior; kilt by a bull, and they was a lot of mournin' goin' on in the camp—reckon they was havin' a war dance—about the same as the Osage war dance, I guess. O' course at the end of the dance they had to have hair. I guess they was afraid o' old Big Chief, so they didn't pay any attention to the Osages, but seems there was some kind of messenger come into camp and the Cheyennes decided to take his hair—the messenger might have been a Crow—or do they come down that fur? Maybe hit was a Pawnee, anyway the feller didn't say. Anyway this messenger lit out past old Big Chief's camp, and the Cheyennes tuk in after him. They said the Cheyenne chief was mad as a hornet as he rode up to the camp and told 'em he wanted that messenger. The messenger had hit the high places, and the chief seen him agoin' over the hill. He started to take in after him but old Big Chief run out in front o' him and grabbed his reins. The Cheyennes was mad as hops—you know how they are after a war dance. The feller said old Big Chief jist stood there, and the Cheyenne threatened him but Big Chief would not let go his holt. By this time Big Chief's band was gathered and the Cheyenne band was talkin' among themselves purty excited. The feller said it sure looked like a scrap. Pretty soon the Cheyenne chief got mad and started to hit Big Chief with his gun, and the feller said old Big Chief—you know how big he is—said he reached up and caught the Cheyenne by the throat and pulled him clean offen his horse, and held him there. Seems like there was a lot o' talkin' and some dirty looks for awhile but nothin' happened. Kinda 'fraid of each other like two roosters peckin' chips—one afraid and t'other glad of it. By golly, that'ud a been a fight, let me tell you."

"The Cheyennes didn't want Osage hair, eh?" said the trader from behind the counter.

Then a tall fellow drawled, "Ain't none of 'em a-wantin' Osage hair fur as I can see."

"Bet if the dog soldiers had a been there they'd been a fight." Again the drawl, "Ain't never seen any dog soldiers a-carryin' Osage hair on their stick neither, hev ye? Them Osages roaches is purty safe I guess." Then the trader spoke again, "I heard Sweeney tell a good one—you remember Sweeney, the trail agent? Wasn't any bigger'n a minit, but he had the nerve. He told me he was with Che Topah's band one year on the buffalo range. Seems like they hadn't had any luck —he said the Cheyennes and Arapahoes had scared away what few there wuz. Che Topah's outfit run out o' meat, an they was several women purty hard up for meat—some of 'em sufferin' I guess, the way Sweeney talked. He said one afternoon they saw a big herd of cattle crossin' the prairie and Che Topah lit out at a dead run followed by the whole band. Sweeney said he had a slow horse and didn't get up to 'em until after Che Topah was talking to the owner. He said that Che Topah tried to explain to him in sign language, as nice as could be, that there was some women in his camp starvin' for meat, and that he wanted about twenty head. He told the fellow he would give him paper sayin' that they had taken so many head, and he could get his money from the agent. The owner wouldn't do it. Sweeney said he rode up then and told this fella that he'd been appointed trail agent for the Osages when they went off the Reservation, and that he kept a strict account of the cattle they took. He told him that that was his job, since there had been so many false claims about the Osage demandin' cattle from the herds crossin' the prairie. He said he would make a note of the number taken and he would give the owner a voucher which the Major would honor. Sweeney said the man told him that he didn't intend to give these goddam Injuns anything—'let 'em starve,' he said—'it'ud be a good thing for the country if they all starved.' Sweeney said they weren't askin' him to give a single hoof—he'd get his money for 'em. Nah, he wouldn't do it. So Sweeney told him they'd probably take 'em anyway, that he would count 'em and the man would get his money jist the same. Sweeney said the man pointed to the Winchester on his saddle, said he'd shoot the first red bastard that touched a hoof. He said Che Topah ask what the white man said and Sweeney told 'im he couldn't take 'em. He had not more than got this out of his mouth when the whole band rushed

« 175 »

out and cut out all the beef they needed, and the owner nor any of the cowboys touched a gun. He said the fella jist went on with the rest of the herd, and he said that he counted twenty-seven head that the band cut out and killed for beef. Afterward Sweeney said he was called to the Major's office and was asked all about the cattle, and he told the Major all about it—he said the Major showed him a claim from this fella for fifty cattle."

"Didn't get any pay for any fifty head did he?"

"Sweeney said they paid him for the number they took—no more."

A deputy marshal came into the store and spoke to the group. "Say, Ed," said one of the group to the marshal, "I seen the Major pushin' them jackrabbits of his'n toward the west—what's goin' on out there, ya reckon?"

"Oh, little fancy horse stealin', I reckon—Pawnees or Osages—don't know which yet. Some ranchers across the river complainin' about horse stealin'. I reported it to the Major this morning and he said he'd attend to it, so I guess he's gone out there to see about it."

"He'll believe it was the Pawnees until he finds the ponies right in the Osage lodges, too—'n'en he'll wish he was blind." The marshal looked over at the speaker, "Don'cha fool yourself. He sure will hate to find ponies in the Osage camp, but he's gonna be fair, he's gonna be fair and do his duty ever time. The way it looks now, from what he said this mornin' they's gonna be some of them young bucks in the Big Hill country, take a little trip to Fort Smith if he finds any stray stock from across the river out there."

. . . .

A Hunting Camp

The Major climbed slowly out of the blackjacks to the prairie. When he reached a high point he stopped the mules and looked back at the little Agency lying among the gayly painted hills; serene in the iced sunshine. Blackjacks crept up the sides of the hills and then stopped abruptly, and the dull coppered prairie began. Their edges were ragged like a crazy quilt that had been dropped from the sky; a crazy quilt with brilliant reds and yellows and browns, and an abundance of minor shades. In the valley where the stone buildings were just visible, the elms and cottonwoods and walnuts of the creek, with their light yellows and pale greens, made a sinuous ribbon among the rioting blackjacks that clothed the hills on every side. Along the edges of the ravines that veined the copper prairie, the sumac flamed, and added another color to the abandoned glory of the scene.

The Major felt the ominous silence; the autumnal silence that was almost audible. It was broken by the cawing of crows flying across the painted woods. The Major clucked to his mules and again took up the trail.

He drove on across the prairie that had the color of dull copper. There was no whispering; no breezes playing over the great expanse; just a silence that seemed sad even though the genial sun flooded everything. The hills stood out clear and distinct and blue in the distance; a deeper blue than the sky that curved down to meet them.

As the mules trotted over the trail, a mere speck on the prairie; across streams fringed with elm and sycamore, meeting over the clear pools of water, the Major thought of his mission to the western part of the

Reservation. There had been much complaining from the settlers along the west side of the Arkansas about horse taking. While some of their claims against the Osages were ridiculous, there were, he felt, some grounds for complaint, and although little had been done about the matter, he was in possession of much information. He was working on the theory that the Osages would gradually adjust themselves and grow out of this old habit of the plains, but he finally came to the conclusion that it would be a very good lesson if some of these Indians were arrested and tried. He believed that the Pawnees were adept at this old game of horse taking and he was sure that the Osages were blamed for the depredation of these people. In fact there had been cases when the Pawnees had taken horses and when hard pressed had placed the blame on their traditional enemies, the Osages. Once he had received a communication from the department enclosing a bill against the Osages for several hundred horses which the Pawnees said the Osages had taken from them. The claim had been carefully prepared giving dates and places, giving the number of horses taken as one hundred.

The agent of their reservation had assisted the Indians in preparing this claim and he personally urged that the claim be allowed and the money paid at an early date. Upon receipt of this claim the Major had at once called the Osages together and asked them if they had any claim to make against the Pawnees. At first they had been silent. It had been their habit to make no claims against the tribes living on reservations around them but they usually took the matter into their own hands and retaliated. The Major had repeated the request that the Osages give him any evidence that they had which would show that the Pawnees had taken horses from them.

They finally said that they could get such evidence but that they would say nothing about it; that they could adjust these things in their own way. However the Major insisted, saying that he wished to show the Pawnees that they had no claims. He got the details of these claims, the dates, places and descriptions of the horses, and when it was added up it was found that it exceeded the claims which the Pawnees had filed against the Osages. In answer to the claim the Major sent his counter claim in detail, and there had been no reply.

He appreciated the fact which most people over-looked; the fact that horses had been considered by the plains Indians as belonging to him who was able to take them. They were, with the wild game of the prairie and woodlands, a gift from Wah'Kon-Tah, and after the advent of the Spaniard the catching and tam-ing of wild horses had gone on continually among the tribes. To take an enemy's horse was the most effective way of embarrassing him; to take the horses of unwel-come white men crossing Indian domain was the best way to put intruders at the Indian's mercy.

So the taking of horses was a well established cus-tom among the tribes of the plains, and they under-stood it as such; the taking of herds of horses and the retaliatory action was a game.

The white man did not view the custom in this light. White men considered that when a band of Indians stampeded their horses, they had stolen them; to them it was not a military expediency. They never realized that the Indians understood themselves to be in almost a perpetual state of war with white trespassers and that taking their horses was the best way of disabling them and discouraging further encroachments on their domain. On the other hand when the white man went in search of his horses, he cursed the Indians for thieves as he followed the long weary trail of his lost herd. If by good luck, he was able to recover it, he seldom stopped with the recovery of his own, but took all the Indian ponies he could possibly round up. He never considered himself a thief, and that he was a trespasser seemed never to have come to his consciousness.

The Osages had brought this custom with them to their last reservation, and the Major, while realizing their attitude in the matter, had decided, after many efforts to show them that they must do away with this custom, to stop these incursions across the river. Not that he had any fear that these two tribes would come into open conflict again, though they had been traditional enemies, he believed that the Pawnees and the Osages could play this game between themselves for years yet; it was his desire to stop the trouble between the Osages and the white settlers. In the case of the claims against the Osages, it was difficult to tell how many of them were based on fact. It seemed to him that every time an Osage appeared across the river, the white settlers began to make claims, knowing that the government was ever ready to listen to any complaint made against their wards, without taking into consideration the character of the accuser or the trustworthiness of his statement.

Yet considering a horse as a gift, as all wild life was a gift; a gift which must be shown consideration in the scheme of things; a gift toward which a certain courtesy must be manifested, the horse was also a possession and an indicator of wealth, his value depending entirely upon the food supply of his master.

One day when the lodge was full, an Indian might refuse a large sum for a very indifferent horse, yet in a month from that day, if the lodge were empty, he would sell the same horse for a ridiculously low price, and feel that he had received fair value for it. Necessity often determined the Indian's actions. When he was hungry, a perfectly natural condition, it was just as natural that he should satisfy that hunger, wherever or whenever he found the means. It was his habit to feed anyone coming to his lodge, and when he went to the other lodges, he expected to be fed. Wherever there was food that was not being used, he felt free to take of it if he needed it, having little understanding of food, the gift of Wah'Kon-Tah as a personal possession.

Often horse buyers asked permission of the Major to come to the reservation, but they usually left puzzled at the attitude of the Indian toward his horse. They could not understand that the Indian should have no idea of market value; why a flattering offer for several head of horses meant nothing to the owner.

Late in the evening the Major arrived at one of the camps near the Arkansas, and went straight to the lodge of one of his friends; a man in whom he had put great trust, who in turn trusted the Major as a friend. He knew if he started any kind of an investigation, no matter how carefully planned, that he would find absolute silence, and his plans would be frustrated. He stayed the night at the lodge of this friend. They talked of the coming winter; of many things pertaining to the conditions of the Osages and the Reservation, but the subject of horse taking was not mentioned, though he felt that his friend had guessed his mission.

The next morning after washing in the icy waters of the stream and breathing for several minutes the exhilarating air, that carried the most delightful of autumn odors, he came back to the lodge to a breakfast of meat, dried corn and black coffee.

After breakfast he and his host sat out in the warm sun. For some time they sat, then the Major said: "My friend, I have come to talk about this thing which makes my heart heavy. For long time we have talked much about this. We have said it is bad. We have said it ought to stop. Yesterday one came to me and said, 'In camps of Osages there are horses belonging to white man who lives across the river.' I said it is bad. I do not want to believe this thing. He said, 'It is so—I know this thing.' I have come now to talk about this. I think it would be good thing if horse taking should stop. I come to you to talk about this. I come to you to get names of these people who have crossed river to get horses. It is bad talk. It is bad to ask you about this, but I believe it is good for your people if you tell me about this."

"It is bad to tell you this thing. It is good for my people if this thing stops. There will be trouble if this thing does not stop, then it will be bad for my people. You are my friend. You have in heart great love for my people, I believe. You will not say that I told you this thing. I would not tell you this thing, but I believe it will be good for my people if it stops." Neither said anything for some time then the Major spoke, "My heart tells me that it is good for your people if this stops."

His host picked up a stick from the ground, and made several marks in the dust; the Major watched him intently: "It is like this," he said, "some young men of this band took those horses," as he drew a map showing the location of the band's camp. Then he went on to describe each horse and the men who had taken it, and as he finished he rose suddenly, as if to dismiss a very disagreeable subject said, "It is bad thing for my people." He walked off into the bushes, and was instantly hidden from view as though he had never been present. The Major got up and arranged the legs of his trousers, brushed his clothes with his hand, then went over to where his mules were tied, hitched them to the buggy and drove away.

TOMSHEH FEASTING

Late in the morning he came to Salt creek and turned down this stream toward an encampment, where he had heard that the Indians were to hold a meeting. At noon he came to the edge of a limestone escarpment, and down in a valley in the midst of the flashing yellows and reds gleaming in the sunshine, he saw a large gathering of Indians. The smoke from the fires drifted lazily up to the tree tops, then was dissipated by little air currents. Horses were moving clumsily about in their hobbles. The camp itself was all color and leisurely activity. Tall men walked about or sat in groups under the trees. The women were busy at the fires.

Suddenly one of the little mules snorted and jumped, and a breathless, half-naked boy broke out from the undergrowth to the right. When he saw the Major he stopped short, then without saying anything he walked gravely off toward camp. The Major looked in the direction from which he had come and saw several boys half concealed by a clump of sumac bushes, watching him. They had been playing some game of hunter and hunted; perhaps the boy who broke from the bushes was supposed to be a Pawnee or a Comanche and the others Osages on the trail. Or perhaps he was a deer and the others hunters. In any case the sudden appearance of this white man had stopped their game, and they stood, filled with curiosity but assuming an effective air of complete indifference.

The Major again looked down at the camp, apparently unnoticed, but he was sure that his presence was known the minute he came into view, or even before. An Indian rider on the prairie seeing the dust raised by the buggy would have had ample time to ride into camp and announce that the agent was coming. He would not have said, "Some one is coming," but would have made sure of the identity of the person before announcing it to the camp.

The Major drove down the steep escarpment, the rear wheels dragging over the platy, ringing limestone, when he held his foot on the brake. He drove up to a tree, tied his team and went over to the gathering. His presence was ignored as though he had not been seen, until an old man whom he knew very well came up to him with eyes smiling and said, "How," and offered his slender hand. The Major replied, "How, my father.

You do not come to Agency. You do not come to see me."

"Ho," said the old man, his eyes still smiling, "I am no good now. I am old. I am like stud horse, who is old. All day I am in shade of tree, and my head is low."

The Major looked over the crowd and said, "I have come to talk about something. Who is in charge here?"

"Ho," said the old man, the creases disappearing suddenly from his eyes, "It is that man over there."

The Major saw the dove pole erected, and the great open lodge, and he knew that they were preparing for the dove ceremony. He felt a little annoyed with himself that he had been so discourteous in coming at this time. He went to the man indicated as the man in charge, and said, "I have come to talk to these people about things which have troubled my mind. But it is not good I see. They will have dove ceremony and I shall go. I did not know that they were going to have dove ceremony." The man looked at him, and his face showed nothing. "You can stay—it will be all right."

"No I will not stay here—I am white man—it is not good that I stay here."

"I believe it is all right. One time you came to making of medicine man with Gray Bird—you are friend of Gray Bird—it will be all right."

"That is good. I want to talk to these people about thing which troubles my mind. I will talk about this thing. I will go then."

"That is good. I will call people. I will tell them that you wish to talk about this thing."

"Good," said the Major. The people had begun to gather around the large pit which was filled with glowing coals, and above which was a framework of hickory bows holding pieces of beef, which sizzled and dripped. On one side some women were cooking round, flat pieces of dough in the fat of the beef. The Major joined the people who had already begun to eat. After he had eaten many of the people came up to him and shook hands, and others he approached and extended his hand, calling them brother or uncle or father, as courtesy dictated.

The master of ceremonies then called the people together, in a long, high-pitched cry. When the people had collected the Major mounted the tongue of a wagon nearby and spoke to them thus, "My friends I have come to talk about a thing which is worrying my mind. Listen to my words that come from heart. I have thought much about these tomsheh feasts. I want to talk to you about this thing. Last payment, when crier called name of man at your camp, this man did not come to window to get his money, and I said, 'Why does this man not come to window to get his money?' They said, 'He is dead, this man.' My heart was heavy. He was young man, 'Why did this man die?' I said, and they said, 'At feast this man ate too much tomsheh, and drank white man's whiskey when weather was hot.' When crier called another name, this man did not come to get his money and I said, 'Where is this man—is this man dead?' And they said, 'This man died.' I said, 'Why did this man die?' And they said, 'This man ate too much tomsheh at feast when weather was hot.' My heart is heavy about this thing. I have come to talk to you about this. I want to talk to you about next payment. My heart will be heavy if man does not come to get his money when his name is called at payment time," He hesitated a moment and from the crowd came several "hows" of approval, and the Major continued, "Now my friends I want to talk about this payment which will come. When crier calls name of man, I hope they will not say, 'He is not here—he is gone away.' This thing makes my heart heavy."

He got down from the wagon tongue, and the old man who had greeted him when he first came into the camp rose slowly, and standing, bending over a little and supported by his cane, spoke, "There is something good in this thing. This thing which our friend said is good. It would be good thing if we did not have these feasts when weather is hot. Osages are great people. When they ride out on prairie, Pawnees and Cheyennes say, 'They are Osages, we do not want to fight Osages.' Osages have counted many coup on their enemies. But some day if they have big feast when sun is hot, and drink white man's whiskey when sun is hot, they will die and there will not be Osages riding over prairie. Pawnees will say, 'Ho, we are not afraid of Osages. Medicine of Osages is small.' There is good in what our friend has said, I believe."

Some of the listeners said, "How," and some said, "Ho-hooooooo" in expressing their approval. The old man sat down on the grass again, carefully wrapping his blanket about him as though to appear occupied un-til the slight thrill which his own words and their approval had given him would have time to die in his old heart. He was an old man and he spoke of the prairie and the activity of his people in the light of his distant youth. The talk of "counting coup," and "good or bad medicine" was being displaced in the thoughts of the younger leaders by the problems of their people's adjustment to the restricted reservation, and the laws of the white man. Although on nearly all occasions, these leaders, especially when talking to their own people, seldom failed to tell them how great had been the Osages in the warfare of the plains, even referring at times, when they had become eloquent, to the stories of battles with the Illini, and to the terror in which the Caddoan tribes held them.

The Major was preparing to go. He had his hand on the rope to untie his mules when the drums began their slow throbbing. Even the first beats had something in them of the incessance with which they would beat as an undertone during the ceremony of the dove. He hesitated a moment. He was filled with that inscrutable something which he had always wanted to express. This language which was so simple; a very part of the earth; like the voice of the earth, held a great power over him, yet annoyed him and made him discontented, because he could not express the emotions which it caused. He jerked the rope purposefully and tied it to the hame, then got into his buggy and drove through the high grasses to the trail which led up to the limestone escarpment. Above the grinding of the rims on the loose stones, and the creaking and cracking of the buggy, he heard the throbbing. Even after he was on top and had flicked the mules into a trot, he could hear the pulsing beats as they came up from the valley on the heavy air of autumn.

The sun was in mid-heaven and the rays seemed to be concentrated through the still air. He stopped by a persimmon tree at the head of a ravine and got out of the buggy, to eat some of the ripe fruit that had squashed on the rocks below. The sun had warmed up some insect into song and his low pitched voice came from the grass roots; almost like a plea for the return of summer.

On having his mouth puckered by a fruit that was not quite ripe, he got down on his stomach and drank from the cold water which had formed a pool on the flat rocks at the head of the ravine. He got up and wiped his mouth, then noticed that both mules had their heads up, their ears forward, and were looking intently across the prairie. He looked in the direction indicated by the mules, expecting from the intenseness on their faces, to see an Indian come riding into view. The mules were too intent to be watching a skulking coyote or a wolf.

Soon he saw a figure coming toward him. It was a man. He had just come up out of a hollow into full view and was walking with great swinging strides. He recognized the man as Stanley, who walked over the reservation at all times of the day or night, during storm or fair weather, with his tweed jacket filled with fruit seeds, preaching the gospel of fruit trees and shade trees to whites and Indians alike. The Indians looked upon him as a queer man, and one to be humored but not necessarily respected. However, they showed him that courtesy which they showed to all white men who attended to their own business, and did not meddle in theirs, or to anyone who did not attempt to patronize them. The Indians were good judges of the purposes of the white man as an individual but where a number of white men became the government, they showed an implicit trust that was poignant.

Stanley was an enthusiast. He could see the Reservation covered with fruit trees, and no laboratory scientist forgot himself more in the subject, than did Stanley in fruit trees. Always he had both pockets full of various seeds and often times he sacrificed space in his pack which should have been filled with articles for his comfort and gave it up to seeds. They were a fetish.

Nearly everyone on the reservation knew the ruddy faced, jacketed Stanley walking with swinging gait across the prairie, or appearing suddenly from the blackjacks. Many times the Major had picked him up, or had volunteered to take him to his destination, but Stanley could never wait until the Major was ready, and he would start off over the trails alone, with his mind fondling a single thought. The Major imagined him detached, and filled with a dream for the future of the Reservation, lying in the sun in geometrical patterns of peach, plum, pear, apricot, apple, and cherry orchards.

When he had come nearer the Major, and was once more coming out of a depression into view, the mules dropped their heads again, quite content as to the identity of this small bit of life that moved so arrogantly over the expansive prairie. When within hailing distance, he waved his hand and then as he came nearer said, "How," affecting the greeting of the Indian. The Major

replied, "How." He came up with the childish irre-
sponsibility of a one-sided scholar away from his work.
Smiling, he seated himself on the limestone ledge and
looked up at the persimmon tree with its burden of fruit,
then smiled up at the Major, "Haw, right here's a hint
as to what man can do on this old earth if he had the
ambition. Here is a tree; a wild tree standing here for
no other purpose than to furnish food for the Indian,
and yet man will starve, and dig all day in the ground
when he might just as well have his food hanging from
trees all along his way. Here's a hint which nature has
given man and he won't take it; nature the great hinter."
The Major smiled and looked at the tree, "Yes, good
'possum food too," but Stanley did not hear him. He
felt in his pockets and pulled out some large pits, held
them out to the Major and said, "What are they?" The
Major received them in his hand and looked at them,
"Peach seeds, I guess—looks like peach seeds anyway."

"Got 'em yesterday. I'm goin' over to the Arkansas and help Riviere plant an orchard. Do well in that
sandy loam on the river—told him I'd bring 'em next
time I come." Saying this, he got on his feet and
continued, "Well, I'll be goin'." He looked at the sun,
"What time you say it is?" The Major pulled out his
watch, "One o'clock."

"Well, it will be late when I get there." He started
out, but turned around with a cheerful face and said,
"By the way I gave Alvin Wood some plants, and showed
him how to plant 'em." Then before being hidden by
the hills he turned and waved his stick.

The Major climbed into his buggy and clucked to
the mules. He thought of Stanley with a smile. He

thought of him as being quite civilized; too much civilized for the comprehension of the people of the Reservation. The whites and mixed-bloods thought of him as being "cracked," but no joke at his expense ever seemed to touch him; never lowered the heat of his enthusiasm.

He had planted mulberries, grapes and peach trees at nearly all the stage stations, and the freighters would say disparaging things about them and laugh at the stories told about his hikes across the Reservation, but the force of the man, the absolute sincerity of his purpose, elicited from them in time a shade of admiration, though they would not have admitted this to their fellow freighters or to themselves even.

Years later those same trees are standing, and mark the location of some of the old stage stands, where the buildings have rotted down or have been torn down, or changed out of all likeness to the original. It is only a group of cedars, or the dead branches of some peach trees, showing above the fringe of green lower branches, or a great mulberry which seems to have exceeded the limits in girth and expansion of its branches. Sometimes there are tangles of domestic blackberries shining like metal in the July sun, far from the original place of plantation, their seeds having washed down the ravines and lodged in the alluvium deposits. In themselves a sufficient monument to one who dreamed strange dreams fifty years ago.

Late in the afternoon the painted blackjacks came into view; creeping up the sides of the hills and reaching up the ravines and streams like fingers, the mad colors seeming to be alive in the light of the late afternoon. A shimmering, abandoned dance at the end of a season, before death and long sleep; a last flare of vibrating life, before winter's repentance; nature's mardi gras.

Before he had descended into the little valley the Major could see the smoke rising lazily from the chimneys; rising high into the still, heavy air, then forming into a ribbon lying against the hills. He could hear the voices of the Agency floating up to him, especially the staccato barking of an Indian dog. As he crossed the ford by the mill he caught the pleasant odor of wood smoke and cooking meat, which when blended was the odor of all Indian encampments; the odor of the Indians, themselves. He thought of one of the older traders who had come down from the Kansas reservation, who one day said in a moment of enthusiasm, "I don't know why it is —I love those fellas—I even love to smell 'em."

There was a dim, red light shining in the trader's house, and another red light gleamed in the window of the store. A tall figure with a blanket wrapped well around him, almost concealing the face, walked directly but leisurely along the darkened road, soundlessly; it seemed to float.

When the Major and his tired little mules climbed the dusty hill, there was a welcoming light in the narrow south window of the big, sandstone house.

"THE HANGING JUDGE"
Chapter Twelve

EVERAL days later the Major heard someone calling up to him from the yard of the residence. He looked out of the window into the early morning light and saw a horse tied to the pickets of the fence. He heard a voice below his window "How," it said, "I have come." He saw a young man from the Big Hill country standing there. "How," he answered, "I will come down."

When he came into the yard he said, "Is everything all right in country of Big Hills?"

"Yes, I believe everything is all right." The Major wondered what this man was doing here at this time of the morning, but he thought it best not to ask a direct question. "You have had long ride," he said, "you will have something to eat."

"Yes. That will be good. What do you want me to do?" The Major thought for some time before he answered, then he said: "They told you to come here?"

"They told me you wanted to see me—I have come."

"Who told you this?"

"The marshal told me this thing."

"Which one."

"Marshal with scar on his face told me this thing."

"That is good. You stay here."

After breakfast the Major went down to the office

and sent word that a certain United States marshal should come to see him. He arrived later in the day, and the Major asked him why he had told this young man to come to see him, and added that he did not remember having authorized it. The man replied that the Indian had been one of the band who had stolen horses and that he had thought that it would be better to tell him that the Major wanted to see him than to go into the camp and arrest him.

The Major was very much annoyed. "I suppose you have evidence and consider this man under arrest for horse stealing?"

"Yeah, that's the size of it, I reckon."

"Well, I can't keep you from taking him to Fort Smith, but I'll go along with you when you go. I want to tell you right now that I don't want you using my name or my influence again. You have no right whatever to do this, and I don't intend having you do it. You're here to arrest anyone who breaks the law, and if you have the evidence that this young man has taken horses, why I can't keep you from arresting him, but remember that you will do your arresting in camp next time, and leave my name out of it. This young man rode most of the night to ask what I wanted. Do you think for a minute that I would play such a low down trick as to tell him that I wanted to see him so that you could arrest him?"

"Awright, Major, when can you leave?" as though he would say, well, anyway, I got him and that's all I'm after.

"I'll tell this young man what you've done and I shall be ready to go with you tomorrow morning—in the meantime I'll answer for your prisoner—he'll stay with me."

The marshal clumped out of the office.

.   .   .   .

It took several days to make the trip to Fort Smith, several days for the trial, and several days for the return. The young man was acquitted by the "hanging-judge," though he did not seem to be particularly impressed by the fact that he was allowed to return to his home.

When they arrived at the Agency the Major sent word that he wished to see the band of Indians that had been accused of taking horses, and about which he had received information from his friend in the big hill country. He felt that since he had gone part of the way, he must now go on. He came to the decision that he must make an example of this band before he could do away with the troublesome habit.

The band came in as requested, and assembled in the council house. The Major stood before them for some time, then he said: "My heart is heavy. I have said many times that it is bad thing to take horses from white man. I have said that it is bad for your people to take horses from Pawnees. Many times I have talked to you about this thing. Many times your chief and older friends have talked about this thing, but you have sat like men made of wood—you have turned your ears away. Now you have taken horses. My heart is heavy. I said, I hope I dreamed this thing. But I know this thing and my heart is heavy." He took out a little book in which he had the name of each young man who had taken a horse, and the description of the horse taken. He looked up from the book to the inscrutable faces about him, "You are Osages," he said, "you know how to be men; you know how to be punished. In my heart is great love for you. Like love of father for children. But children have not thought of love in father's heart, and they have not listened to good words of father, and now father must say to children that his heart is heavy. He must say to children that they must be punished for taking these horses."

He looked at the book again and then walked up to one of the young men and said, "You have horse— you have bay horse." Then to the next young man, "You have taken painted horse." And so on until he had accused each man and described the horse which he had taken, saying that those who had not taken horses could go home and they would not have to come back to the Agency, but that the others must go as well, and on a certain day they must bring all horses which they had taken into the Agency, at which time, he said, he would turn them over to the United States marshal.

One of the spokesmen of the band got up and said: "It is good. We will go to be punished. We will bring horses to Agency. This man who told you these things, who is this man?"

The Major replied, "As long as sun comes up and makes east red, I will hold this name in my heart."

There was silence.

On the appointed day they came into the Agency with the horses and the Major turned them over to the marshal. The next morning when they started for Fort Smith in wagons, accompanied by a marshal, the Major came down into the area and gravely shook the hand of each young man. There was nothing in the expressions on their faces to show that they were moved in the least. As the wagons creaked away along the Rocky ford road, the Major stood and looked after them. The dust lifted from under the horses' feet and floated close to the ground, then suddenly rose and hid the wagons from view; hiding the forms of these solemn, indifferent young men, on a long strange journey. He knew that they were deeply concerned about their probable fate, but he knew also that they would show no emotion. They would face the firing squad or approach the scaffold with the same stoicism, and knowing this he was suffused with unhappiness, even though he also knew that the judge at Fort Smith understood perfectly the nature of the crime, and that a year at Detroit penitentiary would likely be the punishment. He turned back up the steps to his office, sadly, and Duty patting him approvingly on the back did not reassure him. Already in his mind was a plan for appointing each member of the party as a policeman on his return to the Reservation, putting upon them this responsibility as vacancies should occur.

WICHITA CHIEF

As the gorgeous days wore on and each day the blackjacks seemed to become madder in their abandoned display; as the early mornings became keen edged and scent laden, and the yelping of the coyote bands became sharper in the chilly evenings, the air filled with acrid incense of hickory and oak, there was the thrill of purposeful activity in the Agency.

Many of the people from the southern part of the

Reservation arrived, and camped in the bottoms by the mill, adding their lodges to the lodges of the people from the east. Around the encampment there was great activity.

During the evenings, stories of former buffalo hunts were revived, and youths would sit in a circle when the older men talked of the prowess of the Osages and the number of buffalo they had taken; the number of Cheyennes, Pawnees and Arapahoes they had killed, and the number on whom they had counted coup. Faces shining with wonder and admiration, the boys listened. They looked with reverence on their fathers and the older men of the tribe, whose word to them was law. As they went to their pallets of skin in the lodges of their fathers, they dreamed of alkali dust high above the shaggy herds; of swift ponies and taut bow-strings; dreams in which they always played the rôle of hero. The older men before going to bed would stand out from the fires and gaze at the heavens, losing themselves in contemplation of the silent, blinking stars that shone above the tree tops.

Back of the traders' stores wagons stood ready to be loaded with supplies and articles of merchandise which would be needed by the Indians on the plains. Merchandise that would be traded for the robes which might be taken during the hunt. Long into the night the faint red light shone in the windows and on the inside the men smoked and looked at lists and checked goods to be taken. In the thrill of packing there would be stories of former hunts, and there would be anecdotes while the stove crackled and showed a red hot side.

More bands came to the bottoms near the mill and

set up their lodges, and at evenings around the fires that reflected from the white boles of the sycamores and lighted up the under branches of the tall oaks and elms, there was more talk and low laughter. The women moved in and out of the lodges like dark ghosts, appearing and disappearing in the whimsical leaping of the flames; stopping occasionally from the preparations for the long trip, to scold in shrill voices the skulking dogs as they retreated with tails between their legs to sit disconsolately at the edge of the light, hope shining in their eyes and expectation in the slavers from their mouths.

Gradually the lodges in the bottoms disappeared as the bands moved out with their equipment west across the prairie, across Salt creek, and on to the sandy bottoms of the Arkansas, where they crossed at Rock Ford and found themselves in the reservation of the Kaws. As the bands reached the Arkansas and camped for the night, they often found other bands of their tribe there, or saw evidence of their having been there recently.

They moved up the Salt Fork, across the wind swept plains. The few trees that grew along the borders were bent and twisted before the sand-laden wind "like people who are afraid." The short grass of the high plains seemed brown and dead in comparison with the copper colored prairie and the painted blackjacks of their own reservation. In mid-day bands of antelopes flashed their white beacons as they ran away, finally becoming hidden by the distance or by the gentle swells.

On and on they traveled across the high plains that seemed to melt into the sky in the shimmering distance. On and on until they saw the great Salt plains to the north, then they turned south and come in sight of the Cimarron river, its reddish waters flowing lazily in the autumn sun. Sometimes they recognized small bands of Cheyennes or Pawnees against the skyline, the wind playing with their horses' tails and the pale dust clouds coming from their hooves like smoke from the earth.

Somewhere in the valley of the Cimarron they would set up their lodges and prepare for the great herds as they came south.

Sometimes on these hunts, they clashed with the Cheyennes, and almost invariably they clashed with their old enemies the Pawnees. Sometimes they would talk with them and each side would bluff, then they would ride off without striking a blow.

During the day the sun reflected the indolent waters of the Cimarron and the air danced over the plains at noon. In the evening there would be much big talk in camp as the women worked with the buffalo robes. The cold moon would climb out of the sand hills, and make of the lodges spirit homes, and the moving figures strange people of another world. The wolves drawn by the scent of the hunt, would send their long, mournful howls into the night, the horses would snort and strain at their hobbles, and the dogs would slink toward the shelter of the lodges and half-heartedly challenge this song of the plains, as they stood with the hair standing along their backs and the slightest quiver in their legs.

Sometimes during the evenings some of the bands would make medicine, so that Wah'Kon-Tah would be sure to see them as they set out for the herd, and perhaps aid them.

When the herds were sighted the bands would organize and start out under their respective chiefs, and at the proper signal would attack the flanks of the herd losing themselves in the clouds of gray dust. There would be the popping of rifles and the thunder of hooves that seemed to shake the earth.

When the dust finally faded and the thundering was faint in the distance, figures like pygmies appeared on the empty plains; figures moving about among small black bumps scattered over the sparse grass; black bumps like some baleful excretions of the earth. A riderless horse would trot nervously away, his mane streaming in the wind. There would be several horses standing with heads down and sides heaving, while their owners would attempt to cut the hamstrings of wounded buffalo.

Then later the figures would disappear and other figures would take their places; a greater number of figures bending intently over the black bumps. A short distance from them would be the skulking coyotes, nervously quartering the wind, and at a greater distance the gray shapes of wolves exposing themselves in their hungry impatience. On the distant horizon a yellow-gray column of dust would climb to the sky.

When the great herds had disappeared the bands would sometimes settle in a sheltered valley for the winter, to await the return of their game in the spring. Around the lodges would be hickory racks of long strips of meat hanging like ribbons.

Sometimes the wind screamed like a woman who has the evil spirit, and carried stinging flakes of snow, but the dome-shaped lodges were warm and the people were happy if there was much meat in the lodges, and plenty of robes to be taken to the lodge where the trader from the Agency had his merchandise.

One morning during the autumn hunt, a warrior came to the lodge of the chief and said that he had had a dream. He said it was about a man of the beaver band who had died several months before, and that because of this dream his mind was troubled. He said that after the hunt he was very tired and that his throat was dry but he was not thirsty. He said that it seemed to him that there were many little things alive in his body, and as he lay on his bed, he would jump many times when he did not wish to jump but wanted to go to sleep. He heard the talk of many things during the night. Besides the many coyotes that talked to the moon, he heard the wolves who talked like a mourner chanting the song of death. Finally he went to sleep, he said, and soon it seemed that he was riding over the plains, but he could not hear the steps of his horse; he could hear the talk of the wind under the moon and the light of the moon was so bright that he thought the stars must be sick. He said it seemed like the world of Wah'Kon; the world of spirits. Suddenly he saw a figure; a man riding a good horse, but there was no sound except the spirit talk of the wind, and the horse and rider were floating above the earth, he thought.

When the figure approached him it raised its hand and said, "How, my father." And he knew that the figure was a member of the beaver band. The figure told him that his spirit was troubled; he said that he had died and that there had been no mourning dance, and that Wah'Kon-Tah did not know him. His heart was heavy he said, and his spirit was very sad and had no home, and must wander over the earth like a spirit that is lost.

The dreamer said that they talked there on the plains a long time. The talk of the wind stopped and the moon seemed to listen, and a great sorrow came into his heart for this spirit that had no home. And he told this spirit out of the great sorrow in his heart that when he woke up he would tell the people about this thing. The spirit vanished, he said, and yet there was no sound. Now he had come to tell them about this.

The people listened to the man who had dreamed and said it was good. They said it would be good to have mourning dance.

The next morning at sun-up the drums began to beat and the dancers, painted in yellow and red and black, began to dance. Some had bone breastplates edged with wampum, with silver bands on their arms. Some had eagle feathers in their hair.

All day they danced around an open structure covered with branches of the cottonwood. They danced out for some distance and then back; they gyrated, and leaned backwards, and at time traced their course along the ground with a stick which had an eagle feather bobbing on the end, their bodies bent forward and their eyes to the ground as though they were trailing. Some had eagle feathers in fan-shaped groups fastened above their buttocks, and they imitated the dance of the cock prairie-chicken in the spring.

For two days the drums beat like a great pulse and the dancers danced, looking often at the sky, while the singers chanted so that Wah'Kon-Tah might hear and see the prayers of his children.

On the third day a party of the dancers suddenly ran from the structure, jumped on their horses and with a clatter of hooves rode out of camp. Holding their bows with the eagle feathers dangling from the end so that Wah'Kon-Tah might see.

The little party rode west. They had eaten very little since the dance began and their stomachs were empty. For an hour they rode west and in the distance they saw a party of Pawnees but it was a large party. When the Pawnees saw the Osages with the black and yellow paint on their bodies, the stragglers came up with the main party and they stopped and faced their ancient enemies.

The mourning party rode on toward the Pawnees and a Pawnee chief came forward with upraised hand to meet them. When they came up to him they stopped, and the chief began to tell them with language of the hands that there were many more Pawnees over the hill, but while he talked one of the war party rode forward and hit him across the shoulder with a coupstick; he turned his pony sharply and the war party fled in a dead run. The Pawnees did not give chase, believing that it might be a trick to trap them, but they were very angry that this insult had been given their chief.

On toward the west the party rode. As they came over a swell they saw a lone man driving a wagon, a trader who was carrying his goods to one of the hunting parties. He suddenly looked up from the contemplation of his horses' rumps, and after one glance at the war party, cracked his whip over his horses and shouted at them, and soon had them in a dead run across the plains. When his wagon hit a rut or a ravine articles of merchandise bounced out, but he drove wildly on until he disappeared over the hill, and the rumbling of his wagon could be heard for some time.

The party rode on as though they had not seen him, and very likely the incident would not be mentioned among them, until some time later when one of them would get up to tell the story, then there would be much laughter around the fire.

At high noon they came upon a little valley. There were several lodges extending along a little stream, and there was no one visible around the camp, but as they rode down a hill a man appeared, leading some horses to the water. The party dashed down upon him before he was aware and surrounded him. Then a rifle shot; muffled, almost inaudible in the atmosphere of high noon.

The party remounted and came dashing up the side of the hill and over it out of sight, away to the east. On the end of a stick carried by Oh Hunka Moie, a long black tuft of hair waved in the wind.

In the little valley by the stream among the scrub cottonwoods a man lay very still, with three bows, which had eagle feathers floating from the ends, sticking in his body. Wah'Kon-Tah would know that they were the bows of the mourning party. The horses which the man had been leading were drinking and splashing close by.

.   .   .   .

Just before sundown the party rode wildly into

camp waving the tuft of hair and shouting with excitement "We have killed enemy. Ransom has been paid. Spirit of our friend can enter Happy Hunting Ground." Three times they rode around the camp then dismounted. The ponies stood where they were stopped, their heads lowered, their sides heaving; their chests flecked with foam blown from their mouths. The sweat dripped from their bellies.

The dancers washed the paint from their bodies and the women mourners washed the ashes from their hair and there was feasting.

Later when the camp had become silent, the moon climbed out of the earth and seemed to struggle in the branches of a clump of cottonwoods along the river.

.　　.　　.　　.　　.　　.　　.

One morning a messenger came, saying that the agent wanted the Osages to come back to the Reservation. They packed their robes which had not been traded and packed the jerked meat of the buffalo, then traveled back slowly along the Salt Fork to the Rock Ford of the Arkansas. All the way they watched closely for war parties, but they saw nothing except the swelling, rusty brown plains, slinking coyotes, bands of antelopes watching them from a great distance, and flocks of prairie-chicken that flew up cackling before them.

When they reached the Reservation the limbs of the trees were bare and cold winds hissed through the tails of the horses and caught at the loose wrapping of the packs.

The men seemed to sink into their blankets so that only their roaches and spinning red eagle feathers appeared; bending and spinning as they rode silently along.

The women rode behind, dismounting and scolding the whistling wind when it tore at the packs and made reparations necessary, and they would continue to grumble in their blankets for some time after remounting.

To an Osage woman matters of the world were badly adjusted, and they went through life scolding things animate and inanimate, without hope that by scolding matters might be readjusted, but as a sort of perennial protest against a world governed by, and existing for the gorgeous male. Their life was a hard one but they had their brief hours of happiness when their husbands or sons distinguished themselves through bravery or in oratory, and their feminine hearts were full to the bursting when they dressed their men for the dances; arranging the gay trappings just so, and applying the paint with the loving hand of an artist; expressing themselves in what to them was beauty, and thrilling to the jingle of the many little bells and bits of metal, as their tall lords arose with dignity and strode out to the dance lodge.

Then there were children, loved of Wah'Kon-Tah. Little brown, naked bodies climbing over them, and clinging to their breasts; or looking out on the world with large black eyes set in round, brown faces, from the snugness of a baby-board, watching things recede from them as their mothers walked about the Agency or worked around the camp; children who were loved fervently by their mothers and fathers; who grew up to respect their parents and the elders of the tribe, to the point that the young men would risk death at the bidding of their fathers or the chiefs of the bands; taking messages when the winds carried sleet and snow across the prairie, or when the heat devils danced and gave strange forms to distant objects.

When the band reached the Agency they set up their lodges in the bottoms by the mill. In the spot used by visiting tribes as a camping ground, they noticed strange lodges but they refrained from looking intently in that direction, pretending that they did not notice. Several of the people said, "What is this thing?" And an old man answered, "It is lodges of Wichitas, I believe." And the people said, "It is lodges of Wichitas."

Some of the families were still cooking their evening meal when a strange white man appeared, accompanied by the Agency interpreter. As he approached he thought himself ignored as the people pretended that they did not see him. He said to the interpreter: "This looks bad—they seem to be in a bad mood—they are ignoring us." The interpreter said: "They know we are coming. They ain't lookin' at us 'cause it's bad manners when you gawk at people."

They came up to the lodge of one of the head men and the interpreter said, "How," and the head man answered, "How." Then the interpreter sat down and crossed his legs and the Indian sat down by him, but the white man remained standing not knowing just what to do, then finally after looking carefully at the blanket spread by the fire, he sat down. The three sat in silence for some time and the white man looked around the lodge very intently as though he would remember what was in it, so that he could describe it some time to rapt listeners who believed that there was interest in people who came in contact with Indians. The interpreter was vicariously ashamed and he looked to see how their host was taking this lack of manners, but there was nothing on the face of the man sitting on the other side of the fire.

When the white man had satisfied his curiosity he said to the interpreter "Go on, tell him what we came for." But the interpreter remained silent for a while longer, then he began talking with the head man, making use of his long slender hands and pointing to the west. And the head man replied and smiled several times; once they both laughed as though at some witticism. The white man thought the speech seemed lazy, coming with effort from the stomach and becoming caught in the throat, and making deep guttural sounds, which needed to be supplemented with the hands. He wondered why the interpreter did not tell of his mission so that they could leave. He had nothing to do, having had dinner at the agent's residence, but he wanted this thing over. He was about to say something short to the interpreter when through the door of the lodge, he caught sight of a woman with a baby on a board. She was stirring something in a large kettle with a spoon. For some seconds he forgot about the interpreter and sat there watching her. He was about to get up and ask her in pidgin English what she was going, when one of the horses began kicking at another horse tied to the same tree. Immediately the woman began to scold and walked toward the animals with purpose, talking shrilly. The kicking horse stopped as he heard the voice and assumed an expression of repentance. In camp the woman was dominant, and much to be respected, and all dogs and horses and even the mightiest of men understood this. No one offered resistance to a scolding woman.

While she was untying the surly pony, the white man realized that the talk had ceased, and he looked expectantly at the interpreter. Presently the interpreter continued in Osage: "We have come to talk about things which this white man wishes to say. This man wants to talk about two of your young men. He said that it is very bad that these young men killed Wichita chief. He thought it was good to call Osages back from buffalo hunt. He says Wichitas want these young men who went on war party and killed Wichita chief. He says it is very bad."

"How."

"He says if Wichitas do not get these young men there will be trouble. He says it will be bad if Wichitas and Osages fight. Blue Coats will come, he says. To-morrow there will be council—Osages and Wichitas will talk about this thing. He says it will be bad if there is trouble. You ought to tell people this thing, he says."

"How."

The white man spoke up. "What did you tell him? Did you tell him that I was sent by the Great White Father in Washington to talk to the red children?"

"Yeah."

"Tell him how serious this thing is—that the Great White Father will have to send troops if there is fighting —tell him it will be better to have a council and ad-just this matter, even if the Osages have to give up one of these young men who did the killing. It would save the tribe and the the government a lot of trouble. Who is this fella? Has he much influence?"

"Yeah, he's got influence with his band, and they'll all be there at the council."

"Be sure to tell him that we don't want any trouble."

"All right."

"Well, tell him."

The interpreter turned to the head man again. "He says you are great man among your people. He has heard this thing, he says. He says he believes that you will do right thing. He says Osages are great people. He says they love peace. He says Wichitas are small tribe; their medicine is weak, he says. He says at council tomorrow, Osages will act like great people and will give Wichitas few ponies for their chief. He says Wichitas are not Pawnees—that their medicine is weak and Osages are great people—they will not fight Wichitas, he says."

"How. Tomorrow we will talk about this thing."

"How."

"It is all right? Will he come to the council?" the white man asked.

"Sure, he'll come—they'll all be there."

They rose to leave. The white man went over to the head man and shook hands, and as he followed the interpreter out of the light of the fires into the deeper shadows, he looked back over his shoulder at the cluster of lodges. The flaps of many had already been closed to keep out the cold air, and he could see the flames of the fires dancing against the walls. He looked forward with pleasure to the council on the morrow.

The council was held in the bottoms up the creek from the mill. Gradually the people assembled. Mixed-bloods, traders, visitors and interpreters and the people of both tribes. The Osages came from all directions, walking proudly and nodding to each other. The visitors and other officials stood in groups and discussed the trouble, and the mixed-bloods stood around and conjectured with the traders about the outcome.

Some figured they'd be fightin' all right enough—they ain't no Osage 'ud give Three Striker or Oh Hunka Moie over to the Wichitas, they thought. Some said they wouldn't be nothin' to it a-tall—the Osages 'ud probably hafta give 'em Three Striker—or maybe Oh Hunka Moie—some said Oh Hunka Moie done it anyhow. Yeah, but some thought even the fella from Washington bein' there wouldn't have anythin' to do with the Osages —the Osages knew what they was doin', never you fergit it. The fella from Washington was runnin' the whole show, maybe, but you can take a horse to watter, but you can't make 'im drenk, some thought. They all agreed that they wasn't much sense to all this business nohow—the Osages could give 'em a few ponies and everything 'ud be all right.

One old trader remembered the time when an Osage mournin' party had killed a coupla Comanches —the two tribes had got together and settled the business. He remembered they met on the high prairie at the head of Skull creek, in the northeastern part of the Reservation, and they were both in war paint all right, an' they come at each other on the run. They never got off their horses—just set there and wrangled it out. He thought the Osages had given 'em some ponies, but he didn't remember how many it was now.

Soon many of the people were seated; the principal

men of the council in a circle, and the others on the outside of the circle. The white man from Washington stepped up with the Wichita interpreter on one side and an Osage interpreter on the other. He cleared his throat, but just as he began to speak to the seemingly expressionless faces around him, a pileated woodpecker came flying to the dead top of an oak nearby, uttering, "Kuk-kuk-kuk-kuk-kuk-kuk-kuk," as he began to hammer the resounding trunk. The speaker looked up with an annoyed expression as though he were on the point of sending someone up there to stop that infernal noise. The shy bird, however, seeing this strange group of harmful animals below, flew away, shouting his derision.

The white man cleared his throat again and began: "The Great White Father has sent me here to talk to his red children, the Osages and the Wichitas. He is very sorry that there is trouble between them and he told me to settle this trouble. As you all know the Osages got permission to leave their Reservation in order to go to the plains to make their annual buffalo hunt. Unfortunately, while they were there they held a war dance, and a party of their men rode off to the camp of the Wichitas and killed a beloved chief of that tribe. The Wichitas have long ago buried the hatchet with their red brothers, and their white brothers, and they came to their agent and told him of what the Osages had done. Now the Great White Father has sent us to settle this trouble and he is very sorry that this trouble has come among his children. He wants his children to live in peace under the great American flag, and he wants the Osages to live in peace on this great and beautiful Reservation of theirs and not go on the war path, so that they will become civilized like the white man and become a part of the great American people in this great and free land. He wants them to prepare themselves so that someday they can have a voice in the great government at Washington.

"I am sure the Great White Father would like to be here at this time to see his children in peaceful council in this beautiful valley; among these great oaks hoary with age; by this limpid stream that purls its way through these wooded hills. I say I believe the Great White Father would be glad to be here at this time, and listen to the peaceful council of his red children— because it will be a peaceful council I am sure. I am sure that the Osages are sorry for what, in a moment of excitement, when they returned for a few hours to their old ways, have done, and I am sure they will make every effort to come to some agreement with the Wichitas, and live in peace among these beautiful valleys and the rock-ribbed hills of their great Reservation.

"The Great White Father did not send soldiers with us, because he believed that his red children were well disposed toward each other and toward the government, but he has the soldiers close to the Reservation and they can be called—." Here he looked around and saw several of the officials shake their heads; "uh— er—he knows that the Osages will pay for this man that the war party killed and that they will live in peace with the Wichita, and that it will be the last time that the Osages will kill one of their enemies during the war dance. The Great White Father is very proud of the Wichitas for coming to their agent about this matter, instead of digging up the hatchet that has been buried so long."

He sat down and the interpreter for the Wichitas talked for some time, translating the speech, then the interpreter for the Osages translated.

There was a short silence. A Wichita got on his feet. He made a quick movement forward, then stopped. He seemed too full of emotion to speak. Finally he began in a high voice, working himself up to the point where he pointed his finger several times as the Osages, who sat as though they were not aware of him. He stopped occasionally and the interpreter translated what he said into English. Then the Osage interpreter translated into Osage. The speaker spent much time in telling of the virtues of all Wichitas saying that they had always desired peace with the white man and with the Indians, and when he came to the chief who had been killed, he was visibly moved and could scarcely stop talking long enough for the interpreter to translate.

The Wichita interpreter wore the clothes of the white man, his hair falling over his collar and down the front of his coat in two long braids; interbraided with red cloth. He seemed slightly embarrassed, until he began to translate that which his principal had said about the chief who had been killed and he became moved too. He began each translation with, "Mah friend, he says." He translated in regard to the unfortunate chief: "Mah friend, he says, it sure is bad that Osage killed this man. He says he was fine man. He says he didn' bother nothin'. He says, when Indian want fin' out somethin' they go this man, he says. He says he sure was smart. He says he alltime give a'vise to hees people,

he says, he ain't there no more. He says, Osage kill this
fine man, and they gonna haft pay for it, he says. He
says Wichita like great peace. He says Osage gonna
hafta give this man who kill Wichita chief. He says he
sure was good man. He says chulern hold out their
hands when he pass, and he alltime smile, he says. He
says dogs love him; he says they follow him when he go
someplace and he put hees han' on their head he says.
He says ever body love this man. Now he says he ain't
there; the camp of Wichitas is still like lodge where no
one live, he says, and hearts of Wichitas is very heavy,
'cause he ain't there, he says. He says, Osage alltime say
they great people but he thinks they ain't great people
if they do this kinda thing. He says they sure gonna
hafta pay for this man."

One of the Osage councillors arose. He pulled his
blanket close about him in front. He was self-conscious
though no one would have guessed it; only by the un-
certainty of his voice could this be ascertained, as he
started to speak. He said that this thing seemed bad but
he did not think it was. Osages, he thought, would be
willing to give ponies in payment for this chief. He
intimated that since it was a Wichita the matter was not
as important as they made it out to be. He said he
couldn't see why there was so much trouble over this
thing, and he believed the Osages had never claimed the
Wichitas as friends; the old men had told him that the
Wichitas had taken ponies from the Osages. He said
the Osages didn't run; that they had stayed in camp
on the Cimarron and he believed that the Wichitas
knew where the camp was, too. At least, he thought
they could have asked the Pawnees or the Cheyennes,

as they always knew where the Osages were, so as not
to camp too close. He didn't believe that the Wichitas
wanted to know where the Osages were camped, and
he was sure that the Wichitas' medicine was weak, or
they wouldn't run to white man about their troubles.
They made white man believe that they were good and
wanted to take white man's road, but he believed that
it was because their medicine was weak that they did
this thing. The Osages, he believed, would give the
Wichitas ponies for this man; they might give as many
ponies as they would give for a Pawnee or a Cheyenne,
as they didn't want to have trouble with government.
He said every one knew that Osages were great people
—every one knew that Osages were peaceful people.

Following the Osage speaker another Wichita got
up and repeated much of what the first speaker had
said, saying the man who had been killed was much
loved, and that there was great emptiness in hearts of
Wichitas. Sometimes, he said, they thought they heard
his voice, but it was only wind on prairie, and they were
very sad. He said their hearts were like deserted lodge,
and he believed that this man's ponies were unhappy,
and dogs lay about camp with hearts that had shriveled
with great sadness, and that flowers of prairie next
spring would hang their heads when this great man
did not pass any more. He said he believed that birds
would sing with sadness in their voices. It was a bad
thing that Osages had done, but if they would turn
Three Striker over to them, they would go and say no
more about this thing.

All through the day there was much haranguing,
and it seemed that they were making no progress to-

ward a settlement. Many on each side spoke; even Three Striker, the accused, got up and spoke. He readily admitted that he had given the coup that killed the chief, and he seemed proud of the fact. He said that many thought that Oh Hunka Moie had given the coup, but that he had done it. He said he was warrior, that he did not intend to go into hands of Wichitas. He knew he would not die in camp of Wichitas, with women taunting him and spitting on him. He said many times he had died (dreams were temporary deaths wherein the soul went into the spirit world and had many strange and sometimes instructive adventures), and that he had met his soul in spirit world. It was not soul of one who had died in camp of Wichitas; a shriveled soul that had escaped from body killed by Wichitas, and which women had cursed and spat upon, but healthy soul of warrior who had died in battle with enemy. He assured them that he was not afraid to die; that he knew how to die, but that he would not die in camp of Wichitas. He said he knew this thing.

There was a little excitement after this, but the talk soon reached the old, monotonous level.

The sun was casting long shadows across the bottom and the cool air seemed to be creeping along the creek on its first nocturnal wandering. The councillors seemed tired of their ineffective haranguing. There was a quick movement in the circle and Pawnee No Pah She arose and stood for a second. Every one became quiet and looked at him expectantly. He was a great man among his people, and was admired by the whites for his intelligence and for the force of his personality, and when "Governor Jo" spoke everyone listened. No one spoke better Osage and few orators excelled him. His words seemed to live when he wished to impress his audience, but at other times he was blunt, and the expressions given to his thoughts were like hammer blows, smashing mercilessly, unadorned by simile.

He drew himself to his great height and pulled his blanket together in front: "There have been many words. Wichitas have sent many words from their tongues; they have said little. Osages have talked like blackbirds in spring; nothing has come from their hearts. When Osages talk this way, Wichitas believe they are talkers like blackbird. I have listened long time to this talk of blackbirds, and I said when my people talk like blackbirds, Wichitas think they are women. I want to say few words, then Wichitas can go to their lodges and mourn for their chief. I want Wichitas to know this thing. I want them to know that Osages are great warriors. Today they have talked like women but they are warriors. They have those things which Wah'Kon-Tah gave to men, so that he could tell them from women. They know how to die in battle. I want Wichitas to know this thing. We will give ponies to Wichitas for this chief, then they can go home to their lodges. I have spoken."

On the Osage side of the circle there were many how's and oh-oooooo's, and several arose to go, indicating that this was the end of the council. A Wichita arose and almost trembled with anger, but he spoke only a few seconds then sat down. Already the council had begun to break up.

With the aid of the white representative from Washington and several of the head men of the Osages, the later agreed to give the Wichitas quite a number of ponies, and though they were not satisfied, they accepted the settlement.

The mixed bloods and the traders walked back up to the Agency, laughing about what Governor Jo had said to assure the Wichitas that the Osages were not women.

DEATH OF CHE-SAH-HUNKA
Chapter Thirteen

NE COLD autumn evening the Major drove from Independence into the Agency. After first sighting the dim red lights it seemed hours before he was finally standing before the stove warming his stiff fingers. There was a knock at the door and he was called. He saw an Indian runner standing there. He was one of the Hominy Indians and though there was no reading his face the Major felt that there was bad news, or perhaps trouble. A thought flashed through his mind that his little mules were too tired to make the trip that night. Then he said, "How." "How," replied the runner.

"You are cold, I believe."

"No, I am not cold."

"You will come into the fire and we will talk—you wish to tell me something?"

"Che-Sah-Hunka is dying they say. I have come to tell you this thing."

"That is bad. I will go." The information staggered him. He said to the runner, "Go to barn and tell man there that I want team that is not tired. Tell him I must go see Che-Sah-Hunka." He went back into the room and sat down to the meal that had been prepared for him. He looked up at his wife. "I shall be gone a day or two—Big Chief is dying."

"Thee is going tonight?"

"Yes, I am going as soon as I can get a team."

"Thee is warm enough."

"I'm all right."

Through the cold night with the wind rattling the leaves of the blackjacks he drove the thirty miles through the wooded hills to the south; across Hominy creek and on to the Arkansas river, to the camp of Big Chief.

He came on the camp suddenly. There were no fires burning and he could only guess at the outlines of the lodges.

He stopped in the darkness. A feeling came into his stomach and he felt that he would like to sit there until dawn. The calm of the camp with the winds moaning in the tall trees of the bottom, gave rise to a queer weakness that seemed suddenly to flood his body. He took out his watch and by the light of a match saw that it was just midnight. He believed that if only the dogs would bark his courage would return. He sat there for some minutes then he began to shiver. He got out of the buggy and felt in the darkness for a tree. Finding one he led the team over to it and tied them; he did this slowly as though to gain time but he wasn't sure why he wished to gain time. He would walk to the camp. It would not be courteous to drive into the camp if death had arrived and he felt sure that death had come to his friend.

Still he hesitated in the darkness, and the winds seemed to scream in the tops of the trees, at times accentuating the cold. Suddenly he made out a dark form moving among the lodges and he walked slowly toward it. The form stopped and he spoke to it as he came up. "It is friend of Che-Sah-Hunka," he said, "I have come." The figure said, "How," and led him to the large lodge which he knew so well. He came to the entrance and thrust in his head. There was the odor of charred wood of the dead fire. Then he heard a movement and the wife of Big Chief came out. She stood in the darkness for a second, then said, "He is gone. We will talk about things he said." He followed her into the lodge and feeling a blanket under his feet he sat down and she sat down beside him. She started to talk but her voice broke and she put her hands to her head and began to chant the Song of Death. Suddenly he was flooded with sympathy for this woman, and his heart went out to her in his emotion. He instinctively put out his hand, touched her shoulder and at this human touch of burning sympathy the stoic, the spartan of the prairie and the blackjacks became a woman and sank down, resting her head on his lap, wailing, and the Major put his hand gently on her head and stared at the entrance of the lodge. He was scarcely aware of the something in his throat and the hot moisture on his cheeks, he allowed to dry.

On hearing her voice the wailing was taken up along the line of lodges and the wind in the tree tops became an accompanying dirge. A cur raised his nose to the cold stars and howled long and heartbreakingly, the vague emotion, the instinct or the dim thoughts in his mind unguessable, but with the wail from the lodges, his voice carried that same questing; that question that has been asked through the ages from the darkness enveloping dwellers on the earth. Others took it up and there was no scolding woman with uplifted arm and menacing, shrill voice to stop them.

The night wore on and the wailing was spasmodic. The wife of Big Chief would be silent for long periods and the Major knew that she was not aware of his presence. She had lost herself in grief. Then suddenly she sat up and remained there motionless staring at the invisible walls of the lodge; with the silence of a statue, the dark, vague outlines of her body expressing more effectively than action or words the grief that tore at her heart.

Just before dawn the camp had become quiet again and then suddenly the long-drawn chant of the Song of Death came from the blackjack hills, carried on the dawn:

O-hoooooo, it is I who fall upon them unawares,
It is I who attack them thus.
O-hoooooo, it is I who fall upon them unawares,
It is I who attack them thus,
Ah, hoooooooooooooooooooooooooo.

O-hoooooo, it is I who serve them thus,
I who brought these deeds to pass.
A-he the he, Ah, the he.
It is I who cause them to lie blackening on the
    earth,
I who brought these deeds to pass.
A-he the he, Ah-he the he.

It is I who cause them to lie yellowing on the
    earth, etc.

It is I who takes from them their remaining
    days, etc.

« 227 »

Then after awhile the wife of Big Chief seemed to come back to the world of men, as she sat and told the Major of Big Chief's sickness and his death. She told him that he had left a message for his friend. He said that he hoped that his friend's years would be many. He had asked her to tell agent again what he had always felt about the mourning dance and request him to see that there was no mourning dance. He had said that many times they had talked about this thing and they had thought that it was bad for his people, that Osages were always in trouble during mourning dance, that there had been trouble with white man because he had believed that white man because of his power and his tricks was their worst enemy, and when his people were in forgetfulness of mourning dance scalp of white man, their enemy, came to their minds. He said that his people were always in trouble with other tribes during mourning dance. That during forgetfulness of mourning dance people thought of scalp of their ancient enemies—Pawnees and Comanches and Cheyennes. He said they had talked about this thing many times and he desired that there would be no mourning dance after his death; that his people should be true Osages but live in peace with white man and tribes; that they should learn all that white man knows and give white man all they know. In his last talk he had said that he desired this thing and that his wife should tell his friend of these things which he had said.

The Major left the wife of Che-Sah-Hunka and walked out into the cold air. The wind had died slightly but was still blowing through the tree tops and swirling the golden and red leaves before it. It caught the smoke of the fires, twisted and distorted them, lifting them, then pressing them to the ground again. He could hear the voice of a lone dog down the river, probably in the camp of Shon Kah Sabe. It must have been young and excited about something, as surely the older ones were curled up in the shelter of the lodges.

Soon the sun had climbed up above the trees and still he walked about or stood and watched the glittering ribbon of water meandering over a sand-choked bed. The sun felt warm and he stood for some time letting its rays through his clothes. His thoughts would not be concentrated, but he felt vague uneasiness, which he decided was a dread of seeing the ceremony for the burial of his friend. The mourning that tore at your heartstrings; tore your heart because in it was the questing of the ages; the something primitive which stirred the depth of emotion like the screams of a wounded horse; this remonstrance to the Great Mystery.

As the rays of the sun warmed his body he stood and looked out across the sand of the river, and seeing bars and drifts that lay across the bed to the Pawnee side, unbroken except by the glittering, slowly moving ribbon of water, he thought of the time that Big Chief had crossed early one morning to council with the Pawnees. The incident came back to him vividly.

A party of Pawnees had come across the river at flood tide and had taken fifteen head of horses from Big Chief. On learning of the theft Big Chief had immediately crossed over to the Pawnee side and had soon caught up with the band. He had told them in sign language that the horses were his and that he wanted them back. After some talk the Pawnees said that he could have the horses but a young Pawnee who was standing near him suddenly snatched the pistol from Big Chief's saddle and leaping on his horse, ran away toward the Pawnee agency on Black Bear creek.

Big Chief was very angry and rounding up his horses, drove them back to his camp. On arrival he changed horses, rode into the Agency and reported the matter to the agent, the Major's predecessor. After much talk the agent sent word to the agent of the Pawnees that the Osages desired a council and then selected three councillors to accompany Big Chief to the Agency of the Pawnees.

When the party reached the river the yellow waters were in flood, making many channels like fingers among the sand bars. A scout had been sent ahead to find a crossing and he had cut willow sticks and placed them at intervals along the route they were to take in crossing in order that they might avoid quicksand and the deepest water.

They got across but their clothes were wet and they decided to undress and dry them. While they were sitting there an Osage hunter came up and joined them; then another and another, appearing out of the bushes suddenly and silently as In-gro-kah, the panther. And the interpreter had asked Big Chief what these men were doing on the Pawnee side and he said that they were hunters, but when fifty or sixty of these men had joined them the interpreter understood. He told Big Chief that surely he would not take these men to the Pawnee Agency for the council, and Big Chief had replied that they would stay on the bank of the river, but that if he needed them he would send a runner for them.

An Osage Grave

The interpreter could see that they were all young warriors.

At the council Big Chief had given one of his characteristic speeches. The Major could visualize him, rising slowly, pulling his blanket up over his left shoulder and then bringing it together in front under his right arm. He could see him standing there looking over the faces in the council room, announcing gravely that he had come to talk to Pawnees; that he wanted them to listen to words that came from his heart. He told them that Pawnees were great people and that they knew much which Osages did not know; that it would be good if these people could come to visit Osages in friendship. He had said that Osages knew much that Pawnees did not know and that they might visit Pawnees in terms of friendship. It seemed to him that instead of this desire of friendship Pawnees came to take horses from Osages; that certain man had taken horses from him and through guile had taken his pistol which had been given to him by United States cavalry captain who had been his friend. He said that this young man had memory which was very short, he believed; that at one time on plains of west on buffalo hunt he had saved this very man from Cheyennes. He said that he did not believe that Pawnees had short memories but if they did, that it would be bad to have short memories about such things. He said that surely Pawnees knew medicine of Osages. For long time they had fought each other on plains, and Pawnees must surely know about medicine of Osages. He said further that he was peaceful man; that he was Peace Chief, but that he would ask that Pawnees return pistol that had been given him by his friend, captain of United States cavalry.

As he sat down a Pawnee rose and walked quietly out of the council room. Then the Pawnee agent talked for a short time about friendship between the two great tribes and resumed his seat. For a short time no one spoke. There was ominous tenseness in the room.

In this silence a man entered the room and walked up to Big Chief holding out a pistol. Big Chief took it and again there was silence. The agent then said that he believed matters were adjusted and the council was over if there was nothing else to talk about. He said that there would be a feast in the Agency of the Pawnees in honor of the Osages; that the chief of the Pawnees had told him to say this. When he sat down again a head man of the Pawnees got up and made a short talk saying that he wished to be at peace with his neighbors, Great Osages, and to show their friendship Pawnees wanted Osages to attend feast. Without changing the expression on his face, he said that those Osages who were waiting by the river should be told to come to the feast too.

The Major's thought came back again to the gliding, almost imperceptible ribbon of water that ran slowly on through the sand, and above him on the dead top of a sycamore two red headed woodpeckers quarreled with each other about store houses for the winter. The leaves eddied and floated in the chill wind and some fell on the water setting daintily on their voyage and disappearing in the reflected light of the sun. A flock of crows had found a barred owl in the gloom of the tall trees of the bottom, as he dreamed away the day, and were cursing terribly; darting at him or sitting above him, calling him thief and murderer. Life went on around the camps opposite cedar islands the same as when Big Chief walked regally among his people. The Major caught himself wondering why this should be.

There was silence over the camps and the Major knew that they were preparing Big Chief for his long ride to the Happy Hunting Ground and a pang came to his heart and then a queer feeling of dread. If only they would not mourn.

He walked back to the camp and to Big Chief's lodge. There were several people there and he didn't know about the etiquette in such matters. But some force drew him into the lodge. He saw the long body of Big Chief. The painters had finished with him. He was dressed in his best leggings and his best shirt. In his hands he held his eagle wing fan and on his wrists were his bracelets. He had his necklace of bear claws and at his throat was the shell gorget made from the fresh water mussel and representing the sun at noon; the symbol of the god of day. Over his shirt was his bone breastplate with wampum on each side. His face had been painted with red, a symbol of the dawn, symbol of the god of day; the Grandfather. On this were alternating lines of red and black on each side of his face representing the tribe and clan and family and the symbol which designated him as Peace Chief, or chief of the Chesho division of the tribe, the division which represented the sky.

He was gorgeous as he lay there; regal, like some primitive god in austere repose; a sort of oriental gorgeousness like some embalmed pharaoh ready to be taken to his tomb. Somehow this tall figure seemed triumphant and the sorrow which his death had inspired in the Major seemed to disappear as he looked, fascinated by this man dressed for the meeting with Wah'Kon-Tah, the Great Mysteries.

They carried him to the sandstone hill on the back of a pony and placed him in a sitting posture, facing the east, in a cairn of sandstone. They placed in the cairn food for the long journey.

The people followed the body up the hill and stood around in deep grief. The wind whipped their blankets and the prayers of the medicine men were torn from their lips and lost over the wooded hills. The red and yellow leaves floated from the blackjacks on a neighboring hill and drifted past on the quarreling wind that sometimes screamed and at other times sang whining, melancholy songs in the stones of the cairn and carried away the wailing of the mourners.

It took several men to place the United States flag in the top of the cairn where it seemed to take control immediately, as it plopped and crackled occasionally like the report of a gun. It became the dominant sound; above the sobbing of Big Chief's wife; above the wailing of the people; above the chants and the prayers of the medicine man.

The Major looked down the hill and saw three ponies tied to a small tree. He felt sad that these sleek-hided ponies should be sacrificed. But Big Chief must have a mount on the long ride. As he looked intently at them he found himself hoping his friend would use the bay as he undoubtedly was the best horse in the Major's opinion.

He began to move down the hill as he did not want to see the killing of the pony. The people had already begun to descend to the feast which was prepared at the camp on the river.

Before sitting down to the feast he held his hands over the smoke of the little cedar fire as others did before him, then found his place among the friends of Big Chief and ate heartily of the beef, lily roots, squash, fried bread and black coffee.

After the feast the sons of Big Chief and his brother-in-law came to the Major saying that they had heard about message that Che Sah Hunka had left concerning mourning dance. They were sorry about this they said. They didn't know what to do about this thing. They said he was greatest of Osages and that they wished to give him greatest mourning dance that had ever been given. The brother-in-law said: "I have fifty ponies. I will spend all of these ponies. I will spend more than fifty ponies for greatest mourning dance that has ever been given any Osage. I will do this in memory of my brother-in-law."

The Major sat and talked to them for a long time. He said he believed that it was best to remember what this great man had said about mourning dance. He said it would show their respect if they remembered what he wished about this thing. "Many times," he said, "he told me this thing. I have listened to him. I said there will be no mourning dance. I have given my word to my friend. He is not here and I cannot take back from him this word which I have given." They could see that this was so, they said, but surely there ought to be mourning dance for Che Sah Hunka. Many people knew that he was great man.

Finally they said that they could not go against wishes of Che Sah Hunka. They had listened to message that Che Sah Hunka had left with his friend.

The Major went to the lodge of his friend but found that the wife was with relatives and he decided not to disturb her. Already he noticed several women with ashes on their heads. He was glad to be leaving. He knew that he could do nothing more.

He watered his mules. As he hitched them they stood hunched and trembling under the cold harness and he had to speak to them many times to get them to stand still. It seemed that they wished to get out of his cheerless bottom too; out into the winds on the upland. Already the shadows had begun to lengthen though it was about mid-afternoon.

The little mules pressed against their collars with desire to go and the whip bending before the wind in the whipsocket was not needed. On the uplands the curtains flapped and the top of the buggy swayed. As he rounded the hill on which Big Chief had been buried the Major looked intently at the cairn of stone with the flag plopping above it. Partly on the piled stones he thought he saw the form of a horse lying there.

The spirit of Big Chief had started on the long ride.

FIRESIDE "BIG TALK"

Chapter Fourteen

SOON all the glory of the blackjacks was gone and the leaves that still clung to the branches were dull brown and rattled in the cold winds, complaining like restive souls. The great oaks stood in the valley of the Agency with spreading gray arms as though to protect the little settlement from the anger of winter. When the sun shone they made delicate designs on the area in front of the Council House, but when the skies were heavy, the winter found its voice in their branches.

Out on the high prairie and among the blackjacks, the world became steel hard. Above the prairie grasses the winds howled and stung the face of the traveler until it was numb, or tore at the coverings of the freighters' wagons, as though they would sweep such infinitesimal objects from the wild expanse. Into the teeth of the wind the mules lowered their heads, and the drivers walked looking at the ground, moving over the prairie like forlorn insects. Fortunate was the freighter who had his bottle on the seat of his wagon or in his pocket, and could find warmth in frequent nips; a great boon in a world of stinging wind, even though he might grow maudlin, or fall over asleep in his chair when he finally reached the warm fire in the trader's store.

Often the wind carried flakes of snow or sleet that stung like hot needles, and filled the ravines and obliterated the trail, leaving the high spots of the prairie bare to form a pattern of old copper and gleaming white. Flakes that were flung horizontally before the wind, stopping as they came to the blackjacks, to swirl and eddy, and settle on the brown leaves still clinging to the slate-colored branches; making a picture in black and white.

When the bands were not camped for the winter on the plains, their dome-shaped lodges were erected in the sheltered valleys of the streams, where the winds could not strike them; where the wood of the sycamore was available for the lighting of the lodges at night, and the oak and blackjacks furnished the coals for cooking.

On the inside the lodges were very warm, with the fire in the center, and the occupants seated on blankets and skins were very comfortable when the cold prowled over the Reservation like some insatiable animal.

Over the Reservation the younger men sat and listened to many stories told by their elders; they listened with interest and with admiration for the teller. Many of the stories had to do with the prowess of the Osages, in the many clashes with their enemies, the Pawnees, and no doubt there were many humorous stories of the discomfiture of the white man in his relationships with the Osages.

In the camp of Saucy Chief, a few miles up Bird creek from the Agency, the young men sat around the fire of Big Wild Cat and listened to the story of the Battle of the Washita, where Big Wild Cat was with Custer at the defeat of Black Kettle, the Cheyenne. There was honor given to Big Wild Cat for his part in this battle.

In the camp of Pawnee No Pah She of the Big Hills, there were many stories. In the lodge of Paw Hue Skah, the genial son and grandson of earlier Paw Hue Skahs, there were tales of battles of long ago. Though Paw Hue Skah had found the robes of his great ancestors too large for him, he had the respect of his people, and was known as friend to many of the traders.

Fortunate was the young man who listened to the tales of the We Heh Sah Ki (Hard Robe). He was a great war chief, and a sage councillor. He too had been with Custer at the battle of the Washita. It was he who crawled to the top of a ridge in the snow during that cold dawn and located the encampment of the Cheyennes.

In the southern part of the Reservation on the Arkansas river, opposite cedar islands, was the camp of Shonka Sabe (Black Dog), the orator, councillor, and certainly the Apollo of the tribe. Near here was the camp of the younger Grah Moh (Arrow Going Home), called Claremore, where the listeners might hear of battles with the Cherokees, but it is doubtful if they would be left with the impression that the Osages had ever been defeated in any of these battles.

Nearer the Agency was the camp of Striking Axe, the dandy, who affected white leggings and blankets. In other parts the camps of Nunka Wah Hoo, who, one time on the plains during a buffalo hunt, had Little Coon whipped because he killed a buffalo calf that had strayed into camp. Wah Shin Kah Sabe, the medicine man could tell interesting tales too. And there were tales to be heard in the northeastern part of the Reservation, near Caney river, in the camp of Che Topah. The young men might hear of the death of Big Track of the Pawnees, and the great taker of Osage ponies, or the story of the meeting of the Osages and the Comanches, who came together for battle, but stayed to council over the scalping of two Comanches by an Osage mourning party.

In this region was the camp of No Pah Wallo, the chief of the Little Osages, and not far away on Pond Creek was the camp of Alvin Wood.

There were others to tell of the battle of the Washita, besides Weh He Sah Ki and Big Wild Cat. In the lodges of Little Beaver and Eagle Feather, the young men might hear a different version of the death of the great Black Kettle, or Sho Mo Kah Se (Wolf) might convince his intense listeners that the battle of the Washita was fought in quite a different manner, not without the intimation that Wolf had fought as an Osage is ever expected to fight.

Then there were the stories of the delightful Oh Hunka Moie (Walks On End) the Don Juan, who wooed, won and rode away across the prairie, establishing himself as a most prolific ancestor.

The stories were not restricted to the lodges of the people. In the traders' stores men gathered around the stove, whose rounded belly grew red and crackled cheerfully. When the bands did not go to the plains for buffalo, the traders also remained at the Agency, among their ropes and beads and calicos and greasy black harness, dried apples, prunes and candies. Around the stove there were many stories about the prowess of the Osages, of experiences over the trails and conjectures about the "guv'ment."

Perhaps a trader or a mixed-blood would tell of the ride of Big Wild Cat, who, accompanied by a trader, went into Kansas on the trail of horses that had been stolen from him by white men from across the border, and how he had recovered them single handed.

Another would tell of the experiences of taking a dead white man in a pine box all the way to Elgin in July; the pine box having been casually set on the bed of the wagon. Or someone would tell of the wolves and coyotes following the wagon containing the corpse which was being taken across the hills to "the States" for burial. There were discussions as to whether the panther screamed like a woman, or whether he screamed at all, and there were always discussions as to who had killed the Wichita chief; whether Oh Hunka Moie or Three Striker, such discussions nearly always bringing up the former's cleverness and the stories current about him.

There were many stories about Oh Hunka Moie, some of them true, but most of them the figments of romantic imagination.

One of the most interesting stories about him was that he was an ordained priest. It was generally known that he had been educated by the Jesuits at the Osage Mission in Kansas, and there were many traders and mixed-bloods who would swear to the story that he carried with him his cassock and rosary, and other things necessary for saying mass, and around the red stove as the winds howled and the snow fell on the little valley of the oaks, stories of his double life would be told. One trader said he was present when Oh Hunka Moie came into the lodge of Wah Shinkah Sabe with his priest's robe.

The trader said that he had gone with the bands to the buffalo ground and had set up his lodge and unloaded all his goods for trading. Oh Hunka Moie had not gone out with them but had been hiding on the plains in order to avoid the Wichitas who were searching for him as the killer of their chief. The trader was sitting one day in the lodge of Wah Shinkah Sabe when a man came in dressed as a priest, and to his surprise he saw it was Oh Hunka Moie.

"He came in and looked around, then he went out to his horse and came back carrying a bundle. He unwrapped it and I saw that it contained Indian clothes. He took off his priests clothes and wrapped them in a bundle, then he handed them to one of the women and told her to keep them for him until he got back. Then he began to put on his other clothes, and called for a glass, then began to paint his face like they paint 'em for the war path. You wouldn't 'uv thought it was the same man—never saw a man change so. When he finished he went out and got on his pony and rode away. I have never heard where he went to or why, and I'm not ready to swear that he went on the war path, but I know what I saw and you can draw your own conclusions, as the fella says."

Some of the listeners claimed that they had heard about his dressing as a priest, and some even claimed on good authority, they said, that sometimes he went into "the States" and said mass. But some said they thought it was a little too much of a good thing—it might be possible for him to do such a thing but they thought it was just a good story. However, they all agreed that he was a smart one, all right.

A trader from the big hill country would tell of the death of Nee Koh Kon Se (Man Alone).

"Old Wah Shin Peesha (Bad Temper) give me the devil," he said, "because my wife gave Nee Koh Kon Se a little laudanum to ease his pain. She was afraid to give any more, but he kept sending a runner to the house to get 'sleep medicine' as he called it. We had to hide out so that they couldn't find us. When the doctor came over from the Agency—this was over in the Big Hill country—it was too late and the poor old fella was dead. The doctor said that he had given a Big Hill woman some laudanum once so that she could sleep, and had kept diminishing the doses until she had recovered, and he thought that that was what Nee Koh Kon Se wanted. But what old Wah Shin Peesha was mad about was because the Big Hills believed that Nee Koh Kon Se had the evil spirit. Wah Shin Peesha followed me all over the lot scolding me for attempting to save the life of one who had the evil spirit. He said it was good that he had died, and that he ought to die.

"But old Wah Shin Peesha has a nephew just as bad. A strapping, young fella; nice lokin'. He seems all right sometimes but he's a little off and the Big Hills believe that he has the evil spirit. A good lookin' young man like he is ought to be a warrior and a hunter, but for a long time they had him herding horses like some little boy. Now they have cast him out altogether, and he comes to the kitchen door at home and my wife feeds him. He had a bad case of scrofula for some time—I guess it was from livin' in the house—they can't live in houses; they're not used to it. He lives in the open now—sleeps anywhere on the ground, with his blanket wrapped around him, and pulled up over his head. Sometimes he is covered with snow but you know that scrofula is almost cured. When he had it the worst he smelled pretty bad and I gave him the name John Stink. Everybody has begun calling him that now—I wish I hadn't started it. His real name is Ho To Moie."

Another trader spoke up, "Speakin' of Wah Shin Peesha, reminds me o' the time a delegation of 'broad-hats' come down when the Osages first bought the Reservation. These fellas come from Philadelphia—big men in the Quaker church, I guess. They thought the plains of the Kaw country was better for the Osages than all these blackjacks and prairie, and they suggested that the Osages take their reservation on the plain. But they wanted these hills 'cause there was lots of deer and other game here, and it was sheltered and wooded. I believe old Wah Ti An Kah had a lot to do with it. He used to talk to the people ever chance he got—stamp his foot when he thought they were not listening to him. Anyway the 'broad-hats' visited across the river and were on the way back, when they came to the Arkansas—it was purty high. Somehow the horses balked right in the middle of the stream and water come into the wagon bed. The 'broad-hats' were purty scared and were wondering what to do, but didn't seem to be able to do anything. Old Wah Shin Peesha was with the party, as a guide or a representative of the tribe, or something. Anyway you know what a terrible temper he has and how big he is. He'll weigh two hundred and fifty, won't he? He's at least six five or six feet tall. Well, anyway old Wah

Shin Peesha lost his temper at all this muddlin'. He stripped off all his clothes except his breech clout, and got out o' the wagon into the water. Then before anyone knew it he had one of those fellas on his shoulder, and waded out to the opposite bank with him. He carried each one of 'em out, then looked at 'em like they was somethin' the cat brought in, sayin' somethin' in Osage which no one could understand, but they thought they heard him say somethin' about 'women.' I'll bet those 'broad-hats' never forgot that incident for a long time. The old fella looks mean enough when he's not mad, but when he's mad he looks like the giants you read about in fairy books."

"Well," said the trader from the Big Hill country, "that sounds like 'im all right. He got somethin' the matter with him last winter, and my wife gave him some quinine. It seemed to help him, and by golly, everytime he feels bad he comes to the house to get some quinine—he comes in and goes right to the cabinet where she keeps the medicine. She brought different kinds of medicine when she come down, so as to have it on hand. Sometimes, she says, she will be sittin' doin' somethin' or other, when he comes in. She says that big fella comes in like a cat, and the only way she can tell he's there is the slight sway of the floor, not another sound—no squeakin' nor sound o' foot steps—just the swayin' of the floor with his stride."

One of the freighters who had remained silent, spoke to another on the other side of the stove, "Fred, reckon that ain't the Injun that tuk my hair on the Caney trail?"

"May bee."

"Shore sounds like 'im." Then he turned to the group in general: "Me an Fred, here, was a-freightin' some stuff from Caney. We wuz jist a-comin' off the prairie an' droppin' off down into Rock crick, when I thought I seen Injuns comin'. They wuz a good ways off but they rode like Injuns. I looked agin and shore enough, they wuz, all right—I could see they had the paint on 'em too. When they got clost I knowed what it wuz—I knowed it wuz a war party, from the way they wuz painted. I wuzn't scairt exactly, but I shore wuzn't comfortable. They rode up on the run and stopped my team and signed for me to git out. If I'd a knowed ary one of 'em I'd a felt better, but they wuz all strangers to me. Then I seen, I reckon, the biggest Injun I ever seen—biggern ary man I ever seen, I reckon. He wuz as big as a skinned horse. He started makin' signs and I didn't know what he meant. All of a sudden he got madder'n hell and pulled a big butcher knife out of his blanket and caught me by the shoulder. Then he grabbed me by the hair—it come to my shoulders 'bout like it is now. I ain't a-lettin' on I wuzn't scairt, mind-ju—I jist figered I wuz checkin' in. Well, he tuk a bunch o' my hair an' cut it off with his knife, then he tuk a piece o' raw hide an' fixed it on some way, then him and them others rode off across the prairie shoutin' and singin'—sounded like they's singin' anyhow.

"When they wuz gone I felt o' my scalp, an' I shore wuz proud it wuz still there. I looked back at Fred's wagon an' one of his mules had his check rein loose and wuz eatin' grass—the seat wuz empty—by golly." He looked over at Fred. "Fred, I'm a-gonna tell this'n on yu, if yu kill me fer it." Fred expressed his em-

In the Trader's Store

barrassment by spitting into the stove. The speaker
turned to the group again. "Where d'yu reckon ole Fred
here wuz? By golly, he tuk to the blackjacks and t'wuz
a good half hour afore I found 'im. He said he sure
never lowed he'd see me agin. I jist lowed, maybe, that
that there big fella was this here Washin' peachie yu
been talkin' bout."

"Hit might have bin," said one of the group, "but
I doubt—there's lots of big Injuns,—they always look
bigger and meaner when they got the paint on. A few
years ago they'd a tuk that mane of yourn—the guv-ment
has jist about got 'em takin' hair instid o' the scelp.
A man on the Reservation is pretty safe now, but I don't
know 'bout if he is on the plains—might be a different
story."

Sometimes Oh Hunka Moie was present during the
conversation around the stove. He was a great story
teller, whether in English or his native tongue, and
usually when he began to talk the rest listened whether
it was with the group in the trader's store, or as he sat
cross-legged in the lodges of his people. His English was
very good and his Osage was almost perfect, although
he was never known as a great orator. He was tall and
very handsome, and was believed by many to be a gen-
ius. His services as an interpreter were sought, and his
translation of the Lord's prayer into Osage was accepted
as the best one.

His stories had a neat turn to them, much of the
material having been gathered from conversations and
from his own experiences. He would stalk into a trader's
store or among a group of people who were speaking
English and listen without the least expression on his

face that he understood; in this way he learned much. It was said that for a year he had been coming into a certain trader's store to make his purchases, talking with the traders through a "brave," but one day suddenly broke into cultured English to the astonishment of the trader.

One of his favorite stories was about his experience with two white men who were traveling across the Reservation. He had been riding across the prairie all morning and was very hungry. As he rode along he saw two white men stop at a small stream and he watched them for some time and saw that they were preparing to cook their meal. When the meal was prepared he rode up to them, and looked at them steadily for several moments, then dismounted without saying a word and sat down between them. He began to eat heartily. He heard one of the white men say to the other; "What did I tell yu? Didn't I say we ortn't come into the Reservation without guns? Cain't tell what this Injun mought do—cain't trust 'em I tell yu." The other one answered, "Maybe he's jist hungry."

"Hungry, hell, you cain't tell what them bastards'll do—soon scelp yu as look at yu."

"What'll we do?"

"Do? Hell, we cain't do nothin', but set here like a coupla patridges and not make 'im mad."

When Oh Hunka Moie had finished, he didn't even grunt as they expected he might do, but walked calmly to his horse and mounted. He noticed the relief on their faces as he started to ride off, and this was too much for his Indian heart so he turned his pony and came back, watching the expressions change, with a warm appreciation of the situation. He sat on his horse and looked at them, and he said they shook like the leaves of the cottonwood. Then he said to them in English, "I would advise you men to bring your guns next time you come on the Reservation, but come, only in case you have very urgent business here. I s'pose you know you are trespassing? I believe you better stay off, but if you do come, bring your guns next time. Good day."

And he rode off.

This story always pleased any group of his people as well as the traders and the mixed-bloods.

Oh Hunka Moie's colorful career, like a flash across the blackjack hills, was cut short by a prosaic train in the little border town of Elgin. Even in death he was the subject for speculation, and the mixed-bloods, traders, and employes discussed his death as they had discussed his activity, around the big-bellied stove in the traders' store. Many said that he was killed by the Omahas because he had betrayed them in his promise of enrollment with the Osages. Some said that a jealous white woman had in some way contrived his end, and others took the natural conclusion that he was killed by the train. Whatever the cause of his death, a picturesque figure went on its last long ride to the Happy Hunting Ground, and very likely there were prayers in English, French and sobbing appeals in Osage for the acceptance of his spirit by the Great Mysteries.

As the winter wore on the newer stories grew stale, but there were always rumors as to what the "guv'ment" was going to do in certain matters. Even then in that wild valley there were sparks of the pride which the Amer-European ever takes in his community and the progress of his town or village. A new piano or an organ brought in from "the States" over the prairie was of great importance, and certainly an indication of progress. Finally when some of the mail came in addressed not to the Osage Indian Agency, Oklahoma Territory, but with the name that had recently been suggested, they saw in it flattering recognition. The name honored the great Paw Hue Skah, who had been a chief among the Osages before their removal. Letters which bore the new address "Pawhuska, O. T." were handed from one to the other and commented on with pride.

When the winters were especially hard and long, stories around the stove palled on the traders, and as one trader said, "A fella almost had to push those freighters out when he fixed to close up at night—they'd be pullin' mules all night, or tellin' tall stories, that'd keep a-gettin' wilder'n 'n wilder.

But it was not always a snow-bound, wind-whipped world. Often the sun shone genially through the branches of the trees, and made fret-work on the dead leaves and the dark soil of the stream valley; glinting from the leaves of the blackjack and shimmering over the monochrome prairie. For weeks the sun would shine every day, warming the cold air that hung over the hills; melting the ice at the edges of the streams; warming the south sides of the hills and leaving the north sides with gleaming snow patches. Then suddenly the cold winds would stir as though from a sleep into which they had fallen, carelessly. And as though remembering their office, begin to stir in the branches of the trees and ripple the tall, copper-colored grasses of the prairies. The dark clouds would creep up from the northwest and the winds would blow, singing mounfully through the cottonwoods and oaks of the streaw valleys, and cause the leaves of the blackjacks to rattle in half hearted protest.

Then after spitting a few flakes, clouds would roll away to the east, and the sun would set in a splash of yellow, and in tongues of red, like the leaping flames of a fire that had been frozen. The moon would burst over the blackjack-fringed hills, and creep up the sky, making obsidian shadows on the muddy place before the Council House, the other stone buildings and the long rambling traders' stores, standing in ghostly silence as red eyes shone from the doctor's house, the traders' houses and the house of the blacksmith.

In the camps over the Reservation, the dome-shaped lodges were the homes of spirit people, and the cold winds in the naked branches were the voices of the spirits of warriors, wandering unhappily over the earth. The moon shadows of the moving branches of the elms would play on the tops of the lodges, and the interlaced branches of sycamores would rub together and squeak pettishly.

As an undertone to the wailing wind, a screech owl would sometimes complain quaveringly, and at such times a tall courageous warrior in his warm lodge, might walk nervously to and fro with the movements of a caged coyote, finally snatching a brand from the fire, he would pull his blanket close about his head and step into the cold wind, waving the sputtering stick under the neighboring trees until the bird with the voice of evil would fly silently away. Then he would go back into his lodge and roll into his warm blankets, attempting to feel some assurance that he had cut short the message of the evil spirit. Before he slept he might hear the thin yelping of the coyotes, or the howl of the wolf that was the voice of hunger, but they carried no evil; they were brothers, hunting as he hunted. The call might even be good medicine, coming after the voice of the bird with the evil spirit, if they happened to be one of the symbols of his clan.

THE WHITE MAN'S ROAD
Chapter Fifteen

THE MAJOR often wondered if Indian children were benefited as he thought they ought to be by the compulsory schooling. It was obvious that they ought to be taught; that they ought to learn the white man's ways in order that they might be prepared for the traveling of the white man's road in the future. Yet he was sorry to see their ideals displaced by the white man's method, and it was difficult to get the proper instructors in the school; people broad enough and civilized enough to understand the Indian mind. But even with the people who were obtainable he thought the instruction according to the Amer-European method would be better than letting the young people grow up under the old system, and suddenly face the conditions which he saw were inevitable.

It was quite beyond reason to believe that these people could remain isolated until they were able to adapt themselves to the changing conditions. The white man was determined to get into the last Reservation of the Osages. If he could not bring about the allotment and the selling of surplus lands, he could certainly filter into the Reservation where he had no earthly business, and by the force of his numbers impress himself on the Indian; obtain ascendency by the mere force of numbers. Police were kept busy bringing in people who had no permits to live on the Reservation and hunters who slaughtered the game. It seemed that the United States marshals were ever on the long road to Fort Smith, taking horse thieves and murderers to the "hanging-judge." As from the beginning, the so-called civilized white man gave more trouble than the savage Indian.

Thus he considered it a race against time to prepare the younger generation as fast as possible to meet the conditions which the white men were forcing. The government school was the only thing at hand for this preparation, despite unqualified instructors. Many of them were religious hypocrites with little sympathy and understanding, whose education seemed to be based on the importance of using isn't instead of ain't.

For a short time his own children attended a school taught by a lady of the traders' colony. They had for their playmates the children of the traders and employes of the Agency, and the little mixed-bloods and full-bloods. They learned to speak glibly in the tongue of their playmates; using both languages in their games. Later, however, the Major's children attended the government school.

He ever warned his children to observe the courtesies of their playmates. He taught them that to stare at people was ill-mannered; especially to stare at Indians, and that the height of discourtesy was to stare at mal-formed people. He took them to see the end of a mourning dance, only after they had promised him that they would not stare at the dancers in their yellow, red and black paint, or stand looking at the chief mourner, who would more than likely be terribly emaciated after his long fasting. No matter how fascinating were the women with mud on their hair, or the men solemnly washing the paint from their faces; or how horribly fascinating the chief mourner with his ribs like a washboard and his cheeks sunken, they were to pretend that they did not see them.

And thus the children of the Osage families who lived at the Agency, learned as much from their playmates, as their playmates learned from them. The little Amer-Europeans learned not to cry when they fell and hurt their shins, but they also learned to pinch in a most painful and effective manner. They learned that jabbering was the talk of blackbirds and not of people, and their teachings, that lies and careless promises were bad, were confirmed in their relationships with their round-faced playmates.

Some friend of the Major's family, feeling sorry for their isolation in the midst of savagery, had subscribed to a weekly magazine which was sent regularly, that is, it arrived regularly at the borders of the Reservation, and arrived at the Agency several issues at a time. It was a child's magazine of the best class but the Major's wife found it advisable to burn the copies as they arrived. She believed they would not aid her children in understanding, or in making their companionship with Indian children more pleasant if they were allowed to read impossible stories of massacres and scalpings of virtuous white men, and red savages consistently "biting the dust."

Indian parents loved their children; loved them with a tenderness that was appealing, and their insight into matters which concerned their children was often uncanny. Their obvious stubbornness and reluctance to place them in government schools may have had source in their acumen and their often keen judgment of the purposes of the white man.

They approved of their children playing with the children of the traders, and many of them evinced this approval by allowing their little girls to come to the Agency to stay. They were careful of their little daughters, and no greater compliment could be paid to a white man than the trusting to him of a young girl. Nearly always there were little Osage girls in the home of the Major.

NELLIE SAUCY CHIEF

The young daughter of Saucy Chief who lived up the creek a few miles from the Agency spent much time at the residence. She was charming in her modesty and in her queer little quirks in thinking. There was soon an attachment between her and the Major's wife. She had been given the name Nellie for some unknown reason and her Indian name which was probably a pretty one, or even a poetic one, was forgotten and she became Nellie Saucy Chief.

Nellie divided her time between the Agency home and her own home in the upper valley. She took great delight in the occupations of the young lady of that day, and soon began to wear the clothes of the white woman, changing back into her shirt, strouding, leggings and blanket, as the whim came to her. Finally she embraced the ways of the white woman and began to feel interested in their heaven.

As in all young girls there was much romance in her and she had reached that age where young girls were said to dream of a knight on a white charger, but it would be difficult to determine the kind of young man who was the knight of Nellie's day dream; whether he rode across the prairie in breach clout and moccasins, holding the staff with a scalplock dangling from the end, or whether he was a white man in blue coat with impeccable little mustache, with a long knife at his side. From Nellie's position of indecision as to what she wished him most to be, it might be guessed that he was a composite man, but he would very probably be riding a pinto pony instead of a white charger.

In the midst of delightful hours spent in the drawing room with the Major's gracious little wife and the thrill of being a young woman with two homes, she fell sick. In her first illness, inspired by the romance of the thing, she asked the Major's wife to promise that when she died she would be buried in the beautiful white dress they had made, and that she would be buried in the white man's coffin in the ground.

Her parents came for her and took her to their lodge. Nearly every day the Major's wife would go to the camp to see her. She seemed to be improving but one day a runner came to the residence and said that Saucy Chief had told him to say that his daughter was dying, and the Major and his wife were to come.

They went in the buggy up the creek and then into the valley where the camp of Saucy Chief was located. As they jogged along they saw a wagon coming toward them, with an Indian riding alongside. As they came closer they saw that the horseman was Saucy Chief and that the woman sitting in the seat was his wife.

As they approached each other Saucy Chief got off

his horse and walked toward them with the reins over his arm. The Major stopped his mules, and he and his wife got out of the buggy. They knew from the horseman's action what was in the bed of the wagon, and that his dismounting was a courtesy to his dead daughter. The Major and his wife returned the courtesy by approaching him afoot.

When they came together they told him that their hearts were heavy.

As the wagon came up the wife of Saucy Chief got up from her seat and backed down over the wheel. When she approached them they told her also that their hearts were heavy. She told them that her daughter had said to her and her husband that they must tell wife of Major that she should remember word that had been given; word that had been given about being buried as white woman is buried, and that she would wear clothes of white woman and be covered up in earth. The wife of Saucy Chief said she thought it was bad that Indian should be placed in ground where it was dark; where sun could not be seen at dawn, but that her daughter had wanted this thing and they were coming to residence to give body to Major's wife.

The body of Nellie Saucy Chief was laid out in the north room of the residence in a pine box, which was the only white man's coffin available. Her pretty brown face shone in many ruffles and laces of white. There were the restrained prayers of the Friends for her soul, and occasionally there were outbursts and sobbing of the Indian women who had gathered, also restrained. Over the whole there was sorrow that lay heavily, and a silence that seemed charged.

When the services were over and they were preparing for the burial the mother of Nellie could restrain herself no longer, so she came up to the Major's wife, and looking at her with great sorrow in her face, said: "I have looked at my child in white man's coffin, and I said it is good. He wanted to be buried in burying ground of white man. I said it is good to be buried in white clothes of white woman. I do not know about these things. I looked at face of my girl and I said he is Indian, my girl. They will not know who he is. It will be good if we paint the face of my girl."

The Major's wife answered, "It will be good if we paint the face of your girl."

The mourning party left the room except three women. They stayed out for some time, and when they came back into the room to conclude the services, they saw that the daughter of Saucy Chief was ready for her long trip, and that there would be no doubt about her identification in the land of the Great Mysteries.

EAGLE FEATHER

One day several Indians who lived near the Agency came to the residence, walked quietly in and sat down. The Major thought they had come to talk business and he waited for one of them to say something. They sat for some time then one of them said that he had come to tell the Major a thing which his friend Eagle Feather had told him to say. He said that Eagle Feather had died.

The Major was shocked to hear of the death of Eagle Feather. They had been friends and he had appointed him as a policeman when they first came to the Agency. He told them his heart was sad because they had told him this. The spokesman then told him that he had come to talk about a will which Eagle Feather had left, and that these people with him were witnesses to this will. He said that in this will Eagle Feather had given his two little girls to the Major and that he was to bring them up in the way he thought best. He said that he would like to take the little girls and bring them up as his own, as he was a relative to Eagle Feather, but that Eagle Feather had told him to say these things to the Major.

The Major had known nothing of Eagle Feather's family, as naturally, they had never discussed such things. He told the visitors that he would think about this thing and he would let them know later.

He found that the two little girls were in school, and he remembered that Eagle Feather had once told him that he did not think that little girls should go to the government school. After some thought the Major sent them to a school in Philadelphia.

They were away at school twelve years, and when he went east he always went to visit them.

When they grew up one married and went as a missionary to another reservation, where she remained until her husband's death, then she returned and became interested in the education of girls, sending them away to school at her own expense. The other one made her home with the Major's family until her marriage.

THE WHITE GIRL

One morning when the Major came downstairs he found several young men waiting for him. One of them said that they had been talking about a certain thing, and that they had decided that they would like to see the white man's country up in "the States." He said that they had been invited by a Cherokee to go along with him and dance for people who had never seen Osages dance. They said that Cherokee had told them that white man would give them money when they danced, and they thought it would be good to go. They would have money of white man and they would see many things.

After some talk as to where they wished to go, the Major gave them a permit to leave the Reservation for the purpose of dancing.

Some months later they returned and called at the residence to tell the Major of their experiences in "the States." They said they had had a very good time, and had seen many things that would take long time to tell about. They said white man was very much pleased with their dancing, but that they thought white man had very little manners as he would stare at them on the streets of the cities, and sometimes he insulted them by taking hold of their clothes when they were wearing them, and feeling of ornaments on their arms and wrists. They said they were glad to get back and they would have much to tell for long time.

The Major told them that he was very glad that they had enjoyed the visit to "the States," that they had learned much about ways of white man. He said that his heart was glad that they had behaved well, so that white man could not say that they did not know how to act.

When the party left one young man remained behind. He sat for some time then with some embarrassment told the Major that he wanted to talk with him about a certain thing that was worrying him. The Major asked him what this thing was and he said in English: "For long time we were in this Philadelphia. There was a girl there in this Philadelphia who come to see us dance all time. She kep' lookin' at me. Sometime she look at me so much I couldn' hardly dance good. Purty soon we go walkin' together and we talk long time. When we goin' leave we go get married. Now I'm married to this girl."

The Major thought for a long time of the many things that might happen to a handsome young brave in a city. He said: "I'm afraid that you have picked up with some bad girl. You don't know about the bad girls in the city—you better just forget about it." The boy's face flushed slightly.

"Yes I know there are bad girls in this Philadelphia, but I know that this girl is good girl." His sincerity impressed the Major and he asked him many questions as to what the girl had said, and as to where she lived, and where they had been married. By the boy's answers he believed that perhaps some romantic girl had been fascinated by this young man and had married him in a moment of romantic dreams of the thrilling life on the plains. He turned to the boy and asked, "What is this girl's name?"

The boy felt in the pockets of his clothes and pulled out a crumpled piece of paper. "It is on there," he said. The Major read the name and the address which were written in a careful schoolgirl hand, then he said: "I will keep this paper and I will write a letter to this girl —you say she wants to come here and live with you on Reservation—I will write to her and tell her how you live—the kind of house you live in. I will tell her it is not the kind of life she reads about in books—like the pictures the white man makes. I will tell her that your life is not like the life your fathers used to live. I will make it seem bad. It is not bad, of course—you have a nice life here, but I believe it is not like she thinks it is, and I will make it seem bad. If she loves you she will want to come anyway, and if she does not love you so much, she will be glad not to come."

"That is all right—but she will come."

In a few weeks the Major received a reply to his letter. The girl said that she married the young man because she loved him, and that she would come to live with him, wherever he lived. To her, she wrote, he was different from any young man that she had ever met and she thought he was wonderful, closing with the statement that she would be ready to come to her husband when she received the ticket.

The Major and the young man met her at the train in Coffeyville; a charming young girl, very fluttered and embarrassed, because she was very much in love.

THE ARAPAHO GIRL

For some time the Major had been attempting to trace a young man and his wife, whom the department reported as being off the Reservation without a permit. One day he received a letter stating that the young man was becoming quite famous as an orator in Illinois, and was lecturing on temperance. He immediately wrote to the department telling them this and suggesting that the young man be allowed to continue off the Reservation since he might be doing some good.

« 267 »

He received an answer from the department, stating that they were aware of this Indian's activities, but that they had reference to a young man who had been at Carlisle, and who was now reported to be on the reservation of the Arapahos.

After some investigation the Major found this to be true and immediately sent for this young man.

He came into the office and reported that he had come. The Major told him that he was supposed to be at Carlisle, and had been given permission to be off the reservation for that purpose.

"I have been on the reservation of the Arapahos," he said in English.

"The Arapahos are not friends of your people. Why have you been there?"

The young man hesitated as if deciding whether to tell the purpose of his visit or not, then he seemed to gain confidence. "I have gone to the reservation of the Arapahos because there is a girl there. I love this girl—that is the reason I went there."

"Why don't you marry this girl then?"

"I went there to ask her father if I could marry her, and he said that he didn't want his girl to marry an Osage."

"Then that is all there is to it—she will not marry you without her father's permission."

The young man looked at the floor, then around the room. Suddenly he got up, took his black hat from a chair and left. The Major thought he looked handsome even in his school clothes.

The young man went out to the hitching rack and untied his pony, then catching the horn swung himself into the saddle without touching the stirrup. He kicked the pony with his heels and started in a run to the brow of the hill, but slowed down as he began to descend.

The area in front of the Council House and the stores was muddy, the mud partly frozen, though the winter sun was warm on the young man's back. He thought the long, sprawling store of the trader was very ugly, especially to one who had seen the great buildings at Carlisle; this store standing there with its many windows, and painted red, was like an old woman; an old white woman; like the matron at the girl's building who put red on her face to hide the wrinkles and the dead skin.

It was all very ugly. These people here in the Agency didn't know much, he thought. He used to think they knew a lot, but now he believed they didn't know much. They had never heard the Carlisle band playing the school song; they didn't know anything about those long, shiny instruments. They ought to hear some of those Chippewa and Oneida boys play. But they thought it was good here.

He rode on across the ford by the mill, up through the Clear creek valley, through the blackjacks and then on to the high prairie. There was a cold wind blowing on the prairie and he pulled his coat collar up around his throat.

His horse jogged along in a fox trot, and his slim body moved with the movements of the horse. He didn't see the copper grass, or hear the wind talking. His thoughts were far away on the reservation of the Arapahos.

At Little Chief creek he saw a band of deer that had

come up from the bottoms to eat acorns, and he saw a coyote slink out of the trail, though the sun was in his face. When he had passed he instinctively looked back, and the coyote had come back into the trail and stood looking at him with great unconcern, holding his muzzle high in the air, as though to catch the little scent-bearing currents that played above the tall grasses.

Before he reached Salt creek the sun had set and it became colder. When he saw the dark line of trees in front of him, he kicked his pony into a lope.

When he reached the stream he sat for some moments on his pony, then his mind was made up. He didn't want to ride into his father's camp until morning; he thought it would be good to sleep here in the shelter of the stream bottom. He pulled the saddle and bridle off, then hobbled his pony with a large red handkerchief which he sometimes wore around his neck, but which he now believed was not the proper decoration for a man who had been to Carlisle. He gathered some wood and built a fire.

He had no food but he didn't want food. He sat before the fire and looking into the crackling flames, saw the face of an Arapaho girl, with her black hair done up like a white woman. He never doubted the beauty of that magic face, and he thought it was wrong that they should call the Arapaho "Big Nose" in the language of the hands. He felt ashamed when he had to place his right index finger by the left side of his nose, when he wished to indicate Arapaho.

As he sat many thoughts came to his mind. He thought of the day he went to the lodge of the chief to talk about marriage with his daughter. The old chief

had been very pleasant but he had said that the Osages
and Arapahos had fought many battles, and he believed
it would not be good to let his girl marry an Osage. The
young man believed that the old chief didn't know
much; he didn't know about the ways of the white man;
he didn't know about Carlisle. He wanted to tell him
about these things, but he could only sit and listen to
the chief, because he was an old man and a great man
among his people, and he, himself, was a young man
and could say nothing.

He thought with a pang of the picture he had seen.
It was a picture of the graduating class and the Arapaho
girl was in it. Standing by her side was a tall Cheyenne.
He had cut the Cheyenne's picture out of the group with
his knife, but every time he thought of it his heart
seemed to shrivel, and he grew hot and tried to think
of something else.

It grew colder and soon from the prairie came the
high, keen yelping of the coyotes, and very close, somewhere in the bottoms to his left, an old dog coyote
gave several sharp barks, then in crescendo mourned as
though his heart were filled with sadness.

The young man got up and undid his blankets from
the saddle, wrapped them tightly around him, and lay
down by the fire to sleep.

He was up early the next morning. He got on his
horse and rode down the stream to the camp of his
father.

The dogs saw him coming and ran pell-mell out of
the camp to bark in a dozen keys and nip the hocks of
his pony. The little pony lay back his ears and lashed

out at one of the curs, rolling him over the frozen ground. He got up and limped away howling.

He saw his tall father come out of the lodge as he rode up, standing like a statue with no movement of welcome after the young man's two years absence. He dismounted, letting the reins fall to the ground, and walked toward the lodge. One of his little brothers was standing with a greasy rib bone in his hand and his round face was smeared with grease. The young man thought his little brother was ugly standing there holding the rib bone in his greasy fist, and he saw that he didn't know how to take care of his nose either. The little brother stood as though he were not in the least interested, but as the young man passed him he heard him say, "Kosh-she," to himself, then he gave his full attention to the rib bone again. The young man walked up to his father, extended his hand and said, "How." The father's eyes were smiling but he answered only, "How, my son," then turned and went into the lodge and the young man followed. His mother came from the black kettle she had been attending. She laid the spoon down and came up to him and put her hands on his arm, and looked up into his face, her eyes brimming with love, "Kosh-she," and then, "Huhn, Kosh-she is man now; he is back." The young man was embarrassed and looked down at the floor. His mother left him and went back to the kettle, but she said at intervals, "Huhn, he is man, Kosh-she," as she bent over her work.

Father and son sat cross-legged on one of the skins. The father slowly opened a beaded pouch and took out a pipe, then filled it with the ground, dried leaves of the sumac and lit it from an ember. Then he lay down, resting his head on his hand, supported by his crooked elbow. Soon the mother placed food before her son and he ate heartily.

When he had finished his father said "It is good that you have come back from white man's school." There was an expression of assent in the young man's face; he said nothing. His father continued "You have come back—tomorrow there will be feast." There was another silence, then the father spoke again, "You have seen many things—now you are man, and you have no name yet." The young man looked around the lodge; he thought it was ugly. He said, "I have seen many houses of white man; houses many times bigger than Council House."

"Pawnee No Pah She has told me of these buildings," said the father, "he has been to Washington many times." There was a longer silence then the father said, "We must think of woman for you—it is time we were thinking of woman." The young man's heart seemed to shrivel and he felt his face getting hot. He was afraid his father would see his fear so he looked away, but he said nothing.

Soon the father arose and pulling his blanket together in front, left the lodge. The young man went to the door of the lodge and saw him disappear among the trees, then he turned and walked through the camp in the direction of the spring.

He saw a young girl coming down along the trail that led from the prairie; the one which the horses used when they came to water. Behind her was an old woman who walked like a duck. Her face was like the dried apples in the trader's store, and she was watching her steps and did not look up until she was near him; just in time to see the young girl looking shyly over the edge of her blankets at him, with a sort of challenge in her eyes; the way that young girls looked at young men, and which sometimes made them feel happy inside. He didn't feel that way and he pretended that he didn't see her, but the old woman looked at him with her eyes screwed up, and seemed on the point of scolding him for being so close.

These old women always looked mean, he remembered; he'd seen these old women who were guards for the young girls run the young men from the place where the girls went to bathe, with a butcher knife. They always carried butcher knives in the folds of their blankets. He remembered, how one night, a young man had taken off all his clothes except his breach clout and moccasins, and had crawled to the lodge of a young girl with whom he had exchanged looks many times. It had been very funny. Just as the young man was starting to crawl under the edge of the lodge, a dog came up and sniffed his bare back with his cold nose. The young man was so frightened that he crawled under the edge of the lodge and started for the door, but in his fright fell over the old woman who was the girl's guard, and she caught him and slashed him across the back with her knife. That was sure funny. But he remembered they caught the young man later, and after a council, tied him to a tree and made the whipper whip him many times. That was sure bad, and he had felt sorry for that young man then.

As he went on up the trail he felt that all this was of very little importance. He didn't think the girls were pretty; talking crazy with each other, and giggling and looking over their blankets at the young men. And the young men were silly too, he thought. Hiding out in the buck brush and waiting for the girls to come to the spring, and when the old women weren't looking, shining a piece of glass in their faces, and the girls looking around and acting silly. They didn't know any better though; they didn't know what love was. Those young men who went out at night and stood against a tree, wrapped in their blankets so you couldn't see their faces, and played a hickory flute near the lodge of a girl who didn't know any better either; they were silly too, he believed. They didn't know about walking along the walks of the campus of Carlisle, with a beautiful Arapaho girl who had her hair put up on her head like white woman and dressed in clean starched dress of the white woman.

They didn't know about the songs sung by groups, and what a warm feeling came to you when you stood by the Arapaho girl, and touched her hand and felt her body close to yours. She was stiff and clean like the starch that shone in the hem of her skirts. She was always stiff and clean, kinda like iron, and sometimes something squeaked like a stiff thing when she moved; she was kinda like bright, clean iron, he thought. She smelled like soap, too. She smelled much better than the mixed-bloods; they smelled like the white woman, and he didn't like to stand by them during the singing, 'specially that girl who was part Chippewa, who acted like a white woman and put on perfume. He always thought that she knew she didn't smell good or she wouldn't put on perfume that way. He didn't like any kind of perfumes; not even carbolic acid, but that was pretty good, he thought. It kept off white man's sickness.

As he walked he was flooded with memories; silent moonlight nights in the spring, with the shadows of the trees thrown across the campus; the snows that lasted nearly all winter. Many of the incidents of the past two years came to him. Even the time he was put in the guard house for three days because he got drunk and pushed Walking Bear, the Sioux, out of line, threatening him when he attempted to regain his place. Shame flooded him when he thought of this, because she had seen him, when he was made to walk around the campus all afternoon after his release from the guard house, with a placard on his back which read in big letters "JUST OUT OF THE GUARD HOUSE, PUT THERE BECAUSE I WAS DRUNK."

But she was associated with all these memories; memories that swarmed in his consciousness, and among them, yet above them, shining like a light and throwing a golden glow on each incident, was the face of the Arapaho girl with her black hair piled up on her head like the hair of the white woman.

The next day the feast was held and all the relatives came. The young man put on his leggings and shirt and blanket and shook hands with those who gave him presents. But he was very uncomfortable, especially when some old woman would talk to him a long time, telling him of the deeds of his ancestors, and telling him of the road he ought to follow, and how he ought to pray every morning to Weh Tyte Go, the Grandfather, when he made the east red; pray to him for long life and happy children and for prosperity with plenty of food in his lodge. And this old woman would hold on to his hand for a long time telling him these things; telling him that he ought to be thinking of a woman to be mother of his children, and all the time he would look at the ground with embarrassment, and when she spoke of marriage he knew that she did not understand the things which he understood, and that she must be like the leaves that cling to the blackjacks in winter.

The young man stayed at the lodge of his father for the remainder of the winter. Each morning rising with his father before the sun was up, and going to some high point to pray to the dawn, the Grandfather, for prosperity and guidance along the road which they were traveling. Sometimes he prayed fervently, making a sort of song of his petition in his rich voice, and at such times he was an Indian and he believed that the life and lodge of his father was good. But there were times when the face of a black haired girl came before him and he felt nothing except a longing that seemed to devour him, and at such times he would often be detached and surly; he had the feeling that he could easily run his knife into the heart of anyone who crossed him.

During the winter there had been the ceremony of naming him. He had done nothing to distinguish himself, but it was common knowledge that his voice was strong and that he could sing well, so that when he went with his father to the lodge to be named, he was called Ho Lah Go Ne (Good Voice). He had been called Charlie at Carlisle. He thought it was a very bad name at first, but he had no choice in the matter and they called him that for convenience, and then they added for a surname the name of his father to which he had no claim at all. But he liked the way the Arapaho girl said "Cholley," and the name had begun to mean much to him.

Soon the memories of his life of the last two years seemed to fade, and the old life was becoming good again. His parents went ahead with plans for him as though he were not a man, but he did not protest. As to the taking of a woman, he held off as long as possible. He did not argue the matter, though he had told his father about the Arapaho girl and the visit to her father. When his father had given the same reasons why he should not take an Arapaho woman, as the old chief of the Arapahos had given, he said nothing but thought that they must be right; they were old men and he was only a youth, but even these sage opinions of old men could not make that alluring image go out of his heart, and the Arapaho girl became dearer because she was now placed with the things for which men yearn, without hope of possessing; above the things of the earth, almost like the Great Mysteries.

One day when he was in the Agency he went to see the Major again. He felt he could say certain things in English in a way he could not talk with his father or anyone else. He wore the buckskin leggings that came up to his hips, his shirt and blanket. His Carlisle clothes had not been taken from the corner of the lodge where he had placed them on the day of the feast.

He came into the office and told the Major that he would like to talk with him again, and when the Major asked what he wanted he told him that he was still thinking about the Arapaho girl. He could not get her out of his mind, he said. She was in everything and his thoughts were full of her.

"What does your father think about it?" the Major asked.

"He says that an Osage oughtn't to marry an Arapaho. Her father says that way too."

"I wonder if you'd be happy if you and this Arapaho girl married anyway. You might ask the Arapaho girl to marry you and then you can find something to do. I think I could help you. You have written to each other, haven't you?"

"Yes—sometimes we write."

"Well—it's up to you—don't you think?" The young man sat for some time and thought, then he said, "My father and mother do not like it and her folks don't like it either." Then the Major saw the difficulty. The hereditary respect for parents and ancestors and the wisdom of old age; to marry without the approval of his parents would be almost unthinkable to this young man—perhaps to the Arapaho girl as well. The Major almost smiled as he thought of this young man coming to him in his difficulty, to appeal to him as a sort of a confidant, already knowing the inevitable result; knowing that he would follow the customs of his people out of loyalty and respect for age and parenthood. The Major said: "I believe it will be well to follow the advice of your father and marry a girl of your own people. You are a young man and have been away to school. You may be able to do much for your people. Very soon they will need men like you to help them in the many troubles that will come. The old ways have gone and the new ways are coming fast, and soon there will be only one road; the road of the white man. You are young, and now since your people elect a governor, and councilmen from among them, you may have a chance to do much for your people by being elected to their council or by becoming their elected chief, and in this there will be great honor to you. I think it will be best to marry girl of your people and you will not be unhappy thinking you have disobeyed your father."

The young man rode back to the camp with a heavy heart and he felt that he'd like to get drunk.

. . . .

Spring came to the prairie and the blackjacks and the hills looked like undulating green velvet. In the early mornings the sonorous booming of the prairie chicken came over the hills on soft, whimsical little breezes. The blackjacks were hung with tassels of green, like the fringe on a piano cover. Under the trees along the valley, white, yellow and blue flowers sprang up as though they had been sprinkled there by some great hand. Eagles circled high against the blue sky, telling the world that fawns were being born all over the Reservation, and the turkey vultures on unmoving wing, made large circles and told a story as well. In the prairie seepages the frogs set up a chorus that was deafening. The horned larks went through intricate ærial maneuvers in their nuptial flights along the trail, and all day the meadow-larks sang that life was good. A cardinal flitted here and there along the stream bottoms, and sang as though he were filled with the wonder of being alive. Even the crow had softened his hoarse caw, and sat motionless on the tops of blackjacks, not even flying away and screaming murder when you pointed your quirt or your bow at him. There were tracks of In-gro-kah, the panther, always headed toward the buckbrush which sometimes fringed the blackjack ridges; he didn't need to see the circling eagles, or the vultures to know what season it was. All day, earth scents hung heavy on the air, and every voice and movement seemed filled with thrilling promise.

During this time the wedding of the young man had been set. On the request of his father he had taken several head of fine ponies to the lodge of the father of a certain girl, and tied them to the lodge stakes. The next morning when he passed he saw that they were not there, and his heart became very heavy. He walked about the camp or rode out on the prairie, and with him always was the Arapaho girl.

One day when they were erecting the large open lodge for the dance, he saw an old white man standing with an expression of importance on his face. He was almost toothless and everybody made fun of him but he did not understand this. He fancied himself a sort of picture book hero who lived among the wild Indians and he pretended that he could speak the language and made a great show doing so when, at the Agency dances there were white visitors. Some said he had been a freighter and some said otherwise, but no one seemed to know just what he was doing on the Reservation or whether he had a permit to remain. No one knew what he was doing unless he was living off the Indians, and was tolerated by them as a sort of court fool; no one except a few of the young men who were occasionally seen drunk.

The old man was always to be seen when there was any activity, getting his sign language confused and making mistakes in talking that made people laugh. Much later he posed as a sort of authority as more and more white people came to the Reservation, and he made sure that they knew who he was. He affected a large hat of the type that had never been worn on the Reservation. His trousers were tucked into cowboy boots which had steer heads embroidered on the tops, and he wore a wide leather belt made in Mexico, and green or mauve silk shirts. Finally, when the Reservation became a white man's country he opened up a curio shop, where he sold spurious curios and posed as an Indian fighter. He had friends who had a pint or two to spare if any one brought up the subject. Eventually he died in artificial glory without even leaving his name.

On this day the young man approached him, and when the old man saw him coming he turned and extended his hand, saying, "Hi there, Charlie—back, ain'tcha?" In his boisterous insincerity he came near slapping the young man on the back but he stopped his hand in mid air when he saw his face. The young man came to the point—"want a pint—how much?" The old man's eyes grew narrow and he looked around, "Hit'll come highern a cat's back, Charlie, reckon might let yu hev a leetle, see'in' hits yu."

"How much?" the young man repeated. The old man looked at him as though he would see how badly he wanted it. These Carlisle boys were some of his best customers. Then he said, "How a-bout thet there horsehair bridle o' yourn?" Disgust came into the young man's face, "I got money—two dollars, eh?" The old man almost wept, and he began to whine thet hit shore wuz dangerous as hell, now—he jist couldn't do 'er—he'd like to—for Charlie, anyway, but he jist couldn't do 'er.

"I give you three dollars." And the young man forced the silver into his hand. He placed it carefully in his pocket and went off into the woods.

He came back presently and handed the bottle to the young man who deftly slipped it into his blanket and walked away.

.   .   .   .

From the hills back of the camp where the young man was lying, he could hear the throbbing of the drums. Sometimes it came in volume and then the erratic breezes carried the sound away. The young man reached for the bottle and held it to his lips but it was empty. He looked around; it was dark, then he felt of his bare legs and ran his hand over the bare upper part of his body. He was naked except for his breach clout and moccasins, and in the pleasing vagueness that suffused him, he remembered that he had been dressed for the afternoon dances, and that he must have slept through them. The drums he heard were for the night dances. He felt that he ought to go down and dance but he was drunk; he knew he was drunk. He thought he had been asleep but he was drunk. He fumbled with his large, red blanket, but when he found that he could not get it around him he threw it away. He saw a flash of lightning, and heard a low rumbling in the west. It was going to rain and he must do what he started to do before it rained, but he couldn't remember. There was another flash of lightning and he saw the ponies grazing across the ravine. It seemed important for no reason whatever that he go to the ponies. He stood up and made a movement as though he would pull his blanket about him, but he didn't have his blanket. He stood unsteadily for a second and smiled a vacuous smile because he didn't have his blanket. Suddenly the importance of getting to his ponies came to him again and he started across the ravine.

The lightning flashes became brighter and the thunder growled a little louder, and the sound of the drums was in his ears like pulsations at his temples. As he started to climb out of the ravine, he fell. "Ho-ho-hoooo" he said and lay there for a moment. Then he lifted his head and saw the lightning etch a tree with its branches against the western horizon, followed by the growling of the thunder like the throat growl of a wolf. He lowered his head and he could see wolves on the prairie chanting the song of the mourning dance—chanting with their noses to the sky—but they were all there, these wolves—Wah'Kon-Tah had taken none of them. He would ride into them and they would run, these wolves—he would tell them that he would be chief of the Osages. He would tell them that they need not fear him—to fear short gun of the white man. Then he raised his head, the wolves were gone, the trees seemed to reproach him, and he said thickly to the trees, in Osage, "I will show you my head is not sick with whiskey of white man." With much trouble he rose to his feet and felt on a hickory tree for his bridle, putting his hand on it at once. He felt proud of this feat and started toward the herd of ponies. A loud clap of thunder reverberated among the hills, and he said to the thunder, "I'm not sick from white man's whiskey." The lightning flashed and he saw the ponies grazing and started toward them, his feet walking in many places.

He crept up to his pinto and felt of its warm neck, then he fell against it. The pony attempted to move away but he clung to the neck, saying thickly, "My head is not sick." He slipped the bridle on with much fumbling, then he stooped and fumbled with the hobble, and when he got the rope off he fell forward and steadied himself by holding onto the reins. He said to the pony, "You think that my head is sick with white man's whiskey—my head is not sick." He jumped to the pony's back in one try and again came the feeling of triumph. He kicked the pony in the sides with the heels of his moccasins and when the pony kicked up he dug his heels deeper; he kicked viciously until the pony went from a lope into a run across the prairie.

The cool wind in his face seemed to madden him and he laid low over the pony's neck and gave a long whoop. Over the black prairie he raced, and the lightning flashes showed the rolling, unreal hills of a ghost land, and the thunder shook the earth, and rolled over the hills and bounced back again. The large rain drops began to spatter his face and his blood seemed to be afire, and burn him as it raced through his veins, and he thought that the beating at his temples was the sound of the drums—war drums—and he kicked the pony until it was putting forth all of its strength in the mad dash.

Then the rain came down in sheets and roared over the prairie. It was like a gigantic drapery hung from heaven when the lightning flashed. The young man shouted against the earth's shivering thunder and the steady roar of the rain, and in his madness he thought the pony was very slow. He splashed through the little pools of water that had formed on the prairie, and the pony began to breath heavily; with every jump letting out an explosive "huff." The pony's back seemed hot to his legs and the sweat pricked him like needles. Suddenly he seemed to be going backwards and he thought the pony was afraid—he was going backwards. Then madness came over him and he knew why he was riding—he knew that there was a Pawnee just ahead, and he would take this Pawnee's hair. The pony seemed to be going forward again and he kicked its heaving sides, and he became eager and yet cautious. The pony slipped once or twice on the wet prairie sod.

The lightning showed pools of water that reflected its intense light for a moment, then there were no pools and the thunder boomed across the hills. They splashed through the pools and the young man felt the cold water on his thighs. The pony kept slipping. Then there was a splash and he felt the cold water higher up on his thighs. Then suddenly he seemed to be sliding and there was no pony under him. He felt something cold and heavy on the side of his head, and he put up his hand and scraped off the mud. The rain drops splashed on his face and body, and seemed to sputter like rain drops on the hot stones around the fire.

He got up and walked cautiously. He was afraid the Pawnee had heard the noise. He staggered a few steps and his feet slipped into a small ravine and he fell. He felt the cold water gurgling around his body, and he was suddenly helpless and very tired. His pony came to his mind and he thought that the pony must be somewhere near, sleeping. He thought he would rest for awhile. Pawnee is over hill, he thought, and when pony is rested we will go find this Pawnee. Pawnee will be asleep too, and we will wait until the pony is rested. He would remain in the water and the Pawnee could not hear him. Pawnee would say that it was noise of running water. He closed his eyes and lay against the muddy bank. He would sleep there in running water and Pawnee could not hear.

THE MOURNING DANCE

Chapter Sixteen

HE LONG, drawn-out chant of death that came often from the blackjack hills on the early dawn, filled the Major with dread. It was a haunting wail, the primitiveness of it having an effect that the weeping of the Amer-European lacked. However, he feared the consequences even more than he dreaded to hear the chant.

The mourning dance, which the white man called the war dance, had given much trouble, and it got its name from the white man because of the wars that sometimes followed the raids of the scalping parties. On hearing the early morning wailing, the Major would rise and go down into the Agency, where he attempted to ascertain whether or not there would be a mourning dance, and if learning that there would be one, he would go immediately to the people in charge and attempt to get some assurance from them that there would be no trouble.

Sometimes among the arrangements for the dance would be the hiring of a Pawnee or some other Indian, who would let his hair grow long and hide out in the woods, where the scalping party could find him and cut off his hair in lieu of taking his scalp. Sometimes in their excitement the party forgot and came into camp exulting over a real scalp.

One morning the Major was awakened by the familiar wailing, and as soon as he arrived at his office he made inquiry. They told him that there would be mourning dance, and that already Shah Pah Nashee (Standing Buffalo), a friend of the dead Indian, had been appointed by the relatives and had gone into the hills to fast as chief mourner. He got the promise that there would be no trouble, then waited.

Shah Pah Nashee was divested of weapons and sent into the woods to live for thirty days on the food he could get with his bare hands, and a man was appointed to follow him and keep close watch to see that he was not overcome with hunger, and that he was not unduly exposed to danger.

He went away to his fast painted in a certain manner so that Wah'Kon-Tah would take notice of him. As soon as he was far away from camp he began to pray fervently that his friend might be admitted to the Happy Hunting Ground. As the days wore on and hunger gnawed at his belly, and his prayers became more vehement, oftentimes his appeals were frantic. He worked himself into a religious frenzy to the extent that he forgot the discomfort in his belly and was oblivious to every thing about him for hours, finally falling over into a swoon.

Often his nights were tormented. He saw strange forms in the darkness that seemed to skulk about him, and his dreams were filled with monsters that caused him to wake up with sweat dripping from his body. During the long day he would pray until the trees were sometimes turned into fantastic objects that did the most unlikely things, and his eyes saw many things on the

« 289 »

horizon of the prairie or in the blackjacks that were not there at all. And sometimes he heard the voice of the Great Spirit which changed suddenly into the wind playing with the leaves of the trees. As he grew weaker and weaker, and his belly became a depression and his ribs were the ribs of a skeleton, he lost himself more and more in prayer, unaware of that which surrounded him and feeling that certainly Wah'Kon-Tah could not help noticing him.

At the end of thirty days, weak and terribly emaciated, he came wobbling out from the woods to the appointed place for the dance, where there were two medicine men waiting to meet him, in order to conduct him into the lodge set aside for the chief mourner. There they would attend to his wants, giving him that food only which would not harm him, and in very little quantities at first, until he had gained back some of his strength. During this time he would continue his prayers to Wah'Kon-Tah and when the medicine men had attended him they would leave the lodge and chant their prayers to Wah'Kon-Tah, petitioning him to notice this mourner before him; chanting as they walked toward the open lodge that had been constructed for the dance.

The people had begun to assemble the night before, and around the place of dancing there were dome-shaped lodges and open structures for cooking.

From at least two of the clans four or more dancers were appointed and a headman from each clan was chosen to carry the symbols. In case the symbols were in the nature of a buffalo or an elk, they would carry the symbols of the clan symbol, itself.

Mourning Dance

The first dawn after the return of the chief mourner, the dancers came out to the structure. They were naked except for breach clout and moccasins, and on their arms they had bands of silver, and some wore their bone breast plates edged with wampum, and some wore bear or eagle-claw necklaces. Their bodies were painted with thin, yellow paint on a ground color of thin red, the yellow applied only to certain spots of the body. On their faces were symbols painted in red and black usually with a yellow band across the eyes. Each dancer carried a bow on the end of a stick, from which fluttered an eagle feather and which was designed to keep the attention of Wah'Kon-Tah; the stick being held in front of them as they danced. As they danced the drums beat the time, and each dancer was grave of face and devout. They danced around the open lodge and then out from it for some distance, then back again; the dancers of the Chesho clan dancing in one direction around the lodge and the dancers of the Hunkah clan in the other, meeting and passing many times.

On through the day they danced; stopping for a short intermission at noon but taking very little food. There were two sets of drummers and two sets of dancers who relieved each other at intervals. All day the medicine men chanted their prayers and in the lodge apart from the dance structure, the chief mourner prayed.

Near the dancers at the edge of the structure was the wife of the Indian who had died; bowed and praying. She rolled up one of the sleeves of her shirt and put mud on her hair which she renewed as it dried and fell off.

The atmosphere was one of mourning and the faces were grave, as the drums beat incessantly and the chanters prayed fervently through the day.

As the sun was setting the drums stopped suddenly, and the clanking of metals and the jingling of the little bells of the dancers changed tempo as they walked to their lodges, but for many minutes the pulsing of the drums and the jingling sounded in the ears of the people.

At sun-up the next morning the drummers again took their places and the singers began their chant and the dancers appeared again. In the late afternoon they seemed more haggard, and were visibly thinner and more gray. They danced through the third day until sunset, then six dancers suddenly broke away shouting. They ran to their horses and leaping on them, left the encampment with break-neck speed.

They rode across the prairie and in the twilight they saw one of the clerks from a trader's store, but as soon as he saw them he put spurs to his pony and raced away. The party pretended they didn't see him, but later when the clerk told one of the party about the incident, the young man put his hand over his mouth, simulating surprise in the sign language, and said that he thought the horseman whom they had frightened was someone else. "Ho-hoooo," he said, "we didn't know you—we were looking for Pawnee."

The next morning as they came off the hill they saw a lone rider coming up a small stream and they raced up to him and demanded his hair. He looked at them, knowing each one of them by name, and he knew that they knew him but there was no sign of recognition. He was one of the traders at the Agency and it was his custom to let his hair grow long. When he saw that the party was not excited he told them that they could cut his hair if they wished.

They sat on their horses for a few moments, then one of the party rode up to the trader and hit him lightly with the bow stick he was carrying, and turning quickly, the party rode away. They rode up the wooded stream and soon came out on to the prairie again.

They were hungry and surly. A gnawing hunger at the belly does not put one in a happy frame of mind, and since the excitement of the dance was past, there were black thoughts in their minds, and in their hearts were things that displaced the fervency which had been aroused by the dance. They thought of this Pawnee who had been hired, and how the chiefs had warned them that they must cut his hair with the knife, but they couldn't understand this thing. He was one of the enemy people, this Pawnee, and he would be fit ransom for spirit of the man who had died. The ponies they had given him could be payment to his relatives for his scalp, and they couldn't see how cutting hair with knife could be same as taking scalp. But old man had said that this was so now; there were many white men around now and medicine men had said that Wah'Kon-Tah would be satisfied with hair cut with knife.

They crossed the prairie and saw nothing but the green, rolling hills all around them, then they turned again into the wooded hills and down another stream, suddenly coming on to the tracks of a horse, which they followed closely. Sometimes the tracks were deep in the sand and sometimes there was the faintest cutting of the hard soil. In the grass of the valley the trail was plain, and the party urged their ponies to a gallop, going partly by sign in the grass and partly by instinct toward a wild valley which was surrounded by sandstone hills, thickly covered with blackjacks. In the upper end of the valley they rode through grass that came up to their horses' bellies, and here they spread out and rode slowly up the ravine, at the head of which was Dripping Springs.

The season had been a dry one and they knew that the little pools of clear water that extended a short way down the ravine was the only water in the valley, and from all directions the deer had made narrow little trails down from the sides of the hills; radiating in all directions from the water.

The spring was formed in a hollow under a massive sandstone escarpment that had been exposed by the rushing waters of centuries. Where the massive sandstone and the underlying bed of shale met, the water emerged and dripped all along on the underside of the sandstone layer, making a soft tinkling sound. The party stopped and one of them motioned with his lips to a fresh track in the mud.

The Pawnee had heard them and as he crawled up over the edge of the escarpment like some slinking, shadowy panther, one of the party saw him, and let out a whoop, rushing toward him followed by the others. They urged their ponies up the sides of the rock ravine and were upon him before he could get away. The Pawnee looked anxiously over his shoulder in an attempt to read his pursuers' faces. He was in a dangerous position and he realized it to the fullest extent, but they had tempted him with rich gifts, and he was a very poor man.

The party surrounded him and he stood silently looking from face to face like an animal in a trap. What he saw in those faces made his heart shrivel and he looked quickly around at the undergrowth with the alertness of a trapped bobcat.

One of the party got off his pony and pulling out his knife, grabbed the Pawnee by his long hair, making every sign of taking the scalp. He flourished the knife in a menacing manner, but the Pawnee stood still and did not flinch. There was great pleasure in seeing the discomfort of this Pawnee. Finally after prolonged bluffing he cut the hair from near the scalp, and then making a taunting sign which the Pawnee understood very well, he climbed on his pony and rode away with the party.

That evening they rode into camp on a dead run and on the end of a stick waved the black hair of the Pawnee. "We have killed enemy," they sang—"The spirit of our friend can now enter Happy Hunting Ground."

The people began to rejoice. The dancers and the chief mourner washed the paint from their faces, and the wife of the man who had gone away changed to the costume she had worn before his death, and washed her hair.

Sometimes if a woman had mourned much the mud and ashes which she placed on her hair would bleach out a spot which remained very conspicuous during her life time; a symbol of the many sorrows in the life of women of the prairie and the blackjack hills.

Then in mid-summer came the Great Sickness; the people knew it was the white man's sickness. In the mournful questioning of the death-song there was a new note, as it came on the heavy air of dawn; there was a weariness in it approaching despair. All during the summer from every camp came daily wailing, and the people knew that Wah'Kon-Tah was displeased with them.

In the Agency there was one topic of conversation —smallpox.

The traders sent out wagon loads of supplies and left them at some designated spot at the heads of ravines where the location was marked by a lone tree or a conspicuous rock. At dusk tall, blanketed figures would come up to the spot, look around, then begin to take the sugar, coffee and flour to their camps. The Major sent his two oldest children out of the Reservation and the traders sent their families out, when it was possible. There was great fear in the hearts of everyone. The Major and one of the government doctors made every attempt to get vaccine. They made long drives with the Major's mules to towns in "the States" to bring it back, but on arrival they found that it had spoiled in the hot weather.

The Major made trips to the different parts of the Reservation, pleading with the people to bury their dead underground; using every argument in his power to make them see that burial in cairns would only help spread the disease, but they would not see this. They could not bury Indian in ground where he would be lost; where it would be difficult for Wah'Kon-Tah to see him. Wah'Kon-Tah could see stone cairns on hill tops. This Great Sickness of white man did not devour spirits of those who died, they said, that they should be buried in ground like white man.

Like the wounded buffalo which leaves the herd to die in some wash on the plains, and like the sick wolf which leaves the pack to crawl out on some naked rock to end his days in solitude, so the people of the Reservation followed the law that the herd or band must not be impeded. They crawled away from the camps into the woods and the high grasses, and there died alone.

That summer the vultures sailed gracefully against the wind, or stood motionless against the currents of the higher altitudes. In their great numbers, and because of their blackness and their purposeful silence, they became a ghastly symbol. The opossums went about their ghoulish business with that nonchalance so natural to them, and when they were disturbed, or were met in the trails and attacked, they lay over simulating death with their lips drawn over their white teeth in a smile that was grim.

In beautiful valleys stood the hickory framework of lodges, where little breezes played with the gray ashes in the fire holes, and the stridulations of the insects and the chirruping of the crickets became dirges, and hungry, half-wild dogs slunk away, looking back over their shoulders.

When the Major drove up to the deserted camps and called familiar names, his voice seemed to die in the heated air.

Some said there were five hundred of the people who perished during the summer of the Great Sickness, and some said a thousand, but in any case, many of the people of the blackjacks and the prairie went on the long ride to the Great Mysteries, without benefit of the prayers of the medicine men. It is not unlikely that their spirits are still haunting the Reservation, and the sad songs of the prairie during the winter under the moon are the voices of these spirits, and the petitions in the brown leaves of the blackjacks, the remonstrances of wandering, restive souls. Certainly the quavering voice of the screech owl, when the cold moon struggles up through the blackjacks that fringe the hills, must have something to do with that ghastly summer.

"CIVILIZATION" ARRIVES

Chapter Seventeen

HEN a new president came to the White House in 1885, the Major was called from the Agency of the Osages and another man came to take his place. He was sorry to leave but he made himself believe that it was a good thing, inasmuch as his children were growing up and he desired that they should have the advantages of the best schools.

He said good-by to his friends during the activities of packing. One morning he came downstairs and found his friend Gray Bird sitting there awaiting him. They exchanged a "How" and he sat down waiting for Gray Bird to talk. Finally, Gray Bird glanced up with a wolfish movement and said: "They say you are going away. I have come to see you. I have brought pony with me from my lodge; he is tied to thing out there," pursing his lips in the direction of the hitching rack, "I want you to see this pony."

The Major followed Gray Bird out to the hitching rack in front of the house, and there with Gray Bird's mount was a very pretty pony. "I want you to look at this pony," said Gray Bird stepping quickly up to the rack. The Major looked at the pony for some time, and knowing that Gray Bird wanted his opinion he looked it over very carefully; looking into its mouth to determine its age from the teeth and feeling of its forelegs and hocks. When he had finished the inspection he turned to his friend and said: "He is very good horse, I believe. He is young horse. I can see that he is strong." Gray Bird then stepped quickly up to the rack and untied the pony, giving the rope into the hands of the Major, saying, "I want rope; you can keep pony."

He mounted his horse and rode toward the brow of the hill, and the Major watched him until he had disappeared. He stood there until the dust the pony had kicked up, had settled on the buck brush on the side of the road, then he retied the pony and went back into the house. He was not so sure about the necessity of leaving the Agency for the purpose of schooling his children, and he did not know, of course, that he had seen Gray Bird for the last time.

. . . .

Then in 1889, when another president came to the White House, the Major came again as agent to the Osages.

He noted many changes during his absence. The leases to the cattle men had been continued and many more had been made, the revenue enabling the nation to maintain its government; paying all its officers the same salaries which the government paid the Indian police. He also learned that during his absence a commission had visited the Agency and had attempted to get the Osages to consent to an allotment.

They had always been averse to allotment, but the white man was getting impatient on the borders of the Reservation and homes must be found for the winners of the west. In this attempt, many people said that the representatives of the government had presented the proposition of allotment to the Osages, then from the spirit of hospitality and good fellowship had seen to it that several barrels of whiskey were taken to the proper camps. Unfortunately, the Indians had learned how to drink; at least those who cared to drink. They had learned that white man's whiskey, while very warming and transporting, often stole man's reason and made his tongue say things that were not in his heart. They did not enjoy this present from the white man until after the discussions, and they had stood adamant against allotment, then they appointed Och Kee Tah (guards or military police) to collect all the arms and stand guard around the camp, remaining absolutely sober while the others intrusted themselves to the great happiness.

It was also said that before one of the elections on the Reservation the mixed-blood party, who called themselves "the progressives," as opposed to the platform of the full-blood party, followed the example of the commissioners and placed a barrel of whiskey in the camp which was most opposed to "progressive principles," but to their discomfiture the members of the camp came to the polls and voted their ticket, then went back home, appointed Och Kee Tah, and for a few hours were much more than earth bound children of Wah'Kon-Tah.

The government's urge that the Indians be alloted was a constant source of worry to them. There had been a general bill presented in the congress which was for the purpose of alloting Indians on homesteads and throwing the surplus lands open to settlement.

The Osages had sent the Major to Washington to urge that they be exempt from allotment; exempt from all allotment bills that might be presented. He was to say that they had purchased the Reservation from the Cherokees with their own money and they wished to enjoy it in community as their home. He found, when he reached Washington, that the bill had been prepared and hearings on it had been in progress for some time; in fact the bill was before a committee of the house and the hearings had been completed, but the committee accorded the Major an hour in which to be heard.

When he presented himself to be heard he was told that a lady from Oklahoma also wished to be heard, and he was asked if he would give some of his time to her, which he agreed to do, but at the end of her hearing he had only fifteen minutes left in which to submit the claims of the people. He stated the case in simple language and very tersely, and on his return to the Agency he had the pleasure to report to the council that they had been exempt from the provision of all allotment bills.

When they were finally allotted in 1906-7, the surplus lands were not thrown open to settlement and through the efforts of several of their own people, the minerals were held in reserve, remaining in communal ownership.

On his return, the Major found also that the receipts of interest due the people had increased but that the payments had not increased accordingly, though they had increased somewhat.

The tribe desired to increase its holding in cattle, whereupon the Major asked the department to let contract for eight thousand head, the council having previously approved. He believed that by observation and by the fact that they had cattle of their own, they would soon learn much about the industry, and he was highly pleased after the bids were asked that a large number of men offered to deliver cattle, from two thousand to five thousand head, at reasonable prices. He chose the bids on two and three year old heifers ranging in price between eleven and twelve dollars a head, and eight thousand of them were delivered to the pastures and branded; amounting to about five head to an individual. Thus, with the cattle owned by the tribe and the cattle owned by the lessees of the pastures in the Reservation, there were from two hundred thousand to two hundred fifty thousand head on the prairie and among the black-jacks, there being only one spot where they did not do well on account of flies; a section of country of great canyons and blackjack covered hills, along the drainage area of Pond creek, which was called "the strip."

The government was aware of the leases, and though it had never approved them, its silence was taken as consent. However, during a period of increased volume of protest from the would-be settlers along the border, the department wired to the Major that all cattle should be removed from the Reservation immediately, and that he should call on the military if necessary to execute the order, then report progress. He immediately notified the cattlemen to meet on the border of Kansas and there he held a conference. After a day of discussion which extended far into the night, the cattlemen decided that there was nothing to be done and left the matter in his hands.

In a quandary the Major drove back to the Agency. If he attempted to have the cattle moved to the State line he would be met with the quarantine laws and not unlikely, the Kansas militia. He couldn't move them into the Cherokee, Ponca or Pawnee country. The cattle were poor; they had just been shipped in. Sometime during the night as the team found its way over the dark trail to the Agency, he came to a decision, and on his arrival sent a telegram to a man who had been an inspector in the Indian service, but who had retired and had since become a cattleman, a regent of the University of Kansas, and a member of the State legislature. He requested him to come to the Agency at once and hinted of his dilemma.

When he arrived the Major left the Agency after having the council call a meeting, thus leaving the man alone to discuss the problems with the chief and the councilmen. When he returned he learned that the council had delegated this man to go to Washington for them. In a few days he received a wire from the department stating that the order had been withdrawn.

This man had been in the service and knew the workings of the hierarchy known as the Department of Interior, and he also knew the Indians and the cattlemen and their problems. Through these experiences he saw the whole situation very clearly and was able to speak in a language understood by all parties concerned.

INVASIONS

During the Major's absence from the Reservation the number of white people had increased and he saw that the long preparation of the Indian to meet the changing condition must be speeded up, in order to keep them from the influences of the white man until they were prepared to withstand the shock. He noted that after the council had passed a law allowing Indians to employ white people, much better types had come among them. The regulation was approved by the department. A white person desiring to come into the Reservation must furnish the office with a certificate from the county sheriff or some other official of the county whence he came and his character must be guaranteed to the office before he would be allowed to become an employee of the Indians or the mixed-bloods.

This was a mutual benefit, but many white people, some of them of very good character, started coming into the Reservation without permits and there was much trouble. The white man took the stand that he had rights anywhere, and in a characteristic manner he shouted his independence and his freedom.

Soon the whites were equal in number to the Indians and later outnumbered them. The Indian police were inadequate to cope with the new situation and the Major saw that there was no longer an Indian problem to work out; he must now put white men on the police force to supplement the Indians. The Indian problem had become a white problem, and the day of barbarism and outlawry began in the Reservation of the Osages.

It was necessary to issue an order that the children of all white people living in the Reservation must be put in school, and it took time and effort to carry out this order. The police spent much of their time arresting whiskey peddlers, and the old bandits who hung about on the borders, who held up traders and attempted to hold up the Major with the payments, who came in and stole horses from the Indians and got out quickly with them; the old time outlaws who when caught, jested with the United States marshals about their chase and capture as they traveled the long road to Fort Smith where the noose usually awaited them, were displaced by petty thieves, rapists and barbarians who set fire to Indian houses, (at this time the government had begun to encourage the building of houses all over the Reservation) burning some old man in the flames because of belief in some ignorant story about his hidden wealth.

One day two white men crossed the Arkansas into the Reservation and killed an Indian woman, for no other reason than that they had never killed an Indian, and wished to boast that they had done so. They were trailed into the Kaw Reservation by a band of Big Hills and no one ever knew what became of them. No one ever inquired.

After the Cherokee strip was opened (1893) strange caravans came through the Reservation. Covered wagons and buggies with dirty faced children peering out from the curtains, and weary, hard-faced women lolling in the seat beside evil-eyed, bearded men. There were wagons with cows and mules led behind and chicken coops tied to the side; all descriptions of vehicles, some on three wheels and a pole dragging in the dust for the fourth. They often stopped at the Agency pretending to trade, but the Major instructed the police to keep them moving and warned them to watch closely to see that they didn't attempt to camp on the Reservation, with plans for staying. He found the fear of the Indians which many of them had, a great weapon, but in his heart he feared for the Indian.

They often stopped their ox teams or their skinny

mules and horses, and languidly climbed out of their vehicles to look around the trader's stores, where they bought tobacco or some insignificant articles, or slouched around the store with vacuous expressions. The traders also urged them to get on, saying that the Osages were on the war path. Sometimes they were insulted when the traders refused to sell them things (they never refused to sell food) or they argued about the prices, and the trader would usually tell them that they didn't want their trade anyway; they were there to trade with the Indians; this was Indian country, and they'd better get out if they didn't like the prices.

One day a mighty man came into the Agency. He was well mounted and he wore a great hat, boots and long heavy spurs. He had a gun on each hip and wore fringed buckskin breeches and a shirt which had a whole deck of cards, in their original colors, printed profusely on it.

He drew rein with a flourish in front of the trader's store, and dismounted. His boot heels pounded the board walk, his spurs clanked and his leather squeaked as he strode into the store. He posed for sometime without buying anything, and made several very pointed remarks about life bein' a leetle dull in these 'ere diggins, and implied, that of course, he was off for the "strip" whur a feller would find life to his likin'—in them wild leetle towns whur they wuz things a-goin' on, by gawd!

The Major was standing at the window of his office when the mighty man came jogging along the dusty road. When he saw him disappear into the store he called one of the tallest Indians of the police, and motioned for him to come to the window. They stood there until the man came clanking out of the store, then he told the Indian to take his short gun and bring that man to the office. The Indian took off his blanket and tied it around his waist, then smiling at the Major said, "How," in perfect understanding of the part he was to play; nothing pleased him more than seeing a white man frightened.

He stole out of the building, crept along behind the trader's store and came up to the mighty man just as he was surveying the dusty area in the manner greatness always assumes in the presence of the unimportant.

Thrilled throughout his whole being, but with face impassive, the tall policeman stepped up to the bizarre figure, pointed the rifle at his middle and said in English, "Come." The mighty man looked around and his face blanched, as his hands went into the air: "Don't shoot, Chief—Jees Chris', don't shoot—I ain't a-doin' nuthin'—shore nuff——I——ain't——."

"Come."

"I'll go—I'm goin' to the 'strip,' hones'." Then he spoke what some men believed to be "Injun-Amurican" in a quavering voice. "No— shootum——I good white man—see—savve, don't shoot," pointing to his breast, "I good man; I no do bad—frien Injun." The tall Indian was enjoying it immensely but his face was like wood.

"Come," he said again, and this time he poked the barrel of the gun into the middle of the man's stomach and began to back him toward the Council House. The mighty man went willingly and when he found out what the Indian meant he set out in the direction of the Council House very alertly. He began to feel more comfortable when he saw the building—it looked official—he could prove to the white man that he wuzn't a-doin' nuthin.' He climbed the steps to the Major's office with his hands high in the air. The Major saw his face and could scarcely refrain from laughing, but he said, "Well, what are you doing here?" The man gulped and looked at the tall, unmoved Indian. "Colonel, hones' I wuzn't doin' ary a thing—jist a-goin' thru' like—the Chief, here" —he looked at the tall figure and gulped again—"the Chief, here, stuck his gun in my guts and told me to come—I 'us a-goin' to the strip, swhur I'se goin'."

"All right," said the Major, "get out and go—we don't want your kind here. If you don't want an escort of these fellas," pointing to the tall Indian, "to the border, you better be going now."

"Awright, Colonel, I shore will—I don't aim to do nobody no harm—I—."

"All right, get on your way." The mighty man with the deck of cards printed on his shirt left the office, but he tiptoed out and in his shoulders there was a slight droop.

. . . .

The police were kept constantly busy keeping order and sending trespassers off the Reservation; seeing that the whites who had permission to remain were sending their children to school.

But the homeseekers kept coming into the Reservation despite efforts of the police and marshals. They threatened and swore and talked of the rights of "Amurican citizens." The game was fast disappearing, and the walnut logs from the bottoms were being stolen and sold.

One day one of these homeseekers came into the Reservation shouting that Amurica was a free country, and allowing he could live whur he wanted to—he didn't aim to fool with no goddam Injun agent and a passel o' red skin po-leese—that he was white, and free, and a citizen of these here United States, and he'd like to see ary Injun tech 'im.

When the police went to him to order him off the Reservation, he repeated those words and many more, but he was persuaded to come to the Agency at the point of a gun and was brought before the Major, where he again expressed his sentiments and was immediately thrown into the jail at the foot of the hill, across from the traders' stores. The next morning as the Major came down the hill to the office he saw this man walking along the dusty road to Cedarvale on the border. Behind him was in Indian policeman, holding his gun across the front of his saddle, riding along as though he were out for the morning air.

A few weeks later the Major was walking along the road at the foot of the hill, having just come from an interview with a homeseeker who was in the little jail. He heard the singing of a bullet, and immediately ducked behind a pile of stone that had been collected when the traders and mixed-bloods had got together to make a road. The second shot ricocheted off the top of the pile; then there was silence. The Major was boiling with anger, and he knew who his assailant was.

He sat in his office for some time until he could attain tranquillity, as he stared at the window. Then he sent for the "nigger." The nigger came from no-one-knew-where. Perhaps from the Creeks where he might have been a slave. In some way, perhaps because of his happy-go-lucky courage and his knowledge of Indian languages, he had been appointed a United States marshal, and occasionally made his appearance on the Reservation. His appearance in the locality was usually an indication that there was some very disagreeable work to be done. The Major had seen the nigger the evening before, and he thought of him now.

The next morning he came to the door of the office and knocked, waiting for someone to tell him to come in. He came in grinning, with his hat clutched tightly in his hand, and said, "Yassuh." The Major looked at him and said, "You know the white man we had some trouble with a few weeks ago when you were here?"

"De one you-all had in de jail-house?"

"Yes."

"Sho, I know'd dat man."

"Well, I want him arrested and brought here—then you can take him on to Fort Smith. He's a bad actor—better watch him."

"Yassuh, I'll watch 'im—I'll git 'im." Then as an after thought, "I'll git 'im—yassuh." He left the office and went to the barn. He pulled off his hat again and approached the man in the stable. "Mistah Ed, I reckon I'll be takin' ma hoss—got me a little job." The horse was brought out and he rode off down the dusty road.

The next day an Indian came into the office and told the Major that they had a man in the jail and wanted him to come. When he approached the little house he saw a crowd of people standing around looking at something on the grass, and as he came up several of the men looked at him, then moved aside so that he could come into the circle.

There was a man lying there. They had taken his clothes apart and the middle of his body was bare, and in his bowels was a great wound—big enough to put a man's hand in, the onlookers had estimated. When the Major looked at the face he recognized the man who had shot at him, then he looked around for the nigger. He saw him standing by the door of the jail grinning as usual. "Come here," the Major said, "thought I told you to arrest this man." The nigger giggled like a girl, then with a broader grin said: "Yassuh, dat's right— you sho did say dat, but take'm like this'n, I shoots 'em, 'nen I 'rests 'em." There were snickers from the crowd.

Conditions seemed to grow worse and worse and the Major was wondering what the outcome would be; he had begun to believe that all the work of the years would be wiped out by this last invasion of the whites into the last Reservation of the Osages.

GHOST DANCE

The news came to the Agency that the Osages, chiefly the Big Hills, were holding secret councils along the bottoms of Salt creek and on the river. The Major made a trip out there but learned nothing, and when he asked the police they seemed to know nothing about such councils.

In the wild bottoms of Salt creek the Indians were gathering, and were councilling with much gravity. Soon there were few Indians to be seen at the Agency, and in the camps along the bottoms and on the hill, only the hickory framework of the lodges were standing.

Civilization

A strange rumor had come to the camp of the Big Hills and they were much concerned about it; they saw in it a possibility of relief from the steady encroachment of the white man. The old men sat and listened and sometimes talked. They said that it seemed good to them; it seemed good to have buffalo back on plains and deer in blackjacks back in their great numbers; it seemed good to them if all white men were to leave Reservation, and they could live again as Indians had always lived—like their fathers, they could stay where the graves of their grandfathers were. It seemed good, they said, but they didn't know. It seemed good, but in head of white man were many thoughts that were bad which made him talk with crooked tongue. In heart of white man were many things that were bad; white man might have given whiskey to man who had this dream; his mind might have been sick with white man's whiskey, they said. These old men thought that if Indian were to fight white man, white man would come like leaves of blackjack, kill Indians and take their lands. They thought this might be one of white man's tricks.

Others said they thought it was good, and if it were not good why did medicine men keep dreaming that it was good? It seemed good, but they didn't know. This man in land of west; this man who had dreamed and who listened to voice—how did they know that he talked with straight tongue?

The arguments and discussions went on and no white man was allowed in camp. Finally, many members of the tribe collected at the head waters of Sycamore creek, where there was more talking. Then an open dance lodge was erected, and even those who were not sure about the coming of the great Messiah thought that it would not be bad to have religious dances anyway—perhaps Wah'Kon-Tah would see them in their devotion and would tell them if this were true; if it were true about this Indian Messiah who was coming from west, and who would restore buffalo to plains and deer to blackjacks, and run white man away from home of Indian.

Soon the drums were heard sobbing over the prairie from the head waters of Sycamore creek, and each day there was dancing and sometimes the drums were heard far into the night.

There was much talk in the traders' stores when men came together. They talked about the "ghost dance." They talked about it as a child might talk of ghosts; gaining a certain thrill out of imagined possibilities. Some of the United States marshals talked in a manner which implied that they knew more about it than they would jist tell anybody; they intimated that there was much secrecy about the affair, and people in an official position were not telling much jist then. They assumed to know about the trouble with Sitting Bull and the ghost dancers on the Sioux reservation, and they led their listeners to believe that there was the same trouble on the Reservations of the Territories. When asked what was at the bottom of it they would say that it was jist an Injun, who had a dream out west somewhur, and drempt he seen the Great Spirit or somethin' 'er other, and the Great Spirit had told this Injun that they would be a kind of an Injun Christ who would come out of the west, and all the tribes would join together and kill all the white men on their reservations, and this here "Christ" would see to it that all the buffalo was brought back and the Injun wouldn't be troubled with the white man no more.

The traders said they had been warned by their Indian friends to keep away from the camps. One trader said that he had been sent out with a beef they had ordered from the Big Hill trading post, and when he got there with it, no one would notice him; not even his friends. He said they were surly and paid no attention in such a way that he felt like he better get out as soon as possible.

But after a short time the camps at the head of Sycamore creek were deserted and the dried leaves on the branches which formed the roofs of the open structures, rasped sadly, and the wind sang little songs in the framework of the lodges.

Due to the sanity of the older men of the tribe, there had been doubt and a lack of fervency in the ceremonials, and the Osages were lost to the Messiah from the land of the west. The head waters of Sycamore creek saw the last feeble gesture of the Great Osages; it was a ghost dance; the white man had named it well.

THE GREAT FRENZY
Chapter Eighteen

HEN the Major left the Agency of the Osages he was almost glad to go; that is, he believed he was glad to go. It was fast becoming a white man's country, and the hope that he had held for the Indians had become vague and uncertain of realization. But he stayed close to the borders of the Reservation. For a period of years he was in the mercantile business in the little town of Elgin and he was interested in a business of the same character in Arkansas City.

He watched the frenzy grow with a heavy heart from the time the first oil was struck in the eastern part of the Reservation on through the great development. He watched sadly the effects of wealth on the Osages.

Hordes of men poured into the Reservation, bringing with them laboring trucks loaded with pipes and timbers. Young geologists from the State university bounced over the sandstone hills and limestone prairie in decrepit Fords. The derricks sprang up in wild ravines and from the tops of the blackjack hills standing against the horizon of the prairie like some strange fungi. The little Agency spread down the valley with houses on each side of the dusty streets, and brick buildings began to circle like a band the projection of the hill in front of the Council House. The houses spread farther down the valley, then climbed the hill. Then came pavement. The dusty road that had led between the hill and the Council House and which had formed the area, now became Main street, and there was a railroad bridge where Rocky ford had been, and a vehicular bridge up the creek from the old Mill ford, whence a black ribbon of asphalt wound its way up the valley of Clear creek, up through the blackjacks and then on across the prairie, lost, then appearing again like a great, wriggling serpent; wriggling over whispering prairie then through forests of blackened derricks where the pumps chugged and coughed.

The derricks stood black against the red of sunset and where they were thickest, little towns grew among the hills and valleys like excrescences; their single streets muddy under lowering skies and dusty in fair weather, where loaded trucks passed through and shook the buildings, and sometimes stalled in the mud. On each side of the street were frame houses with signs above their doors calling attention to the world that rooms could be had for exorbitant prices, or signs that read, "Eats," "Bill's Place," or "Quick Eats". Rows of quickly built buildings were lighted with glaring lights at night when the extravagantly paid workers came from the fields and danced to the wheezing phonographs, bought corn whiskey, heroin and women, and sometimes were knifed or shot as a consequence.

When these little towns were deserted after the great frenzy, they became the first desolation on the rolling prairie; the first smirch to kill the happiness that the prairie at all seasons inspired. Around them was death and blatant squalor; pieces of rusted pipe, tin cans glinting in the sun, papers imprisoned in tall weeds,

« 321 »

old tires and tin hulks of castaway automobiles. Tin roofs rasping in the prairie winds that seemed to cry out in pain, and loose boards clattered gently against the walls of houses; tobacco signs hanging by one corner and swinging; charred spots where buildings had stood, the origin of the fire that destroyed them having perplexed insurance companies. Around all the grass worn down and killed, showing the brown rocks and the sterile earth.

Into the land of the Osages poured lawyers, doctors and automobile dealers. There were "Art" shops and "Parisian" shops and "Ye Shoppes" of various descriptions, and many drug stores. Most of the old traders had passed on and the old stores had to put on new fronts and assume that which was believed to be the metropolitan air in order to compete adequately with the others. The Agency became thoroughly standardized; its stores and shops selling the same merchandise that was sold in Maine and California.

On sandstone hills and along valleys, ranch houses appeared on the Indian homesteads. There was the main house with subsidiary houses and open lodges for cooking. On a few ranches, those qualified to have them, were built the conical churches of the Peyote worship.

On these ranches many of the old aristocrats remained to sit out the remainder of their lives among their children and grandchildren. They were sons and grandsons of the old chiefs and the leading men of the early days; remaining Indian in their hearts, and accepting what fortune had given them as they accepted all things. Many of them were still religious but followed the new Peyote belief, where the shade of Wah'Kon-Tah is recognized, and the Christ is visible.

Of these tall aristocrats, Wah Tze Moh In (Star that Travels), perhaps because he was a nephew of Wah Ti An Kah, the stormer, and gifted with his ability as an orator, adjusted himself to the conditions that the white man had brought upon his people. He still wore the leggings, shirt, and blanket, and was seldom seen without the gorget made from the fresh water mussel, which was the symbol of the sun at noon, the god of day.

Tall and handsome he stalks through the streets of the Agency or sits in front of the Council House watching the traffic.[1] Whenever there is the opening of a trading post, in sometimes accurate imitation of the posts of other days, or any other festivity or fête where his picturesqueness seems proper, he is called and usually responds. And this nephew of Wah Ti An Kah always speaks, and the sense of his speeches depends frequently on what he had eaten at the previous meal or whether he has eaten; or may depend upon whether his chauffeur has missed the rough places in the road. Standing much as his fathers stood, he at once commands the attention of his hearers, then in flowing Osage talks of what is on his mind. Fortunately he has a very intelligent, diplomatic and discreet interpreter, and his speeches are usually accepted as being in harmony with the bigger and better spirit.

His handsome face has been moulded in bronze, and his picture painted by great artists. His face appears

1. Since this was written, Star That Travels (commonly, though erroneously called Bacon Rind) died, in April, 1932.

on programs, on brochures and as letterheads. His name, an unimaginative interpretation, is known everywhere, and is invariably associated with the word, Osage.

THE MAJOR GOES AWAY

Sometime after the allotment the Major bought a ranch near the head of Rock creek and near the ford on the old Caney trail which he had crossed on his first trip into the Reservation. In a little opening on the side of a sandstone hill, he built his home; doing most of the work himself with the aid of a carpenter. The little house looked across the lines of timber that converged where two branches of the creek came together, and to the blackjack covered hills to the east. Behind the house the blackjacks crept down almost to the kitchen door.

He spent many happy hours measuring and sawing and planning. He believed that one could make a ranch support itself and the family of the owner, even in the sandstone hills cut by ravines, and he was determined to show those who believed otherwise, that it might be done.

But as the years passed there were days when he was restless; he grew sad and his habitual silence was more marked. Around him, dinning in his ears, was the frenzied development and the deterioration, as he thought, of the Osage people. Much of his restiveness was due to the fact that he could do nothing; the feeling of impotence in an active man, especially when it concerns something close to his heart, is a near tragedy.

He had come to believe that this great wealth was the last play of the fate that pursued the Osage people.

Finally when he could sit and watch that which he believed to be the damnation of their souls no longer, he expressed his opinions in words and actions. And after a certain definite action he became more bitter than ever; he found that with the interest of the people at heart he had played into the hands of the white man against whom he had spent years protecting the Indian. He became bitter about the conditions, and the fact that he had been mistaken and misled, did not aid his state of mind, as he did not care to admit that he had been wrong. The obvious coldness of his Indian friends added to his bitterness; he had believed that the action was for their good.

He was an old man and naturally the years of his prime seemed good to him; much happier and of greater importance than the confused years in which he lived. His comparisons between the modern Osage and the great men whom he had known were magnified, and the glamour of youth and activity surrounded the people of the tribe as they were when he lived among them as their agent.

And thus with his thoughts of the past, and the near bitterness that was like an obsession, he would spend a few weeks on the ranch then go elsewhere as though searching for something he couldn't find. Sometimes his hours would become brighter in the possession of a new car; sometimes they would become brighter in the long conversations with younger members of the tribe about their fathers and grandfathers. These discussions of the old days and the men who lived then must have given him great happiness; those personalities must have come up in his mind with a sharpness that took the years from his shoulders. The finality with which he would sooner or later make the statement, in the course of those conversations, that Big Chief was the greatest Osage of them all, often amused his younger listeners and gave their Indian hearts happiness even though they did not agree with him; it pleased them to have their old men and their ancestors praised. The young men would invariably claim distinction for their own ancestors; not with vehemence but with calm pride. Nearly always the Major would attempt to show them that while their ancestors were great men—there had been many great men in his day—that they were not as great as Big Chief. "Wah Ti An Kah," he would say, "was a great man; a man interested in his people and a great leader, but he was too noisy; always wanted to be in front and show himself off. That wasn't Indian— that wasn't Osage," he would say with firm dignity. Then after a pause, "The greatest of your people was Big Chief."

. . . .

Then in a little house in the town that had grown out of the little valley that had once been the Agency; the town that had climbed all over the hills; even up among the blackjacks on Cedarville hill, the Major, in his eighty-seventh year, (April 12, 1931) passed on.

Sometimes during the last years he had been arrested in his stride, as though a hand had been laid gently on his shoulder, indicating that it was time to go; but he impatiently brushed it away and strode on with his head high and his shoulders square, persistent in his independence; refusing assistance as he grew visibly weaker. During the last days as he sat in his chair, fumbling the loose threads on the frayed arms, his eyes would be closed and his thoughts far away. He did not hear the laboring of the motors up the street that climbed the hill in front of the house. He saw a few stone buildings rising above the post oaks and the blackjacks, he saw the prairie that talked and undulated in the breezes; the groups of dome-shaped lodges with figures moving leisurely among them and thin columns of smoke rising lazily.

As the days wore on even these visions became vague and memories would come into his mind; sharp enough at first, only to fade as he made effort to retain them, and just when he was warmed by the pleasure that they brought some trivial thing of recent time would flit into their place and he would make little gestures of impatience.

Sometimes he had visitors and he would attempt to talk with them of the things of the day, keeping locked in his heart the subjects too sacred to bring out for those who did not understand, or whose interest he believed to be inspired by the sensational. Once during the last days, when a visitor came to see him and he learned after several attempts to attribute to him some other name, that he had known his father and his ancestors, the subject came around to the old days of the Agency. They spoke of Big Chief, of Governor Jo and of Black Dog, but in the conversation the Major suddenly seemed far away; his eyes closed and his body was erect in the arm chair as his fingers fumbled.

Then, as from a dream, he mumbled: "I know where Hard Robe was buried—don't let them tell you—."

Then he was silent. Perhaps he believed that he was still talking to someone; to someone who had doubted the place of burial. Then he mumbled:

"My little girl saw them lead the horses up the hill— she can tell you; she watched from the window of the house—she could see the people on Cedarvale hill—they buried Hard Robe on Cedarvale hill. I can take you there—some day I will take you there."

There was another silence, then a frown came on his face as though he were attempting to retain the train of thought; then scarcely audible, mumbling: "Don't let them tell you—I know where Hard Robe was buried and my little girl saw them from the window. The stones are gone now but I can take you there—I know—there's a house there now—I know where— Hard Robe. . . ." He fell silent, and the visitor quietly left the house.

. . . .

When the Major was dressed for his last trip across the Reservation; a trip that would take him up through the blackjacks and across the prairie and on across Salt creek and the river to Arkansas City; over the black road that lies like a great snake, a well-tailored Indian woman of middle age stepped up to look for the last time at the face she had known so well. She stood looking a moment, then lifted her lace handkerchief to her eyes. Then suddenly grief flooded her; took possession of her and she forgot the dainty lace handkerchief; she forgot the modish costume and the place. For what she felt, the tears of the white woman would not suffice; the veneer vanished and she broke sobbingly into the wail of her race. As suddenly she stopped and walked away from the casket, mourning in her heart for the only father she could remember, this daughter of Eagle Feather.

As he lay there in the room waiting for the last trip across the Reservation, there were no marks to indicate who he was, but if his spirit happened to stray to the Happy Hunting Ground, Big Chief would know his friend, and extending his hand with eyes smiling, would say, "How."

EAGLE THAT DREAMS

Chapter Nineteen

O N THE DAY of the Major's death a young Osage climbed indolently into a long, shiny car. "Drive out to the old man's," he said to the slovenly negro chauffeur.

They sped out over the hills and across a small prairie, then dropped into a long valley where there was a group of houses. One large house and several small ones grouped around it. To one side was the conical Peyote church.

The young man stepped out and walked toward the house, and the negro chauffeur climbed out, stretched himself by the side of the car and began chewing a blade of grass with an expression of utter blankness on his face.

The young man went into the back of the house, then through a long hall and into a large room. His father was sitting in an overstuffed chair and his mother sat on a divan, running her fingers along the edge of her blanket. The young man gave a greeting and flopped into a chair. He sat there for some time looking out across the hills while his parents sat silently, the father occasionally lifting a tin can and spitting tobacco juice into it.

The young man said in Osage, "They say old agent went away."

"Huhn-n-n-n," said the mother as she squinted up at her son.

There was a long silence then the father picked up the tin can, spat into it, wiped his mouth, and addressed the little box stove before him, "He was old man. It was time he went away." Again a long silence. Then the mother said, "He was good man, I believe—he was good agent."

"How," said the father, "It would have been good to visit him. I believe. It would have been good to see him put in grave. In his heart there was much that was good. For long time he was friend of Indian. This thing which they say about him was bad. White man put this thing in his heart I believe. In Tah Tze Skah did not know it was bad. For long time he was good agent."

Another silence. After spitting in the tin the father spoke again, "It would have been good to go see him put in grave."

The mother gave a "Huhn-n-n-n," of approval. The young man arose, threw out his chest, thrust his hands into his pocket, and yawned. He addressed his father while his mouth was still open, "You will use wagon-that-moves-by itself today, huh? They are making mine go again at Agency." There was a grunt from his father. The young man walked to the window and looked out. Soon he came back and said carelessly, "I want some money—I need some money for many things."

His father looked at the stove in front of him and said, "I have no money—the agent will give me no more money until next week. You have money at Agency—where is this money you have there?"

A look of disgust and impatience came over the

young man's face. "Old Sick Ear will not give me more money."

"Old Sick Ear is right, I believe. Pet-sah-ne costs much money. White man puts into it evil spirit so he can cheat Indian, when Indian's head is sick. Agent said to Sick Ear, 'You have no more money'."

The young man looked with pity upon his parents. He thought of how old-fashioned they were: his father still wearing his buckskin leggings and his beaverskin bandeau, his pale blue silk shirt and his blanket; his mother in her shirt, moccasins and shrouding. They were certainly behind the time, all right. No matter how swell he dressed he was always embarrassed thinking of his parents sitting out at the ranch. They couldn't even speak English. He wished he didn't have to speak Osage with them—it sure made him feel funny when they talked together in public at the Agency. He walked out of the door, then turned and said, "I go into Agency, I will send black one back with wagon-that-moves-by-itself."

"How," replied the father.

The old people sat for some time. There was some bustle and noise from the kitchen where there were several slovenly negroes preparing the food, and the cars could be heard buzzing along the dusty road a mile away. The mother squinted at her husband. "Our son causes much trouble in my mind. Many times he has broken his wagon-that-moves-by-itself. I believe that he is like one that is filled with evil when his head is sick with Pet-sah-ne, this white man's whiskey." A long pause while she smoothed the edge of her blanket with her forefinger and thumb. Then she continued, "His ears are closed to our talk. He ought to take woman but he has nothing to give for woman. White men have taken much money from him to give to these two white women whom he has taken. Now they are gone, these white women."

They sat silently until their meal was ready; the woman smoothing the edge of her blanket and the man gazing at the stove.

The next morning the car was stopped in front of the main ranch house and Wy Tze Kee Tompa (Eagle That Dreams) came out followed by his wife. There was no greeting from the chauffeur nor did he think it necessary to tell his employers that their son had met young White Horn and had got money from him to buy whiskey. It always seemed to him that they knew these things instinctively. He had readily learned to be silent in their presence.

As he drove to the Agency his passengers sat straight and dignified in the back seat; sat with a dignity that was quite unconscious. They drove through the streets bordered with brick store buildings, busy with the business of the day, then out onto the highway that leads to Hominy.

They arrived at a ranch similar to their own. There were the main buildings and the smaller houses around it. The conical church of Peyote some distance away stood in the shade of a group of elms. Around the main group of buildings was a high wire fence, and within this the people were grouped in the shade of the elms. A short distance away was an open structure covered with the branches of blackjacks, and here and there were the hickory frames of lodges. Under the branch-

covered structure was a long table to which many women and negro servants were busy carrying great plates
of food from the kitchen.

Eagle That Dreams came forward followed by his
wife and when he approached the group he solemnly
shook hands with each person. Some of the men wore
blankets over shirt and trousers, and some wore the
traditional moccasins, leggings and blanket. The host
ordered a chair for him; he muttered a "How" and sat
down.

The voices around him were slow and guttural but
in all the dozen or more people there, only one conversation was going on. An old woman, a tall thin man in
black suit and a black Stetson hat with a flicker tail
feather in the band, and Yellow Horse, in blanket and
leggings, were discussing the funeral of the daughter
of Wah Tze Moh In.

The tall man said: "For many years we have done
honors to those who go away. When they went to
agent he said they could not buy casket with white iron
on it. He said it cost too much. He said it would take
away much money. I do not believe this is good. I do
not believe that this is good for those who go away.
Agent said five hundred dollars is too much for casket."

There was a short silence, then Yellow Horse spoke.
"I have seen many of these caskets with white iron on
them. I believe when Indian buys these caskets it is
good for man at store. He who goes away can be honored by many gifts, but casket that takes away much
money is not good, I believe."

"Huhn-n-n-n," said the old woman, "White man
wants Indian's money." Then the tall man in the black

hat spoke again. "They say that casket of In Tah Tze Skah did not cost much money."

"Huhn-n-n-n, he is gone away, our old agent. There was much good in his heart. My father said he was good to Indian," said the old woman as she looked at the ground.

"How," said Yellow Horse, "he was good man."

The host came up and touched Eagle That Dreams on the shoulder and said, "We eat now." Eagle That Dreams stood up quickly and said, "Send this young man to me."

Soon a young man came across the yard to the group under the tree. He wore an expensive shirt and tie. His clothes were well tailored in the latest mode, with wide cuffs on the trousers. His black hair was parted in the center and slicked down until it shone like black leather. He approached Eagle That Dreams with an air of indifference and carelessness, and extended a limp hand. Eagle That Dreams said to him, "My heart is glad. Now you are man. You have sixteen summers and you stand at place where road forks." The young man looked down at the ground, not so much out of embarrassment as for the purpose of hiding amusement.

The two walked toward the table. Eagle That Dreams went to the head and the young man stood to his right by his father. Soon all were seated.

There were a few young women with their hair beautifully waved, and two of them had too much misplaced rouge. There were a few older women in blankets and shrouding; several older men in blankets and leggings and the remainder were middle aged men in shabby suits and black hats, and young men in duo-colored shoes, expensive shirts and modish trousers. The older men wore their hair long, the roach having been given up after the advent of Peyote worship.

Eagle That Dreams stood and looked for a moment down the long table loaded with beef, pork, mutton and chicken; great plates of bread, fruits and several kinds of vegetables. At each place was a large bowl for soup and coffee, and a plate with forks and knives. In three great piles shone the red cuts of watermelon.

He stood for a moment longer then with a movement of his hand brushed a wisp of graying hair over his ear, pulled his blanket up under his right arm, and in a voice that faltered a little, as though through timidity, began:

"We come here to eat. We come here to honor this young man who has reached forks of road. We come here to ask our Father to let him live long time. We ask our Father to bring good woman to his lodge that he may have many children to honor him. We ask our Father to tell him which road he should follow." Slowly his voice became firmer and he became more assured. He clasped his hands before him and raised his face to the sky with closed eyes. His words flowed evenly and came faster as emotion crept over him, and soon he was praying fervently to a god who was a composite of Wah'Kon-Tah, the stern god of his fathers; Christ, the god of the white man who had proved so powerful; and the peaceful, dreamy god of Peyote, the god of resignation.

"Our Father," he continued, "this young man is in road of white man. Make him carry in his heart memory of his Father. Make his eyes blind to white man's whiskey that his head may be clear like morning. Make his head clear so that he will not make wagon-that-moves-by-itself travel like wind across prairie; so that it will not be broken, and his body broken, and his spirit dark like earth-cloud. Our Father, we come here to eat, to show honor to this young man who is at forks of road. Put into his heart thoughts that are good."

As he prayed the food on the long table became cold. The younger people who had come to the table with an air of nonchalant tolerance were now distinctly bored. The young man in whose honor the feast was given sat on the edge of his chair with his head in his hands and worried a beetle with the toes of his immaculate shoes.

All kept their heads lowered. Three young men whispered to each other across the table. A very fat young man whispered across to the other two in English, "Old Ed got a new Caddy, ain't it?"

"Yeh—got drunk at Tulsa—sure wrecked it."

The third young man whispered, "He's in jail, ain't it?"

"Yeh," said the fat boy.

One of the rouged girls who overheard the whispering, said, "Too much corn."

The boys paid no attention to her but she and her companion giggled. Then the third young man volunteered, "He was goin' to Tulsa to play golf, I guess."

After a short silence the fat boy said, "Bet he ain't goin' nowhere now, ain't it?" At this they giggled so loudly that they almost drowned the voice of the speaker but no one seemed disturbed.

The long prayer finally finished, they began eating. When the meal was over some of the older women brought forth large red handkerchiefs and filled them with food; meat, bread and oranges. The diners moved to the shade of the trees. Some of them sat in small groups and talked for a short time, and one by one the large cars drew up to the gate and the guests departed for their homes over the reservation, each one first shaking hands with the youth who had reached the forks of the road. As each one shook hands he or she pressed money into the palm of his hand. One old woman held his hand a long time and gave him advice. She talked about the bravery of his ancestors and of the great things they had done; how he should keep them in his heart. He stood half amused and half embarrassed as he looked at the ground. He crumpled the twenty dollar note in his hand as she waddled off.

Eagle That Dreams sat with three of the older men for some time after the others had left. The talk was desultory; mostly about the council, the payments and oil. Then Bull Hide said suddenly, "They said I ought to speak in white man's tongue at burying of In Tah Tze Shah." There was a long silence. "Wah Tze Moh In wouldn't go—I didn't want to go alone." Another silence, then Yellow Horse said, "He was good man— in his heart was great love for Indian, I believe." Each one in the group said, "How."

Bull Hide spoke again. "I am much troubled in my mind about church. They say Meh Ompah We Lee (Moon Head) is god too—I don't know about this."

Yellow Horse stirred, then said rather excitedly, "That is so. Long time ago Black Bird told me this. He was father to my wife. He said Moon Head was god. It is so. Black Bird was great man; there was much mystery in him."

"Ho," said Eagle That Dreams, "I do not believe this thing. I remember when Moon Head came to Osages. He was only man. He was Kiowa—Kiowa is not god. He was great dreamer, but he was only man. He said many things that are good, but he was only man. His dreams are good. Osages said his dreams are good; this man who dreamed about Peyote; this Moon Head who dreamed about Peyote, and gave his dreams to Osages. It is good dreaming, but he is man, this Moon Head. He is gone away long time. They think he is God now."

"I do not know about this thing," said Bull Hide.

Yellow Horse let his blanket fall to his waist and tied in there. His face twitched slightly as he bent over from the bench on which he was sitting and picked up a stick. He drew a crescent moon in the dust with the concavity toward the west, "This is altar of Peyote," he said, "Father of my wife, Black Bird, was only Osage who could make Peyote altar this way. Moon Head told him these things. When man goes away he must be buried with face to west. Spirit of man must follow Wah Tze Go as he travels west. Moon Head is also god—Black Bird told me this thing."

The others sat silent, neither approving nor disapproving.

Suddenly Wah Tze Moh In glared at Bull Hide and said angrily, "Many times you make things I say into white man's tongue. You speak white man's tongue very well. You speak with many white men in their tongue; you ought to know better. You ought to know that Indian has only one god who is son of Great Father." He lifted the great cross which he wore suspended from his neck and which hung under the gorget carved from the fresh water mussel, the gorget which represented the sun, the god of day. "This," he said, placing his long brown finger on the silver figure of the cross, "is only man who brings great dreams from Great Father; he is only other god."

Having said this he arose and quickly strode toward the gate, his beaver bandeau disturbing the lower branches of a honey locust.

Before the dust of Wah Tze Moh In's car had settled Eagle That Dreams arose and pulled his blanket about him. He stood for a moment, then he said, "What Wah Tze Moh In has said is true. It is true that altar must face east; it is true that he who has gone away must be buried with face toward east. Moon Head was man, I believe."

He turned and left.

·   ·   ·   ·   ·   ·   ·

Some weeks later Eagle That Dreams got out of his car in front of the sandstone Agency building, wrapped his blanket about him, and walked sedately into the agent's office. Behind him came a younger man as interpreter. They sat down in front of the desk.

"Well, how are you today?" and the young agent smiled pleasantly.

Eagle That Dreams sat without moving and the interpreter said "He's all right."

There was a pause and the interpreter said, "He wants to talk to you."

"All right, this is Wy Tze Kee Tompa, isn't it—I've heard a lot about him."

For some time Eagle That Dreams talked with even, monotonous voice. At the end of his speech the interpreter said, "He says he thinks he's gonna die. He says he sure is worried about everything 'round here. He says long time he tole the people that they should think about time when they wasn't no more oil. Now he says they ain't much oil, and what they gonna do. He said long time ago he had dream about this oil; he said it was bad dream."

The interpreter stopped and Eagle That Dreams continued. He spoke for some time and again the interpreter spoke, "He says he want to know about this casket. He says he sure gonna die. He says he sure wanta be buried on his place, on hill there, and he want good casket. He is great man he says and he wants good casket. He says what you gonna do about it."

The agent was about to reply when Eagle That Dreams began speaking again. At the conclusion the interpreter said, "He says he want to be dressed in his own clothes; he says he want Roan Horse to paint his face, and he wants priest from Catholic church to do like he did at burying of Red Eagle. He says one time when he go to Washington he was in big house there. He says they had many things that belonged to Indian. But he says they didn't have much that belonged to Osage. He said Osages are great people. He says when he die he wants this place to have hees things. He says what you gonna do about this casket. He says he is great man and there will be many people at feast. He says he got plenty of money in office."

The agent replied: "Tell him everything is all right. We will see that everything is as he wishes." There were a few words between the old man and his interpreter, and they arose and each shook hands with the agent and left the office.

. . . .

The air of the early morning was still and cool as Eagle That Dreams got out of his bed. He sat for a moment naked and looked at his wife in the other twin bed. He slowly dressed. He pulled on his moccasins and leggings, and adjusted his breech clout. With his tattooed chest naked to the waist he walked quickly to a glass hanging on the wall. He took up a comb and parted his long iron gray hair carefully—along the straight red line running down the center. For some time he looked at the red line which was the symbol of the straight road which he traveled each day. Each day as he combed his hair he was reminded of this straight road which was red as the symbol of dawn; of the rising sun; red the color of fire which was the Father from which all things came.

He turned quickly from the glass and walked out onto the porch. He stood for a moment, then as Wah Tze Go, the grandfather, peeped over the prairie, he chanted in a clear voice, "Wah Tze Go, Wah Tze Go, may my feet go along road that is straight; may my lodge be filled with meat, may my lodge be filled with children; may I live long on earth, that my feet may travel straight in roads of earth——."

When the lower edge of the sun barely touched the horizon the chant stopped and the early morning world seemed to be listening, except for the coughing of the pumps carried from the oil fields on the heavy air.

NOTES ON THE OSAGES

NOTES ON THE OSAGES

THE OSAGES were known for the first time historically in the year 1673, and by the first French and American travelers were placed on the Osage river, in what is now the state of Missouri. They remained on this river until 1802 when almost half of the tribe was removed to the Arkansas river, the remainder of the tribe moving their permanent camps to the Neosho river in 1822 to comply articles of a treaty with the United States government, in which they ceded land which comprises most of the modern states of Missouri and Arkansas.

Their permanent camps were on the Osage river but they were by no means restricted to so small a region in their activities. They claimed all the territory east of the Mississippi, south of the Missouri, north of the Arkansas and west to the Rocky Mountains. They not only claimed this great territory but were quite able to protect it from the encroachment of other tribes.

They were at war with the surrounding tribes from earliest history and were held in terror by many, being "the scourge of all the tribes within hundreds of miles."[1] They, with the Apache in the west, formed a constant factor in a policy of tribal balance pursued alike by France and Spain, before the Louisiana Purchase in 1803.

---

1 Grant Foreman, *Indians & Pioneers*. New Haven, Yale University Press.

This territory controlled by the Osages was a no-man's land between the French along the Mississippi and the Spanish southwest; two forces attempting to get control of the continent. The French in their desire to open up trade routes to New Mexico via the rivers of what is now the State of Oklahoma, naturally came in conflict with the Spaniard, both sides using Indians in order to carry out their plans; the Osage forming the balance of power. "For many years the powerful Osage were probably more active than any other force in maintaining a state of warfare throughout Oklahoma and preventing its peaceful occupation by either red or white man. They challenged nearly all tribes they encountered on the prairie and east of the Mississippi, but they were long the allies of the French." [2]

There were many skirmishes, raids and retaliatory actions during this period of rivalry. In 1720 an expedition from Santa Fe, New Mexico, under Lieut. Col. Pedro de Villasur planned to visit the Osages to incite them to destroy the Missouri who were then allies of the French. By mistake, however, the Colonel led his expedition into the Missouri camp believing them to be Osages. He naively revealed his plans, and of course his command was killed to a man.

Apart from the fact that the Osages were dominant in the region between the Missouri and the Arkansas, they seemed also to attract the attention of all travelers who came to this region, because of personal characteristics. Nearly all writers mention that they were insolent and very proud, bearing themselves with great dignity at all times. They were a tall people; the men averaging

2 Grant Foreman, *Indians & Pioneers*. New Haven, Yale University Press.

over six feet and their proportions attracted the attention of everyone. They were courageous, aggressive and vengeful, and literature of that period is full of their bloody deeds and the terror in which they were held by neighboring tribes.

It was remarked by one traveler in 1772 that several tribes suffering from Osage raids moved south of the Red river and formed an alliance with the Caddoan people against the Osage on the north and the Apache on the west. The Spanish who had also suffered at the hands of the Osages enlisted the services of these defeated tribes, but there is no indication that these combined forces ever completed any plan for vengeance.

In 1802 the Great Osages became divided. Nearly half of the tribe moved from the camps on the Osage river and settled at the Three Forks, i. e. the Verdigris, Grand and Arkansas rivers, under the leadership of Big Track and Grah Moh (called Claremore). The others remained at the old camp under the leadership of Pah Hue Skah (White Hair).

For some years the government attempted to have these Arkansas Osages, as they were called, move back to the Osage river but they refused, and yearly grew in power and insolence. The division of the tribe was due to the influence of Pierre Chouteau, who had obtained a monopoly on Osage trade before the Louisiana Purchase. In 1802 when this monopoly was given to Manuel Lisa, he attempted to have the whole tribe moved to the Three Forks, but when they would not agree he connived with a very influential and ambitious member of the tribe, one Big Track, whom he created as chief. Grah Moh, the hereditary chief, was only a small boy at that time, but came down to the Three Forks camp with the Arkansas Osages, and later came into his own and this division of the tribe was called Claremore's band. It was this band who for years carried on war with the Cherokees, the Choctaws and the Shawnees.

There are two names which have come down from the early written history of the Osages; names which European writers have stressed in nearly all their accounts. Pah Hue Skah (White Hair) was supposed also to have been a creation of one of the Chouteau brothers, but since that time there has been a chief or a headman in each Osage generation bearing that name. The first Pah Hue Skah, who died in 1808, got his name White Hair through an incident during a battle with European soldiery. It was said that a daring youth during the confusion of the battle dashed in and wounded one of the European officers, who was wearing a white wig. When the officer fell the young man rushed to consummate the coup, taking hold of the wig and drawing his knife. However, before he could use his knife the officer struggled, jumped to his feet and ran away, leaving the young Osage standing in awe with a fluffy white wig grasped tightly in his fingers. So astonished was he that he forgot to shoot at the retreating figure, and when he came to his senses, and after considering the manner in which the officer had been wounded and escaped apparently unharmed, the wig immediately became wah'kon (mystery) to him. Thenceforth the young man fastened the white wig to his roach and no harm could come to him when he wore it in battle, and he was known as Pah Hue Skah (White Hair). The second Pah Hue Skah died in 1833 and Pah Hue Skah the third came with his people to the last reservation in Oklahoma Territory.

Claremore is the other name which has come down in the history of the white man. The name is very likely the result of the Frenchman's attempt to pronounce the name Grah Moh (Arrow Going Home). Grah Moh, unlike Pah Hue Skah and Big Track, was an hereditary chief. He was often called "the builder of towns," and his name looms in the history of the region claimed by his people. He was said to have had a great intellect, a fascinating personality and tremendous force as a leader and a warrior. His wars with the Cherokees alone would have made him famous. The first Grah Moh died in 1828, the second in 1838 and the third was identified as the leader of a large band in the last reservation.

TREATIES

After the Louisiana Purchase in 1803 the domain of the Great Osages came under the sovereignty of the United States and the alliance between this tribe and the French was broken up. In 1808 at Fort Clark was held the first treaty between the Osages and the United States. It was brought about by General Clark who was a member of the Lewis and Clark expedition to the Columbia river in 1804.

The United States claimed that the Osages had made several raids upon white settlers and had caused great damage to property to such an extent that they felt warranted in asking this tribe to cede great tracts of land to them and move farther west. Some of the facts are, however, that white settlers had come over into the Osage domain after the Louisiana Purchase and had incited the Osages so that the government might make such a move, thus leaving these rich lands free for settlement. The immigrant Cherokees also desired rich lands west of the Mississippi; lands which they had been promised by the United States upon its acquisition of the Louisiana country. The government had promised that the immigrant Cherokees might settle upon land west of the Mississippi knowing that the land was claimed by the Osages. Some move was necessary by the United States, and this necessity resulted in the treaty at Fire Prairie on the right bank of the Missouri river, a spot near where Kansas City, Missouri now stands.

This treaty was signed by Pierre Chouteau as representative of the United States and by chiefs and warriors of the Great and Little Osages. It was not unlike the other treaties that followed during the next fifty seven years inasmuch as the most important article was one which referred to the cession of Osage lands to the United States government. As was customary in following treaties Article One opened with the statement that the United States was anxious to promote peace, friendship and intercourse with the Osage tribes and to afford them every assistance in their power. They agreed to pay to all citizens who had claims against the Osages a sum not to exceed five thousand dollars. They agreed to send, to Fire Prairie or to St. Louis, merchandise to the amount or value of one thousand dollars yearly for the use of the Great Osages and merchandise to the value of five hundred dollars yearly to the Little Osages; they having paid the Great Osages eight hundred dollars and the Little Osages four hundred dollars for the signing of the treaty. The government also promised to protect the hunting grounds of the tribe and allow no one to cross the Osage boundary. The tribes, on their part, were to remain friendly and refrain from hostilities and from supplying arms to other Indians not in amity with the United States. By this treaty the Osages ceded to the United States great tracts of land lying between the Arkansas and the Missouri rivers which comprised the greater parts of the modern states of Arkansas and Missouri.

There was another treaty made at Portage des Sioux September 12, 1815. This treaty was for the purpose of reëstablishing peace and friendship between the United States and the Osages after the war of 1812. Injuries and acts of hostility were to be forgiven and forgotten by both sides.

On September 25, 1818, William Clark, governor of Missouri Territory, on behalf of the United States, made a treaty with the Osages by which the latter ceded to the United States government land which was bounded on the south by the Arkansas river, on the west by the Verdigris river, running up that river to the falls, thence northeast to a point marked by the modern Salina, Oklahoma; then east to the Cherokee settlement. The United States government agreed to pay for losses inflicted upon citizens and the Cherokees by the Osages. The government led the latter to believe that if they attempted to settle all claims against them by deductions from annuities agreed upon in the treaty of 1808 they would have nothing left, also stating that the land was to be settled by peaceful citizens who would serve as an example to the Osages in cultivation of the land. As a matter of fact this land was turned over to the Cherokees as a hunting ground, and was known as the Lovely Purchase. This treaty was made at St. Louis.

A treaty at Marias de Cygne, August 31, 1822, relieved the United States of the obligation of maintaining merchandise at Fort Clark under the treaty of 1808, releasing them in fact from the obligations under Article Two of that treaty, and in consideration of this release to pay to the Osages $2,329.40 in merchandise.

In the treaty of June 2, 1825, made at St. Louis, the United States government thus declared that "in order more effectually to extend to said tribes that protection of the government so much desired by them, it is agreed follows": That the Great and Little Osages were to cede and relinquish to the United States all their right, title, interest and claim to lands lying within the State of Missouri and Territory of Arkansas, and to all land lying west of said State of Missouri and Territory of Arkansas north and west of Red river, south of Kansas river, and a line to be drawn from the head sources of the Kansas, southwardly through the Rock Saline. But within the limits of this country there would be reserved for the Great and Little Osages for as long as they chose to occupy same the following described land: beginning at a point due east of White Hair's village, and twenty five miles west of the western boundary of the State of Missouri, fronting on a north and south line, so as to leave ten miles north, and forty miles south, of the point of said beginning, and extending west, with the width of fifty miles, to the western boundary of the lands ceded and relinquished by them. No persons other than the Osages were to be allowed in this reservation except persons attached to the Agency. The government, as one consideration, was to pay to the Osages, at the village or at St. Louis, the amount of seven thousand dollars yearly for twenty years, either in money, merchandise, provisions or domestic animals, at the option of the latter. Further they were to furnish farming utensils, cattle, hogs, chickens and a blacksmith, and there were to be reservations of a hundred and sixty acres each for mixed-bloods in the territory ceded. Fifty four sections of the reservation were to be sold for the purpose of educating Osage children. Claims to the amount of $4,105.80 against individuals were to be paid by the government, and in consideration of this the tribes were to release their claim upon the government for regular troops to be stationed, for the former's protection, at Fork Clark. Other debts to various traders were also paid by the government. Within this reservation there were three sections of land reserved to missionary establishments "employed in teaching, civilizing, and improving, the said Indians." [3]

At Council Grove on the Neosho river, August 10, 1825 the United States government sent its commissioners to the Osages to say that the government desired commercial and friendly relations with the Mexican people, and in order to promote such relations desired to open a road from Missouri frontier to the confines of New Mexico. The commissioners were instructed to get the consent of the Osages as the road which would be surveyed and marked out by them must run through the territory owned by the tribe. In the treaty both sides agreed that the road would be free for the use of citizens of the United States and for citizens of the Mexican

---

3 Kepplers Treaties.

Republic, and the tribe agreed to extend friendly aid and assistance to the citizens of both countries along the road; allowing travelers to draw out of the road and camp. Three hundred dollars was paid to the Osages before signing the treaty and the government agreed to pay five hundred dollars in money or merchandise at the option of the tribe, and at places which they might indicate.

A treaty of understanding was made at Camp Holmes, near Grand Prairie close to the Canadian river. It was signed August 24, 1835. It was really a treaty of peace between the Comanche, Wichita and allied tribes, the United States government, and the Osage, Cherokee, Choctaw, Seneca, and Quapah tribes. The representatives of the United States and the councilors from each of these tribes agreed that all former injuries and acts of violence should be forgiven forever, and in consideration of such agreement the government was to indemnify the tribes for any horses stolen from them, provided that such horses could not be found. It was further agreed that all Indians might hunt and trap in Grand Prairie, west of Cross Timbers to the western limits of the United States, provided that other Indians found on the hunting grounds were not molested by the signers of the treaty.

The Osages were signers of another treaty in 1837 by which they agreed to live on friendly terms with the United States government, the Muskogee and the Kiowa nations and stop their raids against the prairie Indians.

After years of war with the immigrant Cherokees and the Choctaws who were settled on the land west of the Mississippi claimed by the Osages, the government finally got the latter to agree at Fort Gibson, January 11, 1839, that they would cede all title or interest in any reservation heretofore claimed by them within the limits of any other tribe. Under this treaty the tribe must relinquish all claims or interests under the treaties of 1808 and 1825 except the sixth article of the latter (sections sold for school purposes), and in consideration of such cessions and relinquishments they were to be paid twenty thousand dollars; twelve thousand to be paid in money and eight thousand in goods, stock and provisions, and the government was to furnish a blacksmith for the term of twenty years and was to furnish hogs, cows, gristmills, saw mills, hoes and axes, and pay all claims against the Osages up to thirty thousand dollars. At this time the government reimbursed the tribe that which they had deducted from the annuities allowed by a former treaty, and paid to Claremore's band (Grah Moh) their portion of the annuities of 1829 wrongfully kept from them by an agent of the government; a sum amounting to three thousand dollars. They agreed to build houses for the chiefs and headmen and to give them wagons.

Again the United States, desiring to reëstablish friendly feeling among the Indians, and between the government and the Indians, met the Osages at Fort Smith, September 13, 1865. The tribe had been divided during the Civil war and the government desired to reestablish its former relationship. This treaty was said to be unratified, but Pah Hue Skah (White Hair) and Pawnee No Pah She (Man Not Afraid of Pawnees), called Governor Jo, were present, and these chiefs had left the impression with their people that the treaty was

« 355 »

a trick on the part of the government, to take advantage of the Civil war division of the tribe, to impose distasteful conditions on them. At this treaty making with the Indian tribes, many of whom had given their allegiance to the Confederacy, the Osage was not the only tribe present but there were also representatives from the Cherokee, Creek, Choctaw, Chickasaw, Seminole, Seneca, Shawnee, and Quapaw.

Then came the treaty between the United States government and the Osages, September 29, 1865, at Canville trading post, Osage nation, within the boundary of the State of Kansas. Article One started with the statement that the Great and Little Osages had more land than was necessary for their occupation and all payments from the government to them under former treaties had ceased, leaving them greatly impoverished. There was a statement that this tribe was desirous of improving its condition by disposing of its surplus lands and therefore decided to grant and sell to the United States the lands contained within the following boundaries: "beginning at the southeast corner of their present reservation, and running thence north to the eastern boundary thereof fifty miles to the northeast corner; thence west with the northern line thirty miles; thence south fifty miles, to the southern boundary; and thence east with said southern boundary to the place of beginning; provided, that the western boundary of said lands herein ceded shall not extend further westward than upon a line commencing at a point on the southern boundary of said Osage country one mile east of place where Verdigris river crosses the southern boundary of the State of Kansas."[4]

---

4 Kepplers Treaties.

In consideration of the grant the United States agreed to pay the sum of three hundred thousand dollars, which sum was to be placed to the credit of the Osages in the treasury of the United States, and the interest thereon at five per cent per annum, to be paid semi-annually, in money, clothing, provisions, or such articles of utility as the secretary of interior might from time to time direct. The lands ceded were to be sold under the direction of the secretary of interior on the most advantageous terms for cash. The government was to be reimbursed the cost of survey and sale, and the remaining proceeds of sales were to be placed in the treasury of the United States to the credit of the "civilization fund." This fund as stated in the treaty was to be used under the direction of the secretary of interior for the education and civilization of Indian tribes residing within the limits of the United States, but the Osages believed when they signed the treaty that the civilization fund was to be used for all the Indians, referring to all the Osage tribe; that is, including the members of the tribe who had joined the Confederacy and those who remained in Kansas and loyal to the Union. They always maintained vehemently that they would not have signed the treaty if they had understood that money which purchased their land would be used for the benefit of all other tribes in the United States.

In Article Two of this treaty the tribe agreed to cede to the United States a tract of land twenty miles in width from north to south, off the north side of the remainder of its reservation, and extending its entire length from east to west. This land was to be held in trust for the Osages, and was to be surveyed and sold for their benefit under the direction of the commissioner of the general land office, at a price not less than one dollar and twenty five cents an acre, the proceeds of such sales, after deducting all expenses incident to the proper execution of the trust, were to be placed in the treasury of the United States to the credit of the tribe. The interest thereon at the rate of five per cent per annum, was to be expended annually for building houses, purchasing agricultural implements and stock animals, for the employment of a physician and mechanics, and for providing such necessary aid as would enable them to commence agricultural pursuits under favorable circumstances. There was a provision that twenty five per cent of the net proceeds arising from the sale of the land, until the percentage should amount to the sum of eighty thousand dollars, should be placed to the credit of the school fund of the tribe, and the interest thereon, at the rate of five per cent per annum, to be used semi-annually for the boarding, clothing, and the education of the children.

In some of the following articles of the treaty the tribe agreed to pay certain claims of the traders after their examination, and that five hundred dollars annually set apart from the moneys of the tribe were to be paid by the agent to the chiefs. They again acknowledged their dependence on the government of the United States and invoked its protection and care; they promised to abstain from war and to commit no depredations on citizens or Indians, and further agreed to use their best efforts in suppressing the introduction and use of ardent spirits in their country.

Within six months after the ratification of the treaty the tribe agreed to remove from the lands sold and ceded in trust, and settle on their diminished reservation. It was also agreed "that if said Indians should agree to remove from the State of Kansas, and settle on lands to be provided for them by the United States in the Indian Territory on such terms as may be agreed on between the United States and the Indian tribes now residing in said territory or any of them, then the diminished reservation shall be disposed of by the United States in the same manner and for the same purposes as hereinbefore provided in relation to said trust land, except that fifty per cent of the proceeds of the sale of said diminished reserve may be used by the United States in the purchase of land for a suitable home for said Indians in said Territory."

The Osages later bought a reservation from the Cherokees in Oklahoma Territory; land over which they had formerly hunted and claimed as their own. This last reservation consisted roughly of a million and a half acres, was bounded on the west and the south by the Arkansas river, on the east by the ninety sixth meridian, and on the north by the State of Kansas.

After being first mislocated at Silver Lake, just east of the ninety sixth meridian, the tribe later moved to their present reservation. This was in the year 1872.

WAH'KON-TAH: *The Osage and the White Man's Road*
By JOHN JOSEPH MATHEWS has been composed on the Linotype
in twelve point Granjon. This typeface, at once clear and dis-
tinctive, is named for the celebrated printer Robert Granjon,
who was a typecutter as well. Granjon began work around 1523
but it was not until 1545 that his European reputation was es-
stablished. Desiring to create a type representing France, he cut
a typeface known as "caràcteres de civilité," so named from the
titles of two books printed from the new character in 1559 and
1560. This type enjoyed great popularity, especially in the Neth-
erlands. Granjon was fond especially of typographic ornaments
and did much to make their use universal in printed books. The
latter years of his life were spent in Rome, where he cut type
for the Vatican Press, for the Medici and others. The modern
Granjon typeface is not from any of Granjon's but is a
modern recutting by George W. Jones of a type cut
originally by Claude Garamond. ¶The chapter
initials used in this book were especially cut on
wood by P. J. Conkwright of the University Press Staff. Mr. Conkwright also
designed the title page, the spider
appearing thereon being em-
blematic of the Osages.

THE PRINTED PAGE IS EVERYMAN'S UNIVERSITY

UNIVERSITY OF OKLAHOMA PRESS
PUBLISHING DIVISION OF THE UNIVERSITY
NORMAN

Map of
Osage Agency—(Pawhuska Oklahoma)

Mounds

Road To Gray Horse

Old Ford

Cow Boy and Longhorn Steers Road

Government School Garden

Old Mill

Government Barn for Agent's mules

Leland Hotel (Later)

Tisdale House

JA

Delereaux House

Bird Creek

Camp For Visiting Indians

Hide House

Old Green (Hiath) Store

Florer's Store

Road

Water Tower

Skin House

Road

The Hill

Camp For Freighters

Council House

Agent's Office

Payment House (Later)

Doctor's House

Hart[?] Stor[e]

Corn Field

Camp of Black Dog

Beef Drying

Osage Oran[ge] hedge

Co

Cooking Beef

The Lane

Razor Back

To Rock[y] Ford

Baby on Board